Boston Institute of Finance

Mutual Fund Advisor Course

Boston Institute of Finance

Mutual Fund Advisor Course

Series 6 and Series 63 Test Preparation

WILEY

John Wiley & Sons, Inc.

Published by John Wiley & Sons, Inc., Hoboken, New Jersey
Published simultaneously in Canada

Limit of Liability/Disclaimer of Warranty: While the publisher and the author have used their best efforts in preparing this book, they make no representations or warranties with respect to the accuracy or completeness of the contents of this book and specifically disclaim any implied warranties of merchantability or fitness for a particular purpose. No warranty may be created or extended by sales representatives or written sales materials. The advice and strategies contained herein may not be suitable for your situation. You should consult with a professional where appropriate. Neither the publisher nor the author shall be liable for any loss of profit or any other commercial damages, including but not limited to special, incidental, consequential, or other damages.

For general information about our other products and services, please contact our Customer Care Department within the United States at 800-762-2974, outside the United States at 317-572-3993 or fax 317-572-4002.

Wiley also publishes its books in a variety of electronic formats. Some content that appears in print may not be available in electronic books. For more information about Wiley products, visit our Web site at www.wiley.com.

Library of Congress Cataloging-in-Publication Data:

Boston Institute of Finance
     Boston Institute of Finance mutual fund advisor course: series 6 and series 63 test preparation / The Boston Institute of Finance.
     p. cm.
     ISBN-10 0-471-71234-5 (pbk.)
     ISBN-13 978-0-471-71234-3 (pbk.)
     1. Mutual funds—Problems, exercises, etc. I. Title.
     HG4530.B676 2005
     332.63'27' 076—dc22

                                                                    2004027075

Printed in the United States of America

10 9 8 7 6 5 4 3 2 1

CONTENTS

PREFACE

SERIES 6

The Investment Company Products/Variable Contracts Products Limited Representative Qualification Examination (Test Series 6) is a 100-question multiple-choice examination. A maximum of 135 minutes testing time is allowed for candidates to complete the examination. The passing grade is equal to 70% of the total number of questions on the examination. Candidates will be required to correctly answer 70 of the 100 questions on the examination to receive a passing grade.

The examination is administered at the PROCTOR Certification Testing Centers and the results are available immediately upon completion.

The approximate breakdown of questions on the Series 6 examination is as follows:

Investment Companies	45
Variable Contracts and Retirement Plans	25
Securities Industry Regulations	15
Investment Securities and Securities Markets	10
US Government, Money Markets, and Investment Risks	5
	100

Boston Institute's *Mutual Fund Advisor Course's* Series 6 Test Preparation is designed to prepare a candidate for the Series 6 examination. The text should be thoroughly studied by the candidate. All practice examinations should be taken and any questions answered incorrectly should be restudied. The text contains a final examination in addition to questions at the end of each chapter. However, the candidate should thoroughly study the text material and then complete the examinations. **Under no circumstances** should the candidate only do the practice questions without studying the text material.

SERIES 63

The Uniform Securities Agent State Law Examination is prepared by the North American Securities Administrators Association (NASAA) in cooperation with securities industry representatives. The examination consists of fifty multiple-choice questions. The passing score is 70% (thirty-five correct answers). One hour is allotted for the examination. The relative importance given in the examination to particular sections of the Uniform Securities Act is as follows:

20%	Definitions of Terms
15%	Licensing or Registration Requirements for Broker/Dealers, Agents, and Investment Advisors
10%	Registration of Securities; Exempt Securities and Exempt Transactions
45%	Fraudulent and Other Prohibited Practices
10%	Regulatory Oversight, Criminal Penalties, Civil Liabilities, Scope of the Act, and General Provisions

Boston Institute's *Mutual Fund Advisor Course's* Series 63 Test Preparation is designed to prepare a candidate for the Series 63 Examination. The text should be thoroughly studied by the candidate. All practice questions should be answered and any questions answered incorrectly should be restudied. **Under no circumstances** should the candidate only do the practice questions without studying the text material.

Boston Institute has a continued commitment to producing the highest-quality study material available for securities industry examinations.

We also publish study material for various other securities industry examinations. Thank you for your continued support.

Boston Institute of Finance, Inc.

SERIES 6 TEST PREPARATION

INTRODUCTION

OPEN-END INVESTMENT COMPANIES

People face investment decisions during their lifetime. They can choose to place all of their money in a bank certificate of deposit (CD) or savings account. However, this money will grow at a fixed rate of interest. Assume an individual invests $20,000 in a bank CD with a 5% interest rate. At the end of ten years, the money would have grown to approximately $32,578. However, that person would be subject to the purchasing power risk (risk of inflation) over the ten-year period. Any investment with a fixed rate of return is vulnerable to the purchasing power risk.

Assume the same person decided to invest in a growth mutual fund that had an average annual return of 11% over the ten-year period. The $20,000 would have grown to approximately $51,875 over the ten-year period. However, the CD is guaranteed by the bank and additionally by the Federal Deposit Insurance Corporation (FDIC). The investment in the mutual fund is an investment in a security that fluctuates in value. The mutual fund could decrease in value as well as increase in value. To obtain a higher rate of return, the investor must assume a higher risk than he would assume from the CD.

The investment in the mutual fund is an investment in a **security** that fluctuates on a daily basis. A mutual fund is also an **investment company** because it has a managed portfolio of securities. Assume Mr. Lynch invests $20,000 in the ABC Growth Fund, an open-end investment company. He will purchase a certain number of shares and is therefore called a shareholder in the fund. The major assets of the ABC Growth Fund are the cash and securities in its portfolio. The portfolio of the ABC Growth Fund fluctuates on a daily basis. On certain business days the portfolio increases, and on other days it decreases. At the close of business on each business day, mutual funds, such as ABC Growth Fund, computes their net asset value per share (NAVPS). The NAVPS is computed basically as follows:

$$\frac{\text{Assets} - \text{Liabilities}}{\text{Number of shares outstanding}} = \text{NAVPS}$$

Assume ABC Growth Fund's NAVPS is $14 at the close of business on Monday.

$$\frac{\$16,000,000 \text{ assets} - \$2,000,000 \text{ liabilities}}{1,000,000 \text{ shares outstanding}} = \$14$$

If the portfolio increases in value on Tuesday, the NAVPS will increase. If the portfolio decreases in value, the NAVPS will decrease. At the end of each business day, the ABC Growth Fund will publish its NAVPS and its ask price.

The ask price is the price at which an investor can purchase shares. The NAVPS is the price at which the investor can sell the shares. In both cases, the investor will buy the shares from the ABC Growth Fund and sell the shares back to the ABC Growth Fund. The ask price for an open-end investment company is also called the **public offering price** or **offering price**. The NAVPS is also referred to as the **bid price** or **redemption price**. ABC Growth Fund is an open-end investment company since the fund is "open" to continuously selling shares to investors at the ask price and to continuously buying shares from investors who redeem them at the bid price.

Open-end investment companies are sold to the public as either no-load funds or load funds. A no-load fund does not levy a sales charge or load when shares are sold the public. A no-load fund's bid and ask prices are the same. For example, a no-load fund may be shown as follows:

	(NAVPS)	
	Bid	Ask
	$12	$12

The no-load fund could also be reflected as

	(NAVPS)	
	Bid	Ask
	12	NL

NL indicates that the fund is a no-load fund. The "load" is also referred to as the sales charge or sales load. A no-load fund does not levy a sales charge, sales load, or load on the sale of its shares to the public.

A load fund does levy a sales charge on the sale of its shares to the public. Assume a load fund is reflected as follows:

(NAVPS)	Public offering price
Bid	Ask
$12	$13.11

In this example, investors purchase shares at the ask price of $13.11. An investor who redeems shares will receive the bid price (NAVPS) of $12. The difference between the bid and ask prices reflects an 8½% sales charge. The maximum sales charge that can be levied on the sale of an open-end investment company is 8½% of the offering price under National Association of Securities Dealers (NASD) rules.

$13.11   Ask price
 12.00   Bid price
$ 1.11   Sales charge (load)

$$\frac{\$1.11 \text{ sales charge}}{\$13.11 \text{ ask price}} = 8.5$$

The sales charge or load of 8.5% is shown as a percentage of the offering price. Open-end investment companies are referred to as mutual funds. Mutual funds are long-term investments because of the sales charge levied on the purchase. It is a violation of NASD rules to encourage investors to trade load funds on a short-term basis. Short-term trading of load funds would result in excessive sales loads paid by customers.

Open-end investment companies must be sold to customers by means of a prospectus, which is a written communication used to offer shares of an investment company to the public. The prospectus contains information of interest to the ordinary investor. Sales literature relating to mutual funds includes research reports, form letters, market letters, and reprints of previously published articles. Sales literature must be preceded or accompanied by a prospectus. The prospectus must be given to a prospective investor at or before the completion of the transaction. The prospectus is reviewed by the investment company and its attorney to ensure that no material information is omitted.

An investor makes a profit on his or her investment in a mutual fund if the NAVPS increases over a period of time. Assume Tom Murphy invests $15,000 in the XYZ Growth Fund on Monday, January 12, 2004, at 10:00 A.M. The investor will receive the next computed price after receipt of the order. Therefore, the order will be executed at the fund's close-of-business price on Monday, January 12, 2004. Assume Monday's close of business price for the XYZ Growth Fund is as follows:

(NAVPS)	Public offering price
Bid	Ask
$14.00	$15.30

Tom Murphy will purchase 980.392 shares computed in the following manner:

$$\frac{\$15,000}{\$15.30} = 980.392 \text{ shares}$$

To analyze this transaction, the customer invested $15,000 into the XYZ Growth Fund. However, 8½% of the total amount invested was taken out as sales charge.

$15,000   Total amount invested
− 1,275   Sales charge
$13,725   Amount invested in fund

Tom Murphy paid $15.30 per share (ask price), but only $14.00 per share was invested in the XYZ Growth Fund for the customer's benefit. As a percentage of the net amount invested in the fund, it represents 9.3%.

$$\frac{\$1.30 \text{ sales charge per share}}{\$14.00 \text{ bid price (net amount invested)}} = 9.3$$

Therefore, the sales charge on the transaction is 8.5% of the offering price, but 9.3% of the net amount invested in the fund. If the XYZ Growth Fund instead was a no-load fund, the bid price and ask price would both be $14. The customer would have purchased 1071.429 shares.

$$\frac{\$15,000}{\$14 \text{ ask price}} = 1071.429 \text{ shares}$$

With a no-load fund the entire amount invested by the customer ($15,000) would be invested in the fund for the benefit of the customer.

A mutual fund such as XYZ Growth Fund makes two types of distributions to customers. The first type of distribution is an **income distribution,** also referred to as a **dividend distribution**. A dividend distribution is paid from a fund's net investment income. A fund's net investment income is determined as follows:

+ Interest income from portfolio
+ Dividend income from portfolio
+ <u>Short-term capital gains from portfolio</u>
Total investment income

Total investment income – Total expenses = Net investment income

Total expenses are equal to the cost of portfolio management plus operating expenses.

There is no restriction on how frequently a dividend distribution can be paid to shareholders. It may be paid quarterly or semiannually. The second type of distribution a mutual fund can make is a capital gain distribution, which is paid from a fund's long-term capital gains. A long-term capital gain is a gain on an asset held more than twelve months. Capital gains distributions can be paid out by a fund only once a year.

Under Internal Revenue Service (IRS) rules, a mutual fund must distribute at least 90% of its net investment income each year to be considered a **regulated investment company**. A regulated investment company does not pay any tax on net investment income paid to shareholders. The shareholders pay the tax, not the investment company. The investment company will send a shareholder Form 1099-DIV, which designates the amount of dividend distributions and capital gains distributions paid to an investor during a calendar year.

Many investors choose to reinvest dividend distributions and capital gains distributions in additional fund shares. By reinvesting dividend and capital gains distributions, the number of shares owned by the customer in the fund increases. Also the customer's cost basis in the fund increases.

Remember Tom Murphy, who invested $15,000 in the XYZ Growth Fund in January 2004? During 2004, Tom received $1,000 in dividend distributions and $2,000 in a capital gain distribution, and both were reinvested in additional fund shares. Assume that in August 2005, Tom sells all of his shares for $32,000. During 2004, he will pay taxes on the $1,000 dividend distribution and the $2,000 capital gain distribution. The $1,000 dividend distribution will be taxed as ordinary income. The $2,000 capital gain distribution reinvested will be taxed as a long-term capital gain. When Tom sells the shares for $32,000, the gain on the sale of the XYZ Growth Fund shares is $14,000, computed as follows:

$15,000	Original investment
+ 1,000	Dividend distribution reinvested
+ <u>2,000</u>	Capital gain distribution reinvested
$18,000	Total cost
$32,000	Sales proceeds
<u>–18,000</u>	Total cost
$14,000	Long-term capital gain

BASIC INVESTMENT CONCEPTS

Mutual fund portfolios are made up of individual securities. Some investors decide to manage their own portfolio and invest in securities directly. The main types of securities an investor can choose are

- Common stock
- Preferred stock
- Bonds
- Money market instruments

Investors who buy common stock or preferred stock are considered owners in the corporation. Holders of common stock and preferred stock may receive dividends on their stock only if declared by the board of directors. The board may choose not to declare a dividend and reinvest the funds in the corporation.

An investor who purchases a bond directly is a creditor of the corporation. The owner of the bond will receive interest payments from the issuer of the bond. Interest payments on a bond is a legal obligation and must be paid by the issuer. Failure to pay interest on a bond could cause the corporation that issued the bond to go into bankruptcy. Assume an investor purchases a $1,000 par value corporate bond with a 6% interest rate due in 2017. The par value of the bond is also referred to as the **face value** or **face amount** of the bond. The interest rate on the bond is also called the **coupon rate** or the **nominal yield**. When a $1,000 par value bond with a 6% interest rate is initially issued, the nominal yield and the current yield are also 6%. To find a bond's current yield, the annual interest paid to the investor is divided by the market price of the bond.

$$\$1,000 \text{ par value x } 6\% = \$60 \text{ annual interest}$$

$$\frac{\$60 \text{ annual interest}}{\$1,000 \text{ par value}} = 6\% \text{ current yield}$$

The market price of a bond will change based on changes in interest rates. If interest rates in the economy rise, the price of bonds in the marketplace will decline. However, as the market price of a bond decreases, the yield on the bond will increase. Assume after this bond with a 6% coupon rate is issued, interest rates increase to 9%. The market value of the bond will decrease to make the yield competitive with current yields in the marketplace. The market price of the bond will decrease to $666.

$$\frac{\$60 \text{ annual interest}}{\$666 \text{ market value}} = 9\% \text{ current yield}$$

Therefore, if an investor felt that interest rates in the economy will increase over the next year, the investor should not purchase bonds. An investor who purchases a bond assumes an interest rate risk. The interest rate risk is the risk that if interest rates rise, the market price of the bond will decline. The interest rate risk on a bond is directly related to the maturity of the bond. The longer the time period to maturity, the greater the interest rate risk to the bondholder. A long-term bond also subjects the holder of the bond to a purchasing power risk. The bond pays a fixed amount of interest each year. Assume a bond has a 6% interest rate and inflation is increasing at a 4% annual rate. The real rate of return to the bondholder is only 2%.

$$6\% \text{ interest rate} - 4\% \text{ inflation rate} = 2\% \text{ real rate of return}$$

Remember, as mentioned previously, the purchaser of common stock is an owner of the corporation. A common stockholder in a corporation normally has the following rights:

- The right to receive a dividend only if it has been declared by the board of directors
- The right to vote for the board of directors
- The right to subscribe to new issues of the common stock, in order to protect their proportionate share in the corporation from being reduced
- The right to receive a portion of any residual assets upon the liquidation of the corporation

Investors may purchase common stock for capital gains purposes, to receive dividends or for both capital gains and dividends. Assume XYZ Corporation's common stock has a market value of $100 per share. XYZ Corporation's common stock presently pays a $5 annual dividend. The current yield on the common stock is 5%.

$$\frac{\$5 \text{ annual dividend}}{\$100 \text{ market price}} = 5\%$$

Assume XYZ Corporation's board of directors reduces the annual dividend to $3 per share and the market price of XYZ Corporation's common stock does not change (remains at $100 per share). The current yield on XYZ Corporation's common stock is now 3%.

$$\frac{\$3 \text{ annual dividend}}{\$100 \text{ market price}} = 3\%$$

Assume instead that the board of directors raised the annual dividend from $5 per share to $7 per share. The current yield on the common stock would be 7%.

$$\frac{\$7 \text{ annual dividend}}{\$100 \text{ market price}} = 7\%$$

Corporations normally pay dividends quarterly, but the current yield is always computed on an annual basis. For example, assume a corporation pays an annual dividend of $5 per share. The shareholder would receive four quarterly dividends of $1.25 per share.

$$\$1.25 \text{ quarterly dividend x } 4 = \$5.00 \text{ annual dividend}$$

As mentioned previously, some investors choose to manage their own securities portfolio. The investor must decide what securities to buy, and then decide if and when to sell the securities. Assume an investor has $50,000 to invest and purchases the following securities for her own portfolio:

200 shares	Coca-Cola at $80 per share	=	$16,000
500 shares	Disney at $40 per share	=	$20,000
100 shares	Microsoft at $100 per share	=	$10,000
100 shares	CVS Corporation at $40 per share	=	$ 4,000
	Total value of portfolio		$50,000

The investor will receive a customer's confirmation or confirmation statement on each of the purchases. The confirmation "confirms" the purchase of the security to the customer. The confirmation contains the complete details of the transaction such as trade date, settlement date, number of shares, and purchase price.

The management decisions relating to the portfolio will be made by the investor who owns the portfolio. However, many investors do not feel comfortable managing their own portfolio and decide to invest in a mutual fund. The managers of the mutual fund will decide what securities to buy and sell. The investor must choose the type of fund to invest in. The investor might choose a growth fund. The two main types of growth funds are conservative growth funds and aggressive growth funds. Conservative growth funds are also referred to as large capitalization funds or blue-chip funds. Securities held in the portfolio of large capitalization funds are large capitalization companies such as General Electric, Coca Cola, General Motors, Exxon Corporation, and Home Depot. Aggressive growth funds invest their portfolios in midcapitalization stocks or small capitalization stocks. Therefore, investors in aggressive growth funds take more risk in the hope of receiving higher returns. Normally, younger investors seek growth of capital and invest in large capitalization funds or aggressive growth funds.

Assume our investor decided to invest her $50,000 in the Fidelity Large Capitalization Growth Fund instead of purchasing her own portfolio. The bid price and the ask prices are stated as follows for the fund:

Bid	Ask
$15	$16

Our investor will purchase 3,125 shares in the fund computed as follows:

$$\frac{\$50,000 \text{ amount invested}}{\$16 \text{ ask price}} = 3,125 \text{ shares}$$

Assume our investor holds the fund shares for three years. At the time of the sale, the fund's bid and ask prices are as follows:

Bid	Ask
$27	$28.80

Assume the investor sells the 3,125 shares at the bid price of $27 per share. The investor will receive $84,375.

3,125 shares x $27 bid = $84,375 sales proceeds

Assuming no reinvested dividends or capital gains distributions, the investor has made a profit of $34,375.

$84,375	Sales proceeds
– 50,000	Amount invested (cost)
$34,375	Long-term capital gain

If a registered representative (RR) of a broker/dealer recommends a mutual fund to a customer under securities industry regulations, the transaction must be suitable for the customer. **Suitability** means that an investment meets the customer's investment objectives, financial situation, financial needs, and tolerance for risk.

For example, young investors normally purchase growth funds. Older investors normally invest in income funds, short-term government bond funds, or money market funds.

However, before an RR can make a recommendation to a customer, the RR should learn about the following concerning a customer in order to make the recommendation suitable:

- Net worth
- Income tax bracket
- Investment objectives
- Other investments

• Tolerance for risk

Assume an RR receives a telephone call from Ms. Flynn who has $200,000 invested in various mutual funds. She wants to invest an additional $50,000 in "something exciting." She wants the RR to make a recommendation over the telephone. The RR should determine Ms. Flynn's investment objectives, financial situation, financial needs, and risk tolerance before making any recommendation. The more financial information an RR obtains from a customer, the easier it is for the RR to make a suitable recommendation.

1 INVESTMENT SECURITIES

INTRODUCTION

Individuals seeking to invest their savings are faced with numerous financial products and degrees of risk. An individual investor can invest in a corporation as an equity owner or as a creditor. If an individual chooses to become an equity owner, he will hopefully benefit in the growth of the business. He can purchase common stock or preferred stock in the corporation.

Assume an investor purchases 1,000 shares of ABC Corporation common stock. ABC has 100,000 shares of common stock outstanding. Our investor owns 1% (1,000 divided by 100,000 = 1%) of the outstanding shares. He will receive 1% of any dividends paid by the corporation and would receive 1% of any remaining assets upon dissolution of the corporation, after all creditors have been paid.

Our investor would receive a stock certificate evidencing his ownership of 1,000 shares of common stock of ABC Corporation. He could sell his 1,000 shares, or any lesser amount, at any time. Our investor hopes to be able to sell his shares at a higher price than he paid for them. In other words, he hopes to realize a capital gain on the sale of the shares.

Our investor would also like to receive dividends on his 1,000 shares. Assume ABC pays a quarterly dividend of $0.20 per share. Our investor would receive a quarterly dividend of $200 or an annual dividend of $800. The two main reasons an investor buys stock in a corporation are

1. To receive any dividends paid by the corporation
2. To hopefully realize a capital gain on the sale of the shares

However, there is risk associated with owning stock in a corporation. If the corporation goes bankrupt, the investor will lose his entire investment, but his personal assets are not at risk. The investor's loss is limited to the amount invested in the corporation. Therefore, an investor in a corporation has limited risk.

An investor can choose to purchase a debt instrument of a corporation instead of becoming an equity owner. Assume an investor purchases a $1,000 par value 6% bond due in 2008 in ABC Corporation. In this case, our investor has become a creditor of ABC Corporation. ABC agrees to pay our investor $60 per year in annual interest. At maturity in the year 2008, ABC agrees to pay our investor the par value of $1,000. If ABC goes bankrupt, our investor would be paid off before preferred or common stockholders. However, our investor would receive only $60 per year in annual interest regardless of how profitable the corporation becomes.

These are the two basic choices facing an investor. He can choose to invest in a corporation as an equity owner or as a creditor. If a corporation becomes very profitable, an investor would benefit as an equity owner. If a corporation experiences financial difficulties, the investor would be in a better position as a creditor. We will examine in more detail an individual's rights as an equity owner and as a creditor or bondholder of a corporation.

MONEY AND CAPITAL MARKETS

There are two general markets for funds—the money market and the capital market. The **money market** refers to transactions in short-term debt instruments. Commercial banks are the chief source of such short-term funds. The demand for such funds comes from the US government, brokers, and commercial borrowers. The **capital market** refers to the market for long-term debt and equity securities.

The **prime rate** is the interest rate charged on loans made by commercial banks to their best customers (firms with good credit ratings). When interest rates on short-term securities are high enough, individual investors may withdraw their funds from financial institutions and invest directly in the money market. This process is referred to as **disintermediation**.

Money market instruments are any high-grade, liquid debt securities that will mature in one year. Money market instruments include US Treasury bills, commercial paper, bankers' acceptances, and negotiable certificates of deposit. Securities having a maturity longer than one year are normally referred to as **capital market instruments**. Capital market instruments include corporate bonds, municipal bonds, US government bonds, preferred stock, and common stock.

Assume ABC Corporation wants to issue a money market instrument. ABC Corporation would probably issue commercial paper. Commercial paper represents short-term obligations of corporations and normally has a maximum maturity of 270 days.

COMMON STOCK

Securities that evidence ownership in a corporation are called **equity securities**. They can be divided generally into two types: common stock and preferred stock.

Common stock is an equity security because it represents part ownership in a corporation. In general, it presents the greatest opportunity for capital gain to the investor. If the company prospers and grows, the value of the common stockholder's investment will increase. While the possible gain to the common stockholder is unlimited, his loss is limited to the purchase price paid for the shares.

Common stockholders in a corporation normally have rights including

- *Limited liability.* The stockholder is not liable for the losses and liabilities of a corporation and cannot lose more than what he paid for his stock.
- *Proportionate ownership.* The stockholder's ownership of the corporation is in the same proportion as his stock is to all the common stock outstanding. If a company has 100,000 shares of stock outstanding, the owner of 2,000 shares is entitled to 2% of the dividends paid to common stockholders.
- *Transfer rights.* The shareholder has the right to transfer his ownership to another party or give away the shares if he chooses.
- *Dividends.* As an owner, the stockholder may share in the profits of the corporation. Such dividends must be paid out of retained earnings and may not impair capital. Usually, the stockholders cannot force directors to declare dividends even though earnings are sufficient; but, once the directors have legally declared a cash dividend, it becomes a current liability of the corporation and its payment can be enforced by the stockholders. This right, then, is to receive dividends when, as, and if they are declared by the board of directors.
- *Preemptive rights.* When a new issue of common stock is sold, the shareholder frequently has the right to subscribe to that number of new shares permitting him to maintain his proportionate ownership in the corporation.
- *Voting.* The shareholder has the right to vote for directors of the corporation.
- *Dissolution.* The stockholder can receive his share of residual assets upon dissolution of the corporation.
- *Stock certificate.* The stockholder has the right to obtain a stock certificate evidencing his ownership in the corporation. To sell or transfer the shares, the stockholder must sign the certificate exactly as his name appears on the front. The stockholder's signature must be guaranteed by a broker/dealer or bank. The signature and guarantee must be acceptable to the transfer agent, which is normally a commercial bank.

It is important to understand how to calculate the yield on a common stock. Assume ABC Corporation's common stock is selling at $50 per share. ABC Corporation pays an annual dividend on its common stock of $2. What is the current yield on ABC Corporation's common stock?

$$\frac{\$2 \text{ annual dividend}}{\$50 \text{ market price}} = 4\% \text{ current yield}$$

Assume the dividend payment to the common stockholders of ABC Corporation is reduced to $1, but the market price of ABC's common stock does not change. The yield on the common stock will decrease to 2%.

$$\frac{\$1 \text{ annual dividend}}{\$50 \text{ market price}} = 2\% \text{ current yield}$$

Assume the board of directors of ABC Corporation increases the cash dividend to $3 per share and the market price of the common stock remains at $50. What is the current yield?

$$\frac{\$3 \text{ annual dividend}}{\$50 \text{ market price}} = 6\% \text{ current yield}$$

PREFERRED STOCK

Preferred stock is an equity that comes ahead of common stock in the payment of dividends. In the event of a liquidation, preferred stockholders are paid before common stockholders. Types of preferred stock include

- Participating preferred stock
- Cumulative preferred stock
- Convertible preferred stock

Participating preferred stock has a provision for possible payment of an extra dividend above its regular rate. This would happen if the corporation had excellent earnings in a particular year. When common stockholders have received an equal amount of dividends per share, the common and preferred stockholders split any additional dividend payments, usually on a 50–50 basis.

Cumulative preferred stock requires the corporation to pay back dividends that were missed in prior years before any dividends are paid to common stockholders.

Convertible preferred stock allows preferred stockholders to convert to common stock.

CORPORATE BONDS

Corporate bonds issued by a corporation normally have a par value of $1,000. Assume a corporation issues a $1,000 par value bond with an interest rate of 7% maturing in the year 2000. The investor is a creditor of the corporation and is entitled to be paid $70 annual interest and to receive $1,000 when the bond matures in the year 2000.

The investor can sell the bond prior to maturity if he chooses. Corporate bonds pay interest semiannually. Our investor would receive $35 every six months or an annual interest payment of $70. Corporate bonds are long-term liabilities of a corporation.

Corporate bonds are a form of debt and are a promise on the part of the corporation to pay a sum of money (usually $1,000) at a specified future date along with interest payments (usually semiannually) to the holder. Failure on the part of the corporation to make these payments on time is considered to be a default, and the holder of the bonds has the right to take legal action to force the company to fulfill its promises. These bonds are originally sold with a maturity, or due date, of five, ten, or even thirty years in the future. Corporate bonds normally are issued with a par value (face value) face amount of $1,000. Interest on corporate bonds is subject to all income taxes (federal, state, and local).

There are three types of value referred to in discussing bonds.

1. **Par value** (face value) is the amount stated on the face of the bond, which is normally $1,000.
2. **Market value** is the price at which a bond is selling in the marketplace.
3. **Redemption value** (maturity value) is the price at which the bond will be paid off at maturity.

Bonds are not usually quoted in dollars but in eighths as a percentage of face value. Thus, a $1,000 bond would be quoted at 100 when sold at par. Corporate bonds are quoted in points. Each point for a $1,000 bond represents $10 or 1% of par value. Bonds that sell for a price greater than par are said to be selling at a premium. Thus, a $1,000 par value bond quoted at 102¾ would sell for $1,027.50—$27.50 or 2¾% more than par. Bonds that sell for less than par are said to sell at a discount. Thus a $1,000 par value bond quoted at 92½ would sell for $925.00—a 7½% discount from par.

Quote	Market price	Relationship to par
120⅝	$1,206.25	Premium
100	$1,000.00	Par
98¾	$ 987.50	Discount

Assume a bond is quoted at 97⅞. Find its dollar price. A quote of 97⅞ represents 97 full points plus ⅞ of a point, or $978.75.

97 full points	x	$10	=	$970.00
⅞ point	x	$10	=	8.75
				$978.75

Assume a bond is quoted at 103¾. Find its dollar price. A quote of 103¾ represents 103 full points plus ¾ of a point, or $1,037.50.

103 full points	x	$10	=	$1,030.00
¾ point	x	$10	=	7.50
				$1,037.50

To change a bond quote to a dollar amount, an investor can use the point method, as previously illustrated, or calculate it as a percentage of par value. Both calculations will result in the same amount. For example, assume a bond is quoted at 84½. Find the dollar amount at which the bond is selling.

<u>Point method</u>

84 full points	x $10	=	$840.00
½ point	x $10	=	5.00
			$845.00

<u>Percentage of par method</u>
84½% of $1,000 = 0.845 x $1,000 = $845

Other Types of Corporate Bonds

Other types of corporate bonds include

- Mortgage bonds
- Collateral trust bonds
- Equipment trust certificates
- Debenture bonds
- Subordinated debentures
- Guaranteed bonds
- Income bonds

Mortgage bonds are secured by mortgages on real estate. **Collateral trust bonds** are secured by assets other than real estate, normally by marketable securities. **Equipment trust certificates** are issued by transportation companies and are secured by liens on equipment (airplanes, railroad cars, trucks). **Debenture bonds** are unsecured. They are not secured by any specific assets and are backed only by the full faith and credit of the company itself. **Subordinated debentures** are subordinated in their claim on the assets of the corporation. Subordinated debentures are the last type of debt that would be paid off before preferred stockholders and common stockholders. **Guaranteed bonds** are bonds in which the payment of principal and interest is guaranteed by another corporation. **Income bonds** are bonds in which interest payments are made only if the corporation's earnings are sufficient. If the earnings are not sufficient, interest payments on the income bonds will not be made by the issuer.

CONVERTIBLE BONDS

Convertible bonds are convertible into common stock according to the terms stated in the indenture. Convertible bonds in many instances are issued as convertible debentures.

Convertible bonds may reduce the cost of capital to the corporation since it may be possible to sell bonds more easily and at a lower interest rate if an attractive conversion feature is added. This results in an interest saving to the corporation.

The conversion price is the amount of par value exchangeable for one share of common stock; that is, if the conversion price is $50 and the par value is $1,000, it means the holder of the bond will receive 20 shares if he converts). In this example, the conversion ratio is 20 to 1.

$$\frac{\$1,000 \text{ par value}}{\$50 \text{ price convertible at}} = \text{20-to-1 conversion ratio}$$

The face amount of the bond (par value) determines the value of the conversion privilege relating to a convertible bond. The parity price is the price the stock must sell at to be on exact equality with the bond. For example, if the bond above was selling at $1,200, the parity price would be found by dividing the market price by the number of shares into which the bond could be converted.

$$\frac{\$1,200 \text{ market price}}{\text{\# of shares received on conversion}} = \frac{1,200}{20} = \$60 \text{ parity price}$$

ZERO COUPON BONDS

In recent years, a new type of bond called a **zero coupon bond** has become a popular investment. Zero coupon bonds could be corporate, US government or municipal bonds. However, we will describe zero coupon Treasury bonds, which are very popular.

A zero coupon bond is purchased by an investor at a deep discount price, and the bond pays all of its interest at maturity. The difference between the discount price paid by the investor and the value received by the investor at maturity represents the interest received on the bond.

Assume an investor buys a zero coupon Treasury bond $1,000 principal value with fifteen years to maturity. This zero coupon bond costs the investor $189.23. The yield to maturity for the investor is 12%. For an investment of $189.23 the investor will receive $1,000 in fifteen years. However, the Internal Revenue Service (IRS) states that the owner is receiving an annual return on the bond, but the income is being reinvested at the implied yield instead of being paid out. This results in taxable income to the investor even though no money is received by the investor.

Zero coupon bonds are good investments for tax-sheltered vehicles such as individual retirement accounts (IRAs) or Keogh plans. They are available in various maturities and discount prices. Also available are zero coupon municipal bonds on which imputed interest is free from taxation.

Higher-quality debt issues of the same face value, maturity, and coupon, when compared to low-quality debt issues, have lower yields and higher market prices. The reason is that investors are willing to purchase high-quality, low-risk bonds for a lower yield than they would require for lower-grade bonds with greater uncertainty. A lower-quality bond will have a lower market price and higher yield than a higher-quality bond.

INTEREST RATE RISK

The interest rate risk on a bond is the risk that if interest rates rise the market value of the bond will decrease. Assume an investor purchases a $1,000 par value ABC corporate bond with an 8% interest rate maturing in 2018 at par value. If interest rates rise to 10%, the market price of the bond will decrease to $800. The bond will now yield 10%, which will equal the yield of new bonds being issued. The bondholder has an unrealized capital loss of $200. However, if the bondholder holds the bond to maturity in the year 2018, he will receive $1,000. If interest rates rise, bond prices will fall and the yield on the bond will increase. If interest rates fall, bond prices will rise and the yield on the bond will fall. Also, long-term bonds will rise or fall more with changes in interest rates than short-term bonds.

YIELDS

There are three types of yield calculations relating to bonds.

1. *Nominal yield.* This is sometimes referred to as the coupon rate. It is the interest rate printed on the bond. If a bond states on its face that it will pay 6% per year, then the nominal yield is also 6%.
2. *Current yield.* The market value of bonds will fluctuate with changes in interest rates in the economy and the changing attitudes of investors. The face rate of interest—the actual amount of interest paid—will not change. If the bond is a 4% $1,000 par value bond, it will pay $40 per year in interest. If it is a 6% bond, it will pay $60 per year. But if the market value of the bond fluctuates, the current yield will differ from the coupon rate on the bond.

   If the bond pays $40 per annum interest and the bond is currently selling for $950, then the current yield is 4.2% or slightly above the coupon rate of 4%. If the market price was $1,060, the current yield would be 3.77%
3. *Yield to maturity.* The yield to maturity determines the rate of return a bondholder would receive, if the bond is held to the maturity date. The yield-to-maturity calculation on a bond takes into consideration the gain or loss on the principal, in addition to the annual interest paid on the bond.

RIGHTS

Rights are commonly used when a corporation wishes to raise funds through the sale of additional common stock. Rights are also called **subscription rights** because the holder has the right to subscribe to a new issue at less than the present market price. Because the holder of common stock frequently has the right, often referred to as the **preemptive right,** to maintain his proportionate position in the equity of a corporation, a corporation will often sell stock to its own stockholders through a privileged subscription or a preemptive rights offering.

To summarize key points to remember concerning rights

- They allow a common stockholder to subscribe to a new issue of common stock before it is offered to the public. If the stockholder does not subscribe to the new issue of common stock, his proportionate ownership is reduced.

- They normally have a life span of two to four weeks and then expire worthless. They cannot be exercised after they expire.
- They are freely transferable and may be sold by the owner instead of being exercised.

WARRANTS

A warrant is a long-term option to buy stock at a fixed price from the issuing corporation. A warrant allows the holder to obtain shares of the corporation at a fixed price for a certain number of years. The fixed price is normally set initially above the current market price of the stock. However, if the price of the corporation's stock increases, the holder of the warrant will realize a profit.

COLLATERALIZED MORTGAGE OBLIGATIONS

Collateralized mortgage obligations (CMOs) were created to solve a major disadvantage of Government National Mortgage Association (GNMA) certificates, which is an unpredictable maturity. CMOs avoid this problem by dividing their pool of mortgages into separate securities with different maturities. Interest and principal payments are first applied to the security with the shortest maturity. When the shortest maturity is retired, payments are made to the next maturity until all the securities are retired.

CMOs are debt securities collateralized by a portfolio of other securities such as a portfolio of GNMA modified pass-throughs. CMOs are normally issued in denominations of $1,000. They pay interest on a semiannual basis, as well as semiannual partial repayments of principal.

CMOs normally separate mortgage pools into short-, medium-, and long-term portions. The different time frames the mortgage pools are split into are called **tranches**. The greater certainty of the payment size is offset by slightly lower yields to investors, compared with ordinary pass-through securities.

INTEREST RATES AND BOND CONCEPTS

A clear distinction must be made between the rate of interest on a bond and its yield. The interest rate is stated on the bond and indicates the amount the owner of the bond will receive periodically from the issuer. If the interest rate is 8%, the holder will receive $80 per year. However, the yield to maturity on this bond is the relation of the total interest that will be received, plus any capital gain on the investment, to the average amount invested until the bond matures. Obviously, if the interest rate is 8% but the purchaser pays only $900 for the bond, the yield to maturity will be greater than 8%.

There is an inverse relationship between interest rates and bond prices. The market price of outstanding bonds declines when interest rates rise and increases when interest rates decline. This permits the yield on these outstanding bonds to equal (or at least approach equal yields) the yield on newly issued bonds with higher or lower interest rates.

Short-term interest rates respond more quickly and fluctuate over a wider range than long-term interest rates. The same can also be said for the fluctuation of yields on short-term issues compared to yields on long-term issues. The price of long-term bonds is more greatly affected by a change in the level of interest rates than is the price of short-term bonds. The longer a bond has before maturity, the greater the leverage effect of a shift in the level of interest rates on its price. For a specific change in yields, the fluctuation in the market prices of bonds will be greater the longer the period to maturity. If interest rates rise, the price of long-term bonds falls more than the price of short-term bonds. If interest rates fall, the price of long-term bonds increases more than the price of short-term bonds.

To minimize the interest rate risk in a bond portfolio, an investor should purchase bonds with short maturities. Bonds are also subject to the purchasing power risk or the inflationary risk. If an investor purchases an investment-grade bond, the risk of default is not high. However, he will be taking a purchasing power risk. Assume the investment-grade bond has ten years remaining to maturity. When the investor receives the principal amount in ten years, the purchasing power of the dollars received will be less.

All new issues of US government, federal agency, municipal and corporate bonds are now being issued in fully registered or book-entry form only, as a result of changes in federal tax law. However, many bearer bonds and bonds registered as to principal only are outstanding and will be for many years. If a bond is described as **safe,** this means that interest and principal will be paid on time.

If there is an increase in current yields on outstanding bonds, it is normally a result of

- A decrease in the market prices of currently traded bonds
- An increase in general interest rate levels

If a corporate bond is selling at a premium over par value, the current yield on the bond is less than the nominal yield. Assume an investor purchases a corporate bond with a par value of $1,000 in the marketplace and pays $1,200 for the bond. The interest rate on the bond is 5%. Therefore, the nominal yield on the bond is 5%, since the nominal yield is the same as the interest rate stated on the face of the bond. However, the current yield on the bond is 4.2%.

$$\frac{\$50 \text{ annual interest}}{\$1,200 \text{ market price}} = 4.2\%$$

Therefore, we have proven that a corporate bond selling at a premium has a current yield less than its nominal yield.

A convertible bond may be converted by the bondholder into shares of the same company's common stock. Assume a convertible bond has a par value of $1,000 and a conversion price of $50. The par value of the bond is also referred to as the face amount of the bond. To determine how many shares of common stock the bondholder will receive on conversion, divide the conversion price into the par value or face amount.

$$\frac{\$1,000 \text{ par value (face amount)}}{\$50 \text{ conversion price}} = 20 \text{ to } 1$$

In this example, the bondholder will receive twenty shares of common stock for each $1,000 par value bond converted.

Assume a corporate bond is quoted in the marketplace at 104¾. This represents a dollar price for the corporate bond of $1,047.50.

$$
\begin{array}{lllll}
104 \text{ points} & \text{x} & \$10 & = & \$1,040.00 \\
\text{¾ point} & \text{x} & \$10 & = & \underline{7.50} \\
& & & & \$1,047.50
\end{array}
$$

This corporate bond is trading at a premium (above par value of $1,000). If a corporate bond was trading at 87⅝, its dollar price would be $876.25. A corporate bond selling at less than par value is trading at a "discount." Therefore, a corporate bond trading in the marketplace is trading at a "premium," at "par value," or at a "discount from par value."

US GOVERNMENT SECURITIES

The main types of marketable US government securities available to investors are

- US Treasury bills
- US Treasury notes
- US Treasury bonds
- Federal agency bonds

Treasury bills are short-term direct obligations of the federal government. They offer an investor an extremely liquid investment of the highest quality. Treasury bills bear no interest and the holder does not receive an interest check. They are sold at auction at a discount from par. They are marketable but not redeemable until maturity. The interest received is the difference between the discounted price paid and par, and is taxed as ordinary income. The lower the price of the bills, the higher the yield to maturity. Treasury bills are an excellent choice for a person who wants to invest funds in a high-quality security for one year or less. Treasury notes and Treasury bonds are direct obligations of the US government and are normally issued at par value with an interest rate on the note or bond. Treasury notes have a maturity of two to ten years. Treasury bonds have a maturity of over ten years.

Federal agency bonds (federal agency issues) are issued by various government agencies such as the GNMA (Ginnie Mae) and Federal National Mortgage Association (FNMA—Fannie Mae). Federal agency bonds are considered low-risk investments and are not backed by the US government. Ginnie Mae obligations are an exception to the rule since they are backed by the US government.

The two main types of nonmarketable government bonds are Series EE and Series HH savings bonds.

Series EE bonds are nonmarketable and nontransferrable and cannot be used as collateral for a loan. They can be purchased at most banks and post offices and can be redeemed wherever they are sold. They can be registered in the name of one person, in the names of two co-owners, or in the name of one person and a beneficiary who will automatically become the owner if the registered owner dies. They are purchased at discount from par, with denominations ranging from $50 to $10,000. For Series EE bonds, yields are scaled down in the early years to encourage purchasers to hold them to maturity.

Series HH bonds are similar to Series EE bonds except that they are sold at face value and interest is paid semiannually by check. They are redeemable at par any time after the first six months, but, like Series EE bonds, the actual yield increases the longer they are held. Interest is paid by the US Treasury semiannually.

MUNICIPAL BONDS

Municipal bonds are popular with investors since interest paid is exempt from federal income taxes but may be subject to state income taxes. Municipal bonds may be issued by

- States
- Counties
- Cities
- Towns
- Turnpike authorities
- Port authorities

The main types of municipal bonds are general obligation bonds, and revenue bonds. **General obligation bonds** are backed by the full faith and credit of the issuer. **Revenue municipal bonds** are backed by a specific municipal enterprise, such as a toll bridge or a turnpike. The after-tax yield on a municipal bond is an important concept for a municipal bond investor to understand. Assume an investor is in the 28% tax bracket and purchases a municipal bond yielding 3.7%. What is the investor's after-tax yield on the municipal bond? To find the after-tax yield on the municipal bond, the formula is

$$\frac{\text{Yield on municipal bond}}{100\% - \text{person's tax bracket rate}} = \text{After-tax yield}$$

$$\frac{\text{Yield on municipal bond}}{100\% - \text{Tax bracket rate}} = \frac{.037}{100\% - 28\%} = \frac{.037}{72} = 5.1\% \text{ after-tax yield}$$

Therefore, an investor would have to obtain a 5.1% yield from a taxable bond to be in the same after-tax position as a 3.7% yield from a municipal bond. This is true because the return on a municipal bond is tax-exempt, while the return from a corporate bond or US government bond is taxable.

MONEY MARKET INSTRUMENTS

The main types of money market instruments available to investors, other than US Treasury bills, include

- Bankers' acceptances
- Commercial paper
- Negotiable certificates of deposit (CDs)

Bankers' Acceptances

These short-term instruments are used primarily to finance international trade. A buyer of goods draws an order on his bank instructing the bank to pay a specified amount at a specified time to the seller. The bank which accepts this draft is, in effect, guaranteeing it. The seller of the goods can present this draft at his own bank and receive payment in full, minus a discount reflecting current short-term interest rates. Acceptances, then, trade in the secondary market at a discount and are purchased by investors who receive payment in full from the accepting bank at maturity date. The accepting bank charges a fee for this guarantee, but runs only a small risk, since the seller's bank has already forwarded draft and shipping documents to the acceptor.

Commercial Paper

These securities are unsecured promissory notes issued with maturities from 30 to 270 days. Notes are issued from $5,000 to $5 million or more. Other corporations, commercial banks, insurance companies, and mutual funds are major purchasers. This paper is frequently issued by finance companies, and major finance companies sometimes place the paper directly with the purchaser instead of selling it in the marketplace. These securities are issued both directly by borrowers to the lenders and indirectly through dealers who underwrite the paper and, in turn, sell it to ultimate lenders. Commercial paper is normally issued at a discount from par.

Commercial paper is the most common money market instrument issued by a corporation to borrow money on a short-term basis.

Negotiable Certificates of Deposit

These are negotiable certificates issued by banks in return for time deposits. They have been issued in amounts ranging from $100,000 to $1 million. The minimum amount must be $100,000 to be traded in the money market. The maturity is normally negotiated directly between the purchaser of the CD (actually the depositor or lender) and the bank. If the holder of the CD needs his funds before maturity date, he can sell this instrument in the open market since it is negotiable.

INTERBANK MARKET FOR FOREIGN CURRENCIES

Major banks throughout the world trade American dollars and foreign currencies on a daily basis. The interbank market for foreign currencies is a decentralized market. The market is essentially free from government regulation. Trading in the interbank market for foreign currencies is normally conducted in large amounts ($1 million to $5 million).

It is common for central banks of leading industrial nations to take actions that affect their own currencies and other currencies. For example, if the American dollar is falling in relation to the German mark and Japanese yen, central banks might buy American dollars. The Bank of Japan might sell billions of yen in exchange for American dollars. The US Federal Reserve, the central bank of Germany and Britain, might also sell yen or marks in exchange for American dollars.

Assume the American dollar declines from 158.6 yen to 121.2 yen and from 1.95 marks to 1.57 marks. The top officials of the US Treasury and the Federal Reserve Board decide to intervene and stop the falling dollar. The New York Federal Reserve Bank will buy dollars in exchange for yen or marks by placing orders with large banks or foreign currency traders in the US or overseas. If the Federal Reserve is short of yen or marks to carry out the deal, it will borrow them from the Japanese or German central banks and repay them at a later date. The Federal Reserve, by placing the order to purchase dollars, raises the demand for dollars and raises the supply of yen or marks. This action tends to boost the price of American dollars in relation to the Japanese yen and the German mark.

The Federal Reserve must be careful since interest rates tend to increase when the central banks purchase dollars and take money out of circulation. Central bank intervention will not turn the dollar upward for long if economic and political events have convinced banks, businesses, investors, and speculators that the currency will lose buying power in the future.

At certain times, the US dollar is said to be "cheap." This means that the exchange rate allows more dollars to be purchased for a given amount of foreign currency.

EURODOLLAR BONDS

Eurodollar bonds are bonds issued by American or European corporations outside of the United States. Interest and principal on these bonds is paid in Eurodollars, not in any foreign currency. Eurodollars are American dollars held on deposit in banks in European countries.

Eurodollar bonds are *not* registered with the Securities and Exchange Commission (SEC) and, therefore, cannot be initially offered for sale in the United States. Eurodollar bonds are normally sold at lower than US interest rates. Eurodollar bonds could be issued by American corporations, foreign corporations, domestic and international banks, and foreign governments.

ADDITIONAL CONCEPTS

If an investor wants to become an owner in a corporation, the investor can purchase preferred stock or common stock. The investor will receive dividends on the preferred stock or common stock, only if the dividends are declared by the board of directors. Preferred stock comes ahead of common stock in the payment of dividends and has a claim on the assets prior to common stockholders. (See Exhibit 1.1.) In a liquidation, creditors are always paid off ahead of owners. Secured creditors are paid off prior to general creditors, and preferred stockholders are paid off prior to common stockholders.

Exhibit 1.1: Order of payment in corporate liquidation

1. Taxes
2. Secured creditors
3. Bank loans, accounts payable, debentures, and other unsecured debt

4. Subordinated debentures
5. Preferred stock
6. Common stock

If an investor purchases a corporate bond, the investor is a creditor of the corporation. Assume an investor purchases a $1,000 par value ABC Corporation bond with a 6% interest rate maturing in the year 2012. The par value of the bond is also called the face value or face amount of the bond. The interest rate on the bond is also referred to as the **nominal yield** or **coupon rate** of the bond.

The ABC Corporation is obligated to pay the bondholder $60 a year in annual interest ($1,000 x 6%). To find the annual interest paid on the bond, the par value of the bond is multiplied by the interest rate on the bond.

$1,000 par value x 6% = $60 annual interest
(face value)
(face amount)

There is a major difference between the annual interest paid on the bond and the current yield on the bond. If the bond is selling at par value, the current yield on the bond will be exactly equal to the nominal yield or interest rate on the bond.

$$\frac{\$60 \text{ annual interest}}{\$1,000 \text{ par value}} \quad = \quad 6\% \text{ current yield}$$

When this bond is selling at par value, the current yield, nominal yield, and interest rate stated on the face of the bond are all at 6%. However, the market price of bonds fluctuates in the marketplace. As the market price of a bond decreases, its current yield increases. As the market price of a bond increases, its current yield decreases.

Assume the market price of this bond decreases to $900. The current yield on the bond will increase to 6.7%.

$$\frac{\$60 \text{ annual interest}}{\$900 \text{ market price}} \quad = \quad 6.7\%^*$$

6.66% rounded to 6.7%

Notice that the nominal yield and the interest rate on the bond is still 6%. However, the current yield on the bond is now 6.7%. If the market price of the bond increased to $1,100, the current yield on the bond would be 5.5%. The market price of a bond will change as a result of changes in interest rates. If interest rates rise, bond prices will fall. As the price of a bond falls, its current yield will increase. If interest rates fall, bond prices will rise. However, as the price of a bond rises, its current yield will decrease.

Assume an investor buys a AAA-rated $1,000 par value corporate bond of XYZ Corporation with a 7% interest rate maturing in 2015. A corporate bond rated "AAA" means that the corporation's financial condition is excellent and the default risk is extremely low. However, the purchaser of this bond is taking two risks.

1. Interest rate risk
2. Purchasing power risk

The **interest rate risk** is the risk that rising interest rates will cause the market price of the bond to decrease. The **purchasing power risk** is the inflationary risk. The investor will receive $70 a year in annual interest. However, if inflation is 3%, the real rate of return on the bond is 4% (7% interest rate – 3% inflation). Also, when the investor receives the $1,000 return of principal in the year 2015, the $1,000 will buy less as a result of inflation. A $1,000 par value bond of XYZ Corporation with a 7% interest rate maturing in the year 2015 would be listed in the financial pages of a newspaper as follows:

XYZ Corporation 7s15

The name of the corporation is listed, followed by the interest rate and maturity. The number "7" refers to the interest rate on the bond. The "s" is used to make a space between the interest rate and the maturity. The number "15" refers to the bond's maturing in the year 2015. The issuer is obligated to pay the bondholder $70 a year in annual interest and to pay the $1,000 principal to the bondholder in the year 2015.

REVIEW QUESTIONS

1. Which of the following is true concerning warrants?
   a. They are often issued with common stock as a method of reducing the interest rate associated with the issue.
   b. They are considered to be good quality investments even if the corporation's common stock is considered to be speculative.
   c. They are securities that may cause outstanding shares to decrease.
   d. They are long-term options to buy stock at a fixed price from the issuing corporation.

2. XYZ Corporation wants to issue a money market instrument. It would probably issue which one of the following?
   a. Treasury bill
   b. Commercial paper
   c. Bankers' acceptance
   d. Common stock

3. Common stockholders have all of the following rights **except**
   a. To vote for directors
   b. To receive their residual share of assets on dissolution
   c. To receive dividends annually
   d. To subscribe to new issues proportionately

4. Fluctuations in corporate earnings will normally have the greatest effect on the price of a corporation's
   a. Debentures
   b. First mortgage bonds
   c. Preferred stock
   d. Common stock

5. Which of the following are money market instruments?

   I. Negotiable certificates of deposit
   II. Bankers' acceptances
   III. Commercial paper
   IV. US Treasury bills

   a. I and II
   b. III and IV
   c. I, II, and IV
   d. All of the above

6. Which of the following bonds have yields scaled down in early years to encourage purchasers to hold them to maturity?
   a. Treasury bonds
   b. Commercial paper
   c. Series EE bonds
   d. Federal agency bonds

7. Municipal bonds are issued by which of the following?

   I. Turnpike authorities
   II. States
   III. Counties
   IV. Cities

   a. I and II
   b. III and IV
   c. I, III, and IV
   d. All of the above

8. Which of the following debt obligations are backed by the full faith and credit of the issuer?
   a. Revenue bonds
   b. General obligation bonds
   c. Common stock
   d. Preferred stock

9. Assume an investor in the 28% tax bracket purchases a municipal bond yielding 4.8%. What is the investor's after-tax yield on the municipal bond?
   a.   4.8%
   b.   6.7%
   c.   9.6%
   d.   11.5%

10. Which of the following bonds pays all of its interest in one payment at maturity?
   a.   US treasury bonds
   b.   Corporate bonds
   c.   General obligation bonds
   d.   Zero coupon bonds

11. If a corporate bond with a 7% nominal yield has a current yield of 5.6%, the bond is selling at
   a.   A discount
   b.   A premium
   c.   A substantial premium
   d.   Par value

12. If a corporate bond with a 6% nominal yield has a current yield of 7.4%, the bond is selling at
   a.   A discount
   b.   A premium
   c.   A substantial premium
   d.   Par value

13. A corporate bond is quoted at 102. The corporate bond is selling at
   a.   A discount
   b.   A deep discount
   c.   Par
   d.   A premium

14. A customer owns a corporate bond with a 9% coupon rate and a $1,000 par value. The bond is quoted at 103. What is the current yield on the bond?
   a.   8.7%
   b.   9.0%
   c.   10.3%
   d.   12.6%

15. Which of the following bonds are issued by cities, towns, states, and counties?
   a.   Corporate
   b.   Municipal
   c.   US government
   d.   Federal agencies

16. Assume XYZ Corporation's common stock is selling at $40 per share. The annual dividend on XYZ's common stock is raised from $1 per share to $2 per share and the market price of the stock remains the same. Which of the following statements is true?
   a.   The yield on the common stock will increase.
   b.   The yield on the common stock will decrease moderately.
   c.   The yield on the commons stock will remain the same.
   d.   The yield on the common stock will decrease substantially.

17. Corporate bonds are normally issued with a par value or face amount of
   a. $ 1,000
   b. $ 10,000
   c. $ 50,000
   d. $100,000

18. Assume a customer purchases a $1,000 par value corporate bond with a 7% interest rate. The current market value of the bond is $920. What is the current yield of the bond?
   a.   7.0%
   b.   7.6%
   c.   10.0%
   d.   13.1%

19. Assume an investor in the 28% tax bracket purchases a municipal bond yielding 4.9%. What is the investor's after-tax yield on the municipal bond?

    a.   3.5%

    b.   4.9%

    c.   6.8%

    d.   17.5%

20. If interest rates in the economy increase substantially, what will be the effect on the price of long-term bonds?

    a.   They will not be affected in any way.

    b.   They will increase in price.

    c.   They will decrease in price.

    d.   They will increase in price substantially and then gradually decrease.

21. The New York Chicken Corporation went bankrupt. Place the following in order of payment in a corporate liquidation.

    I. Preferred stockholders

    II. General creditors

    III. Common stockholders

    IV. Secured creditors

    a.   IV, I, II, III

    b.   II, IV, I, III

    c.   I, II, III, IV

    d.   IV, II, I, III

22. A corporate bond listed in the newspaper as "IBM 6¼s14" means that the bond has an

    a.   Interest rate of 14% and matures in 2006

    b.   Interest rate of 6¼% and matures in 2014

    c.   Interest rate of 6¼% and no maturity date

    d.   Interest rate of 14% and no maturity date

ANSWERS TO REVIEW QUESTIONS

1. d	5. d	9. b	13. d	17. a	21. d
2. b	6. c	10. d	14. a	18. b	22. b
3. c	7. d	11. b	15. b	19. c	
4. d	8. b	12. a	16. a	20. c	

SECURITIES MARKETS

INTRODUCTION

Securities trading in the United States takes place on stock exchanges and in over-the-counter (OTC) markets. Stock exchanges, such as the New York Stock Exchange (NYSE), are in a central location where trading occurs on an auction market basis. Bids and offers are called out on the floor of the exchange and public buy and sell orders are executed. Trading occurs around a specialist, who is a stock exchange member. The specialist must make sure that an orderly trading market exists in a security.

Trading in the OTC market is done on a negotiated basis through competing market makers. The OTC securities market is decentralized and consists of brokerage firms trading with each other by telephone or computer. Investors can compare prices among the competing market makers to obtain the best price for a security. OTC securities are divided into those that are traded on NASDAQ and those that are not. NASDAQ is an automated quotation system operated by the National Association of Securities Dealers (NASD). The highest-quality OTC securities are quoted on the NASDAQ system. The more speculative OTC securities are not traded on NASDAQ. Trading on stock exchanges and in the OTC market represents secondary market trading of securities, which refers to trading between public investors and market makers in securities that are already outstanding. The NASD regulates the OTC securities market, and the stock exchanges regulate trading on their individual exchanges.

In the new issue market, primary securities offerings take place. For example, a corporation such as General Motors sells securities to an investment banker. The investment banker reoffers the securities to public investors. In a **firm-commitment underwriting,** the investment banker buys the securities from the issuing corporation and takes the risk on resale of the securities. In a **best-efforts underwriting,** the investment banker acts as agent for the issuing corporation in the distribution. There is more risk to the investment banking firm on a firm-commitment underwriting than a best-efforts underwriting. An **all-or-none underwriting** requires the issuer to sell all of the shares or the underwriting is canceled. A **standby underwriting** occurs when the investment banker "stands by" and purchases any securities not purchased by stockholders in a rights offering.

TYPES OF INVESTMENT RISK

The main types of investment risk facing investors purchasing securities include

- Business/credit risk
- Purchasing power risk
- Interest rate risk
- Market risk (systematic risk)
- Social and political risk
- Currency exchange risk

The **business/credit risk** is the risk that an issuer of securities will not make interest or principal payments when they are due and is also referred to as the **default risk, business risk,** or **financial risk**. An investor can minimize the credit risk by investing in high-quality securities such as

- US Treasury bills, notes, or bonds
- Most federal agency issues
- AAA- or AA-rated municipal bonds
- AAA- or AA-rated corporate bonds

An investor would be taking considerable risk investing in

- New issues of unseasoned companies
- Highly speculative growth stocks
- Low-rated corporate or municipal bonds

The **purchasing power risk,** also referred to as the **inflationary risk,** is the risk that money will lose its purchasing power over time. Fixed-income securities are most susceptible to the purchasing power risk. (See Exhibit 2.1.)

Exhibit 2.1: Purchasing power risk (inflationary risk)

Investments most susceptible include

Savings accounts
Life insurance
Series EE and HH bonds
Face-amount certificates
Fixed annuities
US government, municipal, and corporate bonds
Certificates of deposit

Investments less susceptible include

Common stocks (especially growth stocks)
Variable annuities
Growth mutual funds

Assume an investor purchases a AAA corporate bond in ABC Corporation. The ABC corporate bond has a $1,000 par value with a 7% interest rate and has a maturity of ten years. The investor purchases the bond at par value. Each year the bond will pay $70 in annual interest. At maturity, the investor will receive his $1,000, which is a return of his principal.

Since the bond is rated AAA, the investor is not taking a credit risk. However, the investor is taking a significant purchasing power risk. When the investor receives his $1,000 in ten years, it will certainly buy less in goods and services. The fixed-interest payments are also susceptible to inflation. Assume the inflation rate in the economy is 4%. The real interest rate is the current interest rate minus the inflation rate. The bond has a current interest rate of 7% minus the inflation rate of 4%. This gives the investor a real interest rate or real rate of return of 3% on the bond.

Any investments with a fixed rate of return are vulnerable to inflation. Savings accounts; certificates of deposit; US government, municipal, and corporate bonds; and fixed annuities are examples of investments that are affected by the purchasing power risk.

Common stock is an investment that is least susceptible to the purchasing power risk. Assume an investor purchases 100 shares of XYZ Corporation at $65 per share. XYZ is a high-quality security. The XYZ common stock pays an annual dividend of $3.20. The current yield of XYZ's common stock is

$$\frac{\$3.20 \text{ annual dividend}}{\$65 \text{ market price}} = 4.9\% \text{ current yield}$$

The **interest rate risk** is the risk that rising interest rates will cause the market price of debt obligations to decline. The interest rate risk affects debt obligations such as US government bonds, corporate bonds, and municipal bonds. The interest rate risk has a greater impact on long-term bonds than on short-term bonds. If interest rates in the economy rise, the long-term bonds fall more in price than short-term bonds. If interest rates in the economy fall, long-term bonds rise more in price than short-term bonds.

In order to minimize the interest rate risk, an investor can purchase short-term securities. Assume an investor buys $10,000 of US Treasury bills maturing in three months. The interest rate risk associated with this investment is very small. The investor purchases the Treasury bills at a discount from par value and receives full face value at maturity.

Assume a customer invests in a municipal bond unit investment trust, which invests only in high-quality bonds with long-term maturities. Assume there is a substantial change in general interest rates. The portfolio will exhibit the following characteristics:

• The market value will fluctuate substantially
• Investment income will remain relatively stable

The **market** or **systematic risk** an investor faces is the risk of a decline in the price of securities because of a general falling market. Investors have certain choices to make when building an investment portfolio. How many different securities should be purchased and how many shares of each security? Diversification can lessen risk in a portfolio. However, diversification cannot completely reduce risk. Certain investment periods have been very difficult for investors. During these periods, the general stock market has declined and investors have experienced losses. Market or systematic risk refers to the risk of loss because of a general decline in the stock market.

Social and political risks are risks associated with possible adverse government legislation or by changing social factors. The **currency exchange risk** is the risk of incurring a loss on foreign currency exchanges. Foreign securities are susceptible to the exchange risk.

ECONOMIC FACTORS

The US government attempts to control and influence the economy by means of fiscal and monetary policy. **Fiscal policy** relates to the government's influence on the economy through federal taxation and spending programs and is controlled by Congress. **Monetary policy** refers to the government's attempt to control the money supply and is handled by the Federal Reserve System.

The **Federal Reserve System** attempts to influence the level of interest rates to help meet the goals of the government. The goals of fiscal policy and monetary policy are maximum growth with full employment and low inflation. Increasing interest rates tend to slow down the economy, and decreasing interest rates tend to stimulate the economy.

If the economy is in recession, then the Fed will make credit more available by increasing the money supply. This will decrease interest rates and thereby make it easier for firms to borrow and invest in projects that will put people back to work producing more goods and services. Increases in the money supply lead to lower interest rates and higher domestic inflation. If gross national product (GNP) and the consumer price index started to decrease, the Federal Reserve would normally increase the money supply. The Federal Reserve attempts to slow down the economy if inflation is rising and expand the economy if deflation is present.

The tightening of money and credit by the Fed is usually followed by a decrease in securities prices because fewer funds will be available for investment, and economic activity will be slowing down. An expansion of credit by the Fed usually results in increases in securities prices because more funds will be available for investment and it is anticipated that economic activity will increase.

To summarize, the following are functions of the Federal Reserve:

- Lending to commercial banks
- Auditing member banks
- Regulating bank credit
- Regulating the overall money supply
- Acting as agent for the US Treasury
- Being the lender of last resort

Fiscal policy refers to the spending and taxing policies of the federal government. The fiscal policy of the US government is set by Congress. US government fiscal policy would be concerned with changes in government spending and income tax rates. If the US government wanted to stimulate the economy by using fiscal policy, it would increase government spending and lower income tax rates. If the US government wanted to slow down the economy by using fiscal policy, it would decrease government spending and raise income taxes.

The theory of active manipulation of government taxation and spending to control the business cycle is the **Keynesian Theory,** named after English economist John Maynard Keynes.

To summarize, fiscal policy refers to the spending and taxing policies of the US government. Fiscal policy is controlled by Congress. To stimulate the economy, Congress would vote to increase government spending and lower income tax rates. To slow down the economy, Congress would decrease government spending and raise income taxes.

SUITABILITY AND RISK FACTORS

The term **suitability** in the securities industry means that a customer's securities investments fit his investment objectives, financial situation, and needs. A registered representative (RR) obtains information from a customer concerning estimated annual income, estimated net worth, liquid assets, employment status, age, marital status, dependents, investment knowledge, other investments, and income tax bracket.

A customer's investment objectives may be long-term growth, aggressive (speculative) growth, or current income with protection of principal. The allocation of a customer's assets between equities, bonds, and money market instruments must be determined. In other words, the principles of asset allocation are applied to a customer's overall financial situation.

A customer's assets consist of cash, money market funds, other mutual funds, common stocks, cash value of life insurance, and real estate. Liabilities a customer may have include mortgages, credit card debt, and automobile loans. An available line of credit at a bank is a contingent liability for a customer and should not be considered an asset. When the customer draws on the available line of credit, the amount obtained by the customer increases his cash position and increases his current liabilities. A customer's net worth is equal to his assets minus his liabilities.

To minimize risk, an investor will normally diversify his investments. Diversification occurs when an investor spreads his investments among securities in different industries. In order to obtain higher returns, an investor must take higher risks. An aggressive investment strategy concentrates investments in smaller capitalization common stocks and aggressive growth funds. An investor seeking a defensive strategy would invest in money market instruments and money market funds.

Normally, a younger investor will have a high percentage of his assets in common stocks or equity funds. As a person moves into middle age, his portfolio will normally include some of his assets in debt obligations and a smaller percentage in equity investments.

Assume Mrs. Jones has $60,000 to invest but will need the money in five months to pay college costs for her daughter. Mrs. Jones should invest in 90-day Treasury bills or money market funds. Treasury bills and money market funds are appropriate investments for a person seeking income, preservation of capital, and high liquidity. Retired persons seeking current income and protection of principal would purchase Treasury bills or money market funds.

An investor seeking nontaxable income would normally invest in a municipal bond fund, since the income is exempt from federal income taxes but may be subject to state income taxes. If an investor's investment objectives are conservative growth, he would normally choose a growth fund. An investor seeking aggressive growth would normally invest in an aggressive growth fund. If an investor's investment objectives are a high yield, the investor would normally choose an income fund.

Assume Mr. Smith does market timing analysis to decide when to switch funds from money market funds to growth funds. Mr. Smith's investment timing model forecasts a peak in interest rates and the beginning of a major economic expansion. In this case, Mr. Smith should buy growth funds. If the investment timing model was forecasting declining interest rates and the beginning of a major economic recession (downturn), Mr. Smith would sell growth funds and invest in money market funds. If the market is expected to move upward, more market appreciation is normally obtained from common stock funds than money market funds, balanced funds, or income funds. However, in a down market, common stock funds normally decline more than money market funds, balanced funds, or income funds.

Investors can obtain information to compare the performance of various funds through **industry comparative sources** such as Value Line or Morningstar. Industry comparative sources are an excellent source of information for investors who want to compare different mutual funds.

REVIEW QUESTIONS

1. A customer who purchases a fixed annuity would be subject to
   a. Market risk
   b Interest rate risk
   c. Purchasing power risk
   d. Currency exchange risk

2. When the government attempts to stimulate the economy by reducing taxes and increasing spending, it is using
   a. Recessionary policy
   b. Bearish policy
   c. Monetary policy
   d. Fiscal policy

3. When a customer opens an account to purchase securities, the registered representative should obtain information relating to

   I. Liquid assets
   II. Net worth
   III. Annual income
   IV. Other investments

   a. I and II
   b. III and IV
   c. I, III, and IV
   d. All of the above

4. If an investor expects interest rates to increase dramatically and a major recession to begin shortly, he should
   a. Sell growth funds and buy money market funds
   b. Buy growth funds
   c. Buy aggressive growth funds and buy bond funds
   d. Sell money market funds and buy growth funds

5. The concept that a customer's securities investments fit his investment objectives, financial situation, and needs refers to
   a. Churning
   b. Arbitrage
   c. Suitability
   d. Hedging

6. A customer has $50,000 to invest, which she will need in approximately four months. The best choice for this customer is
   a. Common stocks
   b. 90-day Treasury bills
   c. Growth funds
   d. Long-term bond funds

7. Monetary policy is the responsibility of the
   a. Congress
   b. Federal Reserve
   c. Treasury Department
   d. Securities Investor Protection Corporation

8. A retired person in need of income would invest in
   a. Growth funds
   b. Special-situation funds
   c. Money market funds
   d. Speculative growth funds

9. All of the following represent assets to a customer **except:**
   a. Common stock
   b. Cash value of life insurance
   c. Credit card debt
   d. Mutual funds

10. A customer whose investment objectives are nontaxable income would purchase a
   a.   Municipal bond fund
   b.   Corporate bond fund
   c.   Growth and income fund
   d.   US government securities fund

11. Assume Mr. Lynch is a market timing analyst relating to mutual funds. Mr. Lynch's investment timing model forecasts that interest rates are at a peak and the US economy will begin a major expansion. Based on the investment timing model, Mr. Lynch should
   a.   Sell growth funds and invest in money market funds
   b.   Sell growth funds and leave the proceeds in cash
   c.   Buy growth funds
   d.   Buy money market funds only

12. Assume an underwriting firm buys an entire securities issue from ABC Computer Corporation. The underwriting firm will take all of the risk in distributing the shares to the public. This type of underwriting is best described as
   a.   All or none
   b.   Firm commitment
   c.   Standby
   d.   Best efforts

13. All of the following represent assets to an individual investor **except:**
   a.   Treasury bills
   b.   Real estate
   c.   Shares in a growth fund
   d.   Available line of credit

14. All of the following would be suitable investments for an older person with limited resources seeking current income and preservation of capital **except:**
   a.   Money market fund
   b.   Treasury bills
   c.   Long-term aggressive growth fund
   d.   Short-term government bond fund

15. Assume a customer expects a serious stock market decline that will last for several years. The customer owns a substantial number of growth funds, both conservative and aggressive. Which of the following is the best strategy for the customer given his market forecast?
   a.   Buy conservative growth funds
   b.   Buy aggressive growth funds
   c.   Sell the growth funds and buy money market funds
   d.   Sell the conservative growth funds and buy more aggressive growth funds

ANSWERS TO REVIEW QUESTIONS

1.	c	4.	a	7.	b	10.	a	13.	d
2.	d	5.	c	8.	c	11.	c	14.	c
3.	d	6.	b	9.	c	12.	b	15.	c

3 OPEN-END INVESTMENT COMPANIES

INTRODUCTION

Investment companies are subject to federal securities laws and state securities laws (blue-sky laws). The Investment Company Act of 1940 regulates investment companies to make sure that fund shareholders are fully informed and fairly treated.

The three main types of investment companies registered under the Investment Company Act of 1940 are

1. Face-amount certificate companies
2. Unit investment trusts
3. Management companies

Face-amount certificate companies issue certificates at less than face value to investors, which are worth face value at maturity. An investor makes periodic payments to the face-amount certificate company. The face-amount certificate company will pay the face value to the investor at maturity. An investor will receive the surrender value of the certificate if it is redeemed prior to maturity.

Unit investment trusts are closed-end trusts that issue redeemable securities representing an undivided interest in the unit investment trust. Unit investment trusts purchase a fixed portfolio of securities (corporate bonds, municipal bonds, or common stock). The portfolio of securities remains fixed until the bonds mature or if common stock, when the shares are sold. Unit investment trusts are normally sold with a low load (3 or 4%). The unit investment trust *does not* pay a management fee to an investment advisor, since the portfolio is not managed. The unit investment trust has a board of trustees to handle the affairs of the trust.

The two main types of management companies are closed-end funds and open-end funds. **Closed-end funds** are investment companies that trade either on a stock exchange or in the over-the-counter (OTC) market. Closed-end funds trade in the same manner as corporate securities and must be registered under the Securities Act of 1933 because they are securities, and under the Investment Company Act of 1940 because they are investment companies. Closed-end funds have a fixed number of shares outstanding and do not continuously sell new shares. A registered representative (RR) with a Series 6 license can sell closed-end funds on an original distribution, but not when they are selling in the secondary market (stock exchange or OTC market). To sell closed-end funds in the secondary market, an RR must have a Series 7 license (general securities representative) or a Series 62 license (corporate securities representative).

Closed-end funds and open-end funds have a bid price and ask price, which are available at the close of business (4:00 P.M.) on each business day. For a closed-end fund, the bid price is the net asset value per share (NAVPS), which is computed as follows:

$$\frac{\text{Assets} - \text{Liabilities}}{\text{Number of shares outstanding}} = \text{Bid price (NAVPS)}$$

Assume the XYZ closed-end fund's bid price (NAVPS) is computed as $16 per share. The ask price is the price the closed-end fund trades at on a stock exchange or in the OTC market. The ask price could be substantially above or below the bid price. This is an important concept to understand with closed-end funds. The ask price is determined by market demand on a stock exchange or in the OTC market. The bid price is determined by a mathematical computation (Assets – Liabilities ÷ Number of shares outstanding). Therefore, the XYZ closed-end fund may be reflected as follows:

Bid	Ask
$16	$30

In this case, the closed-end fund is trading at a substantial premium to its bid price. The marketplace is looking favorably on the prospects of the XYZ Closed-End Fund. Assume that the XYZ Closed-End Fund's bid and ask prices were as follows:

Bid	Ask
$14	$6

In this case, the XYZ Closed-End Fund is trading at a substantial discount from its bid price. The marketplace is not looking favorably on the prospects of the XYZ Closed-End Fund. A closed-end funds could be trading above, below, or even at the same price as its NAVPS.

Open-end investment companies (open-end funds) are also referred to as **mutual funds**. They continuously offer new shares to the public and will redeem customer shares on demand. Closed-end investment company shares trade on stock exchanges and in the OTC market and their price is determined by market demand. An open-end investment company is defined by the Investment Company Act of 1940 as "either a corporation or a trust through which investors pool their funds in an investment portfolio to obtain diversification and supervision of their investments."

The term *mutual fund* is the most popular name for open-end investment companies. Open-end investment companies continuously offer new shares for sale to investors and provide a continuous market for the redemption of shares from investors. Thus, the investor buys the mutual fund from the issuing company and sells the shares back to the issuer, either directly or through broker/dealers. Shares of open-end investment companies are not traded on organized exchanges as are corporate shares.

Mutual funds are normally purchased in dollar amounts (buying $1,000 of a fund). Sales charges, in the case of **load** funds (no-load funds levy no sales charges), are deducted from the investment and the net investment results in full and fractional shares in the fund. Purchases of investment company shares are carried to three places after the decimal. Assume a customer invests $1,000 in the XYZ Fund. The ask price of the XYZ Fund is $12. How many shares will the customer purchase?

$$\frac{\$1,000 \text{ amount invested}}{\$12 \text{ ask price per share}} = 83.333 \text{ shares}$$

Assume instead that the ask price of the XYZ Fund was $14 per share. How many shares would the customer purchase?

$$\frac{\$1,000 \text{ amount invested}}{\$14 \text{ ask price per share}} = 71.429 \text{ shares}$$

The shares purchased represent the investor's undivided interest in the mutual fund's portfolio and give the investor the right to vote on certain basic issues similar to the voting rights accorded to common stockholders.

The very nature of mutual funds is that risks are pooled into a common portfolio to minimize the risks associated with the smaller portfolio of the individual investor. There are various ways in which the open-end investment company can reduce risks. The most common way is to diversify its investments in the portfolio.

The fund is managed by full-time professionals, and it is likely that their expertise will be greater than that of the individual investor. Moreover, since they are full-time, it is also likely that they will have more time to devote to the management of the fund than the individual investor. It is the primary responsibility of the fund's full-time management to meet the objectives of the open-end investment company, as described in the prospectus.

One of the functions of fund management is to obtain the appropriate diversification of the securities in the fund's portfolio while at all times attempting to meet the fund objectives. Another of their responsibilities is to decide on the proper timing of the investment decision. It is management who must decide whether to buy, sell, or hold securities. In addition, the fund's management identifies the tax status of the fund's distributions. A mutual fund generally makes two types of distributions: **income distributions** and **capital gains distributions**.

Therefore, the fund management should be more competent and skilled than the average individual investor. It is forbidden, however, under Securities and Exchange Commission (SEC) rules to allege or imply that the fund's management or its diversification will guarantee the investor against loss of his investment. Neither can any statement be made that the fund's management or diversification will assure a capital gain. In fact, the SEC forbids any extravagant or misleading claims as to the management ability of the open-end investment company.

TYPES OF FUNDS

The main types of mutual funds offered to investors include

- Growth funds
- Sector funds
- Income funds

- Balanced funds
- Municipal bond funds
- US government securities funds
- Money market funds
- International funds
- Hedge funds

Growth funds have as their investment objective, growth of capital. Their portfolio consists mainly of common stocks. Growth funds may be conservative growth funds, which invest in "blue-chip" or large capitalization companies such as General Electric, IBM, and Coca-Cola. Growth funds may also be **aggressive growth funds,** which invest in small capitalization or emerging companies, have more risk to an investor. The greater the risk an investor assumes, the greater the potential gain or loss.

Sector funds invest in companies in a specific geographic area or a specific industry. For example, the Asia Pacific Fund, Japan Fund, and Korea Fund are funds that invest in a specific geographic area. Sector funds also invest in specific industries such as health care, biotechnology, or telecommunications.

Income funds attempt to provide shareholders with a high yield by investing in bonds and stocks that make liberal dividend payments to shareholders.

Balanced funds have a conservative investment policy and "balance" their investments in common stock, preferred stock, and bonds.

Municipal bond funds are attractive to investors whose investment objective is nontaxable income. These funds appeal to investors who are in a high tax bracket. The income received by a shareholder from a municipal bond fund is federal tax-exempt, but may be subject to state taxes. However, a capital gain distribution from a municipal bond fund is taxable to a shareholder on both the federal and state levels.

US government securities funds invest in securities issued by the US government, such as Treasury bills, notes, and bonds. US government securities funds may be short-term funds or long-term funds. A short-term government bond fund has less interest rate risk and less purchasing power risk than a long-term government bond fund.

Money market funds first appeared in the early 1970s when rates in the money market rose above rates on savings deposits. These funds offered investors high return and high liquidity. Their funds are invested in high-yield, short-term debt securities and attempt to maintain a constant $1 net asset value.

Money market funds are no-load funds with no redemption fee. They *do not* issue certificates, but send out statements at regular intervals showing deposits, withdrawals, and interest credited to the account. The investor can withdraw funds from such a fund on demand at any time without penalty. Many funds, in fact, provide checks that the investor may make out and cash or use to pay bills, just as he can with bank checks.

Money market funds invest in financial instruments with maturities of twelve months or less. A money market fund's portfolio might consist of Treasury bills, certificates of deposit, bankers' acceptances, and commercial paper. Money market funds must illustrate their effective annualized yield. Yields for money market funds are shown for seven-day periods, expressed as annual percentage rates. A money market fund must use the SEC standardized method to calculate yields.

International funds invest primarily in common stocks of foreign corporations. International funds must also be concerned with the value of the dollar against foreign currencies. When the dollar declines against foreign currencies on foreign exchange markets, foreign stocks and bonds become worth more in terms of dollars and the net asset value of the funds rises. When the dollar increases against foreign currencies, the value of international fund shares declines.

Hedge funds attempt to hedge against market declines by engaging in aggressive trading techniques such as short selling. They also customarily allow for borrowing money and place few restrictions on the types of securities they may hold. Hedge funds are very risky and suitable only for individuals of very high net worth who clearly understand the risks.

CLASSES OF SHARES

Funds may offer investors different classes of shares such as

- Class A
- Class B
- Class C

Class A shares charge the investor an up-front sales charge that cannot exceed 8½% under NASD rules. **Class B** shares have a contingent deferred sales charge. For example, the deferred sales charge (back-end load) may decrease from 5% in the first year and disappear after five years. Therefore, an investor who holds class B shares more than five years will pay no deferred sales charge on a liquidation. An RR might recommend class B shares to an investor who wants to avoid an up-front sales charge.

However, class B shares have higher operating expenses than class A shares. A mutual fund's main expenses are

- Cost of portfolio management (management fee)
- Operating expenses
- 12b-1 fees

Expenses of class B shares are higher than class A shares because class B shares do not have an up-front sales charge. Over the long-term, class B shares may be more expensive to own for investors. Funds may convert class B shares to class A shares after a certain number of years. Some funds may offer **class C** shares which have no up-front sales charge and no redemption fee but the highest annual expenses of the three types of shares.

When an investor decides to redeem shares held by a transfer agent, the transfer agent may require a stock power (written statement to sell the shares) and a signature guarantee. Under normal business conditions, the investment company or its agent must make payments to the investor not later than seven calendar days after acceptance of the shares. However, mutual funds are securities that fluctuate in value and upon redemption the investor may receive more or less than the amount invested.

MUTUAL FUND ACCOUNTS

An investor must be of legal age to open a mutual fund account. An account can be opened in the name of an individual, joint tenants, tenants in common, trust accounts, or a Uniform Gifts to Minors account. When a person purchases investment company shares, a customer confirmation is sent to the purchaser. The investor normally receives account statements on a quarterly basis. Investors receive Form 1099-DIV for the calendar year stating which portion of the distributions were dividend distributions which were capital gain distributions. Investors also receive Form 1099-B, which shows the amount of fund shares sold during the year. The information contained on Forms 1099-DIV and 1099-B is reported to both the fund shareholder and the Internal Revenue Service (IRS).

An account in the name of an individual is controlled by that individual only. Instructions concerning purchases and sales can be taken only from the individual unless discretionary power is given to another person. Assume John and Victoria Nixon own fund shares as **joint tenants with rights of survivorship**. If John Nixon dies, Victoria Nixon will become the sole owner of the shares. Victoria Nixon must only present certain legal documents, such as a death certificate.

In a **tenants-in-common account,** on the death of a tenant, ownership passes to the estate of the deceased person. For example, assume two sisters, Helen and Florence MacDonald, own mutual fund shares as tenants in common. If Helen MacDonald dies, ownership of her shares will pass to the estate of Helen MacDonald.

Assume an individual wants to invest in a mutual fund. The individual can set up an open account (voluntary account, which is very popular with investors, since money can be sent in at any time and the shares can be redeemed at any time. When an open account is set up by an investor, the investor must invest the minimum required amount. The investor must then choose either to reinvest dividend distributions and capital gains distributions in additional fund shares or to receive them in cash.

An investor can decide to invest in a mutual fund under a contractual plan. In a contractual plan, the investor agrees to invest a certain amount of money in a fund on a monthly basis. The investor is engaging in **dollar cost averaging**. Dollar cost averaging is investing the same amount of money in the same security at the same interval. For example, investing $300 a month in XYZ Growth Fund for ten years is an example of dollar cost averaging. Contractual plans normally have large sales charges in the early years. Over the life of a contractual plan, the maximum sales charge under NASD rules is 8½% . However, contractual plans can be sold as either a 20% plan or a 50% plan.

Under a 20% plan, 20% of the first year's payments can be taken out as commission. Under a 50% Plan, 50% of the first year's payments can be taken out as commission. If an investor cancels a 20% plan or a 50% plan within forty-five days after the custodian bank mails him a notice of that right, the investor will receive the current value of his account plus all sales charges paid. In a 20% plan, if an investor liquidates after the forty-five-day period, the investor will receive only the current value of his account. Under a 50% plan, the investor has up to eighteen months to receive the current value of his account on liquidation, plus a portion of the sales charge refunded.

It is important when an RR sells a contractual plan to an investor to make clear that this is a long-term investment plan. The RR must explain to the investor how sales charges are deducted from payments in the early years and the total sales charge over the life of the contractual plan. The consequences of liquidating a contractual plan in the early years is that the customer could lose principal. A large portion of the commissions are deducted in the early years and fewer commissions are taken out in the later years. Also, any sales charge refund provisions applicable to a contractual plan must be explained to an investor.

Investors may also decide to set up a **withdrawal plan** when they retire. Under a withdrawal plan, an investor may decide to receive $800 a month. However, the investor must be careful not to exhaust the capital. Assume a customer has $100,000 invested in a mutual fund. The customer is sixty-five years of age and is a single person. He wants to withdraw $2,000 a month. In this case, the customer should realize that invested capital may be exhausted. The customer would be withdrawing $24,000 on a $100,000 investment. The customer should consider withdrawing less per month and could adjust the amount based on the performance of the fund.

DISTRIBUTIONS BY FUNDS

Mutual funds make two types of distributions.

1. Income distributions
2. Capital gains distributions

Income distributions are also referred to as **dividend distributions**. Income distributions are paid from a fund's net investment income, which is derived from gross investment income less operating expenses. The three principal sources of gross investment income are: (1) dividend income the fund receives from its holdings of common and preferred stock; (2) interest income from the debt obligations in its portfolio; and (3) short-term capital gains realized on the portfolio. The fund subtracts expenses from gross investment income to determine net investment income.

There is no restriction on how often dividends can be paid out by an investment company. Dividends are paid as often as they are declared by the board of directors. Dividends could be paid out daily if declared by the board of directors. Certain money market funds declare dividends daily and pay them to shareholders monthly.

Capital gains distributions are paid from long-term capital gains realized on the sale of securities in the fund's portfolio. Capital losses are used to offset capital gains. The net long-term gain is distributed to shareholders according to their proportionate holding of shares. Capital gains distributions can normally only be paid out once a year by an investment company.

When the fund makes distributions, the assets of the fund are decreased. If, however, the fund shareholder reinvests these dividend and capital gains distributions, the number of shares owned will increase and will have a compounding effect on his investment. Even though a mutual fund shareholder reinvests capital gain distributions and dividend distributions, he is still taxed on the amount of the distribution.

Capital gains distributions are based on realized gains or losses. The price of fund shares is also affected by unrealized profits or losses on stocks and bonds that have not been sold. The holder of mutual fund shares is not taxed on unrealized capital gains.

Advertising statements regarding fund distributions are carefully monitored by the SEC. There cannot be any implication that mutual funds will increase the investor's capital or preserve his original capital. Nor can any statement imply that mutual funds can assure a particular return. Even if a mutual fund has increased in value 30% in each of the past three years, the fund's prospectus or an RR cannot state that the fund will increase 30% in the present year.

Mutual funds offer shareholders certain conveniences, including

- Investment decisions are made by full-time investment managers.
- The investor can invest in full or fractional shares.
- The fund shares may be used as collateral for a loan.
- Automatic reinvestment of income dividend and capital gains distributions is available to fund shareholders.

- Some funds offer a conversion privilege. This allows the investor to change from one fund to another, within the same **family** as his investment objective changes. For example, an investor may change from a growth fund to an income fund without incurring any additional sales charges, but would be subject to tax on any capital gain realized on the sale of the growth fund.

TAXATION OF MUTUAL FUNDS

Mutual funds make two types of distributions to shareholders, as previously mentioned: income distributions and capital gains distributions. The source of a fund's income distributions are interest income, dividend income, and short-term capital gains. Capital gains distributions are taxed to an investor as dividends under federal tax law. Dividends are taxed as ordinary income at the investor's tax bracket rate. Capital gains distributions are taxed as long-term capital gains. Mutual funds send shareholders and the IRS a statement at the end of the year showing dividend and capital gains distributions paid during the year on Form 1099-DIV.

A mutual fund will qualify as a **regulated investment company** under subchapter M of the Internal Revenue Code if it distributes at least 90% of its net investment income and meets certain other requirements. A regulated investment company does not pay any taxes on income it distributes. The shareholders of the fund pay the taxes since the mutual fund is acting as a "conduit" or "pipeline." Mutual fund shareholders are not taxed on unrealized capital gains, as previously mentioned.

Income distribution (dividends) and capital gains distributions paid to fund shareholders are taxable even if the amount of the distribution is automatically reinvested in additional fund shares. Also, assume an investor sells Manhattan Growth Fund and purchases Manhattan Income Fund in the same family of funds for a nominal fee. A gain on the sale of the shares in Manhattan Growth Fund is taxable to the investor.

An investor should be informed that capital gains distributions from municipal bond funds are taxable even though the income distribution received is tax exempt.

An investor who inherits securities, such as mutual fund shares, as a beneficiary must value the shares for tax purposes on the date of death of the decedent.

MUTUAL FUND EXPENSES

The major expenses incurred by a mutual fund are

- Cost of portfolio management
- Operating expenses
- 12b-1 fees
- Service or administrative fees

The **cost of portfolio management** refers to payments to an investment advisor to manage the fund's portfolio of securities. A mutual fund enters into an investment advisory contract with an investment advisor. The investment advisory contract must be approved by the fund's board of directors and a majority of the fund's outstanding shares.

Operating expenses are costs the fund realizes for salaries, telephone expenses, and costs of printing and mailing prospectuses and sales literature to investors.

Fees used to pay distribution expenses of the fund are known as **12b-1 fees**. The 12b-1 fees must be clearly stated in the fund's prospectus. They are levied or charged against the assets of the fund and are therefore borne by the shareholder. Fund expenditures from 12b-1 fees are used to pay advertising expenses, compensation to underwriters, and costs relating to printing and mailing prospectuses and sales literature to customers.

Some funds levy **service or administrative fees** to compensate brokers for servicing the accounts of customers. The payments may be made pursuant to an administrative services agreement. These expenses are also charged against the assets of the fund. An expense ratio can be computed for a mutual fund as follows:

$$\frac{\text{Cost of portfolio management} + \text{Operating expenses}}{\text{Average net asset value}}$$

The operating expenses of the fund in the ratio includes 12b-1 fees and administrative fees. The lower the fund's expense ratio, the more beneficial the fund is to the shareholder.

REVIEW CONCEPTS

Closed-end investment companies are different from open-end investment companies in several ways (see Exhibit 3.1). Closed-end funds have a fixed number of shares outstanding. Closed-end funds are listed on stock exchanges and in the OTC market. A closed-end fund computes its NAVPS at the close of business on each business day.

Exhibit 3.1: Comparison—Open-end funds vs. closed-end funds

Open-end funds	*Closed-end funds*
Shares are continuously offered to the public.	Have a fixed number of shares outstanding.
Shares are purchased from the fund and sold back to the fund.	Shares are bought and sold from other investors and through broker/dealers.
An investor buys at the ask price and redeems shares at the bid price.	Investors buy at the ask price plus a commission and sell at the ask price minus a commission.
Shares must be sold with a prospectus.	New issues must be sold with a prospectus.
Can borrow or lend money, purchase put or call options.	Can borrow or lend money, purchase put or call options.
Cannot issue senior securities.	Can issue senior securities.
If the bid and the ask price are the same, it is a no-load fund. The ask price cannot exceed the bid price more than 8½% under NASD rules.	The ask price may be substantially above the bid price (premium) or substantially below (discount) the bid price (NAVPS).

However, the important price for a closed-end fund is the ask price, which for a closed-end fund, is the price the fund is trading at in the marketplace. Assume that a closed-end fund's NAVPS is $22 at the close of business on Monday. The ask price for the closed-end fund could be $31 or $6; it is determined by market demand and could be above, below, or even the same as the NAVPS on a given day. When an individual buys closed-end funds, he does so through a broker/dealer from another investor. An investor would, for example, buy 100 shares of the ABC Closed-End Fund and pay the market price (ask price) plus a commission. The investor *does not* buy and sell from the investment company as he would with an open-end investment company. He buys and sells closed-end funds from another investor through a broker/dealer.

Open-end investment companies (mutual funds) continuously offer new shares to the public and continuously redeem shares sold by investors. An investor buys shares at the ask price and sells shares at the bid price. The investor buys and sells shares at the next computed price after receipt of the order by the dealer. An open-end investment company can issue common stock only. The common stock can be divided into class A shares, class B shares, and class C shares. The class A, class B, and class C have different sales charges, redemption fees, and annual expenses. However, an open-end investment company cannot issue preferred stocks or bonds under the provisions of the Investment Company Act of 1940. Open-end investment company shares are new issues and must be sold with a prospectus. Any sales literature used to sell shares of an open-end investment company must be preceded or accompanied by a prospectus.

IMPORTANT POINTS

To summarize important points relating to investment companies

- When a customer purchases an open-end investment company, he pays the ask price or public offering price next computed after receipt of the order by the dealer. If it is a load fund, the sales charge is added to the bid price to obtain the public offering price. In a no-load fund, the bid and ask prices are the same.
- The term *mutual fund* refers only to open-end investment companies, not closed-end investment companies.
- If an open-end investment company has increased in value, this is referred to as appreciation; if it has decreased in value, it is called depreciation.
- Unit investment trusts are not managed investment companies. They do not have a board of directors. They are issued at par and not at a discount. A board of trustees sets overall policies. Unit investment trusts have a fixed portfolio, normally corporate or municipal bonds.
- Most mutual funds offer quantity discounts. The breakpoint is defined as the point where the percentage sales charge is reduced.
- Investment companies must send out financial statements to shareholders at least semiannually. The income statement must itemize each category of income or expense if it is more than 5% of total income or total expenses. Mutual fund expenses include management fees, legal fees, accounting fees, and advertising costs. A money market fund's largest operating expense is normally the management and advisory fee.

- Quantity discounts on the purchase of investment company shares are not available to investment clubs.
- If an investor liquidates an open-end investment company (mutual fund), the redemption value is based on the next computed bid price on the day the order is received. The redemption price for an open-end investment company is equal to the net asset value minus any redemption fee.
- The payment of a cash dividend decreases a mutual fund's NAVPS.

ADDITIONAL CONCEPTS

The following information is critical to understanding how mutual funds work:

- The custodian of a mutual fund is normally a commercial bank. The custodian holds the assets of the fund for physical safekeeping. However, the custodian bank does not protect investors against loss on a purchase. Also, the custodian bank does not engage in selling fund shares and is not involved in the management of the fund. The custodian does not protect the investor against unsuitable investment policies.
- Mutual fund shareholders are not taxed on unrealized capital gains. They are taxed on dividends and capital gains reinvested in additional fund shares. Mutual fund shareholders are taxed on income distributions and capital gain distributions received from the fund. Shareholders in a mutual fund share proportionately in the fund's income, profits, and losses. If a shareholder switches from one fund to another, the switch is a taxable event.
- If a customer sells mutual fund shares at a loss and repurchases the shares within thirty days, the loss is not deductible for tax purposes. Assume a customer realizes a loss on the sale of 100 shares of ABC Growth Fund. Twenty-seven days later, the customer buys 100 shares of the same fund (ABC Growth Fund). In this case, the customer cannot take a loss for tax purposes since it is considered a "wash sale."
- If a mutual fund's portfolio increases in value, the fund's net asset value will increase. Assume XYZ Growth Fund's net asset value has increased from $12.62 to $14.21 over a seven-month period. This indicates that the fund's portfolio has increased in value over the seven-month period.
- Mutual funds may require shareholders to make initial minimum investments for open accounts, contractual plans, and withdrawal accounts (plans). Also, mutual funds require customers to provide the fund a tax certification form. If a customer does not provide a tax certification form to the fund, the customer may be subject to tax withholding.
- When a customer redeems investment company shares, the redemption price may be more or less than the cost to the customer. If the customer has the mutual fund certificates, the transfer agent normally requires a stock power and a signature guarantee to redeem shares he is holding. The redemption price the customer will receive for the shares is the next computed net asset value after receipt of the request for redemption by the broker/dealer or RR. When a customer tenders mutual fund shares for redemption, the investment company or its agent must make payment to the investor, under normal business conditions, not later than seven calendar days after acceptance of the shares.
- Customers with investment objectives of current income, stability of principal, and high liquidity normally buy a money market fund, which invests in short-term financial instruments with maturities of twelve months or less. Money market funds illustrate their effective annualized yield. They are required to use standardized methods to calculate the yield. Customers with an investment objective of current nontaxable income normally invest in a municipal bond fund.
- The transfer agent of an investment company cancels shares redeemed by investors, issues new shares to investors, and makes dividend and capital gains distributions to investors. However, the custodian bank will safekeep the physical assets of the investment company, which are the cash and securities of the fund.
- When opening a new account for a customer, certain information must be obtained, including the customer's name, and address, whether the customer is of legal age, the signature of the RR introducing the account, and the signature of the principal accepting the account. If the customer is associated with or employed by another member, this fact must be noted. Some customers choose to maintain a mutual fund open account. Mutual fund open accounts allow customers to elect to receive dividends in cash or to reinvest dividends, which may or may not be subject to sales charges. A customer must invest a certain minimum amount to open the account. Customers with open accounts normally invest certain dollar amounts and do not normally purchase a certain amount of shares (share amounts).
- Customers, at certain times, exchange one mutual fund for another fund. Assume a customer is about to retire and wants to redeem shares in XYZ Growth Fund and purchase shares in XYZ Income Fund under

different management. The customer will probably obtain a higher yield in the income fund. However, the customer will realize a capital gain if the growth fund shares are sold at a profit. Also, a sales charge may be incurred when the customer buys the income fund. Customers who are considering exchanging one mutual fund for another should consider the following factors:

- The tax consequences relating to the exchange
- The objective of the fund to which they are transferring to
- Whether they have a desire for more current income and whether the exchange meets that objective
- Recent movements or changes in the stock market and economy

- RRs who have only a Series 6 license may sell mutual funds, variable annuities, and shares of a closed-end investment company on an initial offering. However, they may not sell shares in a real estate investment trust, limited partnership interest, or a closed-end fund currently traded on a stock exchange or in the OTC market. A closed-end fund's ask price is based on market demand. Open-end investment company shares differ from closed-end shares because the shares bought by individual investors are normally newly issued shares of the fund.
- Assume a customer is sixty-four years of age and he wants to invest $30,000 in a mutual fund withdrawal plan. The withdrawal plan will pay the customer $600 per month. The customer should clearly understand that invested capital may be exhausted. The customer can increase or decrease the amount to be withdrawn.
- Assume a fund has a $16 bid and $14 ask. This type of fund must be a closed-end fund. The bid price is the NAVPS for the fund. The NAVPS is computed by the following formula:

$$\frac{\text{Assets} - \text{Liabilities}}{\text{Number of shares outstanding}} = \text{NAVPS (bid price)}$$

The ask price is the price at which the closed-end fund is trading, either in the OTC market or on a stock exchange.

- Assume a fund has an ask price of $15 and a load of 6%. What is the bid price? The bid price can be found in either of the following ways:

$$
\begin{array}{lll}
\$15 \times 0.06 & = & \$0.90 \text{ sales charge} \\
\$15 - \$0.90 & = & \$14.10 \text{ bid price}
\end{array}
$$

or

$$\$15 \times 0.94 \quad = \quad \$14.10 \text{ bid price}$$

- Assume a fund has a bid price of $18 and a load of 6%. What is the ask price? The ask price can be found by finding the bid price in percentage and dividing it into the bid price in dollars.

$$
\begin{array}{ll}
100\% & \text{Ask price} \\
-\ 6\% & \text{Sales charge} \\
\hline
94\% & \text{Bid in percentage}
\end{array}
$$

$$\frac{\$18.00 \text{ bid price}}{0.94 \text{ bid in percentage}} \quad = \quad \$19.15 \text{ ask price}$$

$$
\begin{array}{lll}
\$19.15 & \text{Ask price} & 100\% \\
\underline{\$18.00} & \text{Bid price} & \underline{94\%} \\
\$\ 1.15 & \text{Sales charge} & 6\%
\end{array}
$$

REVIEW QUESTIONS

1. All-American Fund has a $14 bid price and a $12 ask price. The All-American Fund is a(n)
   a. Open-end growth fund
   b. Open-end bond fund
   c. Closed-end fund
   d. Face-amount certificate company

2. Mr. Buffet's investment objective is nontaxable income. Which of the following funds should Mr. Buffet invest in?
   a. Growth fund
   b. Growth and income fund
   c. Corporate bond fund
   d. Municipal bond fund

3. A senior citizen has $60,000 to invest and her investment objectives are preservation of capital and current income. She should invest in a(n)
   a. Money market fund
   b. Aggressive growth fund
   c. Special situation fund
   d. Growth fund

4. Each of the following statements describes shares of a closed-end fund **except:**
   a. The number of shares is fixed.
   b. The shares may be traded over the counter or listed on an exchange.
   c. There is a continuous public offering of shares.
   d. The shares are not redeemable by the issuer.

5. Market demand determines the ask price of a(n)
   a. Money market fund
   b. Closed-end fund
   c. Open-end bond fund
   d. Open-end growth fund

6. Place the following funds from most risk to least risk:

   I. Bond fund
   II. Money market fund
   III. Common stock fund

   a. II, III, I
   b. I, III, II
   c. III, I, II
   d. III, II, I

7. In general, the most conservative investment policy would be followed by an open-end investment company classified as a(n)
   a. Balanced fund
   b. Growth fund
   c. Income fund
   d. Special situation fund

8. In a rising stock market, you would expect the most market appreciation to be shown by a(n)
   a. Money market fund
   b. Balanced fund
   c. Income fund
   d. Common stock fund

9. All of the following would normally be a risk associated with an Aggressive Growth Fund **except:**
   a. Increasing interest rates
   b. Increasing inflation
   c. Falling stock prices
   d. Redemption liquidity

10. A client is doing market timing to decide when to switch between money market funds and growth funds. The client's investment timing model forecasts at the present time a peak in interest rates and the beginning of an expansion. The client should
   a. Buy money market funds
   b. Buy growth funds
   c. Sell growth funds
   d. Sell growth funds and buy money market funds

11. All of the following are characteristics of open-end funds **except:**
   a. They sell and redeem shares of the fund.
   b. Shares are continuously offered to the public.
   c. They can issue senior securities.
   d. They can borrow or lend money.

12. A customer has $20,000 to invest in the ABC Fund. The bid price of the fund is $18.00 and the ask price is $18.56. How many shares will the customer purchase?
   a. 1077.586
   b. 1094.092
   c. 1111.111
   d. 1856.000

13. A person who purchases a long-term US government bond fund should be concerned with
   a. Default risk
   b. Purchasing power risk
   c. Currency risk
   d. Liquidity risk

14. An investor who purchases class B shares may be subject to a
   a. Front-end load sales charge
   b. Contingent deferred sales charge
   c. Lower annual expense than class A shares
   d. Front-end sales charge and a redemption fee

15. The XYZ Growth Fund's Net Asset Value has increased from $14.92 per share to $16.30 per share. Which of the following statements is true?
   a. The fund's portfolio must consist entirely of bonds.
   b. The fund has sold more shares to the public.
   c. The fund's portfolio has increased in value.
   d. The fund's portfolio has remained constant.

16. XYZ Growth Fund's Net Asset Value has decreased from $24.50 to $21.80 over a six-month period. This indicates that the fund's portfolio has
   a. Increased in value
   b. Doubled in value
   c. Decreased in value
   d. Remained the same

17. According to NASD rules, a registered representative who possesses only the Series 6 License is qualified to sell
   a. Shares of a closed-end fund currently being traded on the NYSE
   b. Limited partner interests which are exempt from SEC registration
   c. Shares of a closed-end fund on an initial offering
   d. Shares of a real estate investment trust during the initial offering period

18. The term *mutual fund* refers to a
   a. Closed-end investment company
   b. Open-end investment company
   c. Unit investment trust
   d. Real estate investment trust (REIT)

19. Mr. Jones is purchasing shares in ABC Growth Fund, which offers class A and class B shares. The RR is recommending that Mr. Jones purchase class B shares. On the purchase of the class B shares, Mr. Jones will
   a. Pay a sales charge which will not exceed 9½% .
   b. Pay an up-front sales charge and a redemption fee if he liquidates within ten years.
   c. Avoid an up-front sales charge.
   d. Pay an up-front sales charge but the annual expenses will be less than those associated with class A shares.

20. All of the following customers would find a long-term aggressive growth fund suitable for purchase **except:**

 a. A young restaurant owner with a substantial income investing for growth
 b. A young single doctor with substantial funds set aside for retirement
 c. A young lawyer and spouse investing for their two-year-old's college education
 d. A retired person with limited resources in need of current income

21. If a customer invests in a mutual fund with a 50% sales charge in the first year, refunds on the sales load are available for

 a. Seven calendar days
 b. Forty-five days
 c. One year
 d. Eighteen months

22. A customer purchases the Lexington Growth Fund when the fund's bid price was $15 and ask price was $16.30. The difference between the bid and ask price represents

 a. Sales charge
 b. Management fee
 c. Redemption fee
 d. Expense ratio

23. Mr. Smith sells 100 shares in the Pacific Growth Fund at a loss. He purchases 100 shares of the Pacific Growth Fund twenty-eight days later. Under federal tax laws

 a. The loss is fully deductible.
 b. It is considered a "wash sale" and the loss cannot be deducted for tax purposes.
 c. The loss is only 50% deductible.
 d. The customer may deduct twice the amount of the loss.

24. A real estate agent tells you, an RR, that Mr. Campbell made a $300,000 profit from the sale of his condominium. The real estate agent suggests that Mr. Campbell invest in an aggressive growth fund and wants you to recommend one. Which of the following statements is true under securities industry regulations?

 a. You should recommend an income fund and a money market fund instead of an aggressive growth fund.
 b. You should not make any recommendations without learning about the customer's investment objectives, financial situation, and needs.
 c. You should recommend that the entire $300,000 be placed in an international fund.
 d. You should recommend that the money be moved frequently among conservative growth funds, aggressive growth funds, and municipal bond funds.

25. If an investor wants to redeem shares held by a transfer agent for the investor, the transfer agent will normally require

 a. An oral confirmation to sell the shares from the customer
 b. A stock power and signature guarantee from the customer
 c. Written permission from the fund allowing the investor to sell the shares
 d. A copy of Form 1099-B from the previous calendar year

26. Assume John and Gail Adams own a mutual fund account as joint tenants with rights of survivorship. If John Adams passes away, which of the following is true?

 a. John Adams's percentage ownership will pass to Gail Adams.
 b. Ownership of the account will pass to Gail Adams.
 c. The estate of John Adams and Gail Adams will jointly own John Adams's interest in the account.
 d. John Adams's next of kin, exclusive of Gail Adams, will inherit his percentage ownership in the account.

27. Mutual fund shareholders are not taxed on

 I. Income distributions
 II. Capital gains distributions
 III. Unrealized capital gains

 a. I only
 b. II only
 c. III only
 d. I and II

28. Which of the following is not an investment company registered under the Investment Company Act of 1940?

 a. REIT
 b. Face-amount certificate company
 c. Unit investment trust
 d. Management company

29. Information contained on Forms 1099-DIV and 1099-B is reported annually to the fund shareholder and to the
   a.   NASD
   b.   IRS
   c.   SEC
   d.   State securities division

30. Miss Ryan is considering exchanging one fund for another under the same family. She should consider which of the following factors when making her decision?

   I.   Recent increases or decreases in the stock market and the economy
   II.   The tax consequence relating to the exchange
   III. Whether she desires more current income and whether the exchange meets that objective
   IV.   The objective of the fund she is transferring to

   a.   I and II
   b.   III and IV
   c.   I, III, and IV
   d.   All of the above

ANSWERS TO REVIEW QUESTIONS

1. c	7. a	13. b	19. c	25. b
2. d	8. d	14. b	20. d	26. b
3. a	9. d	15. c	21. d	27. c
4. c	10. b	16. c	22. a	28. a
5. b	11. c	17. c	23. b	29. b
6. c	12. a	18. b	24. b	30. d

4 REGULATION OF INVESTMENT COMPANIES

INTRODUCTION

Investment companies are subject to federal securities laws and state securities laws (blue-sky laws). The Investment Company Act of 1940 regulates investment companies to make sure that fund shareholders are fully informed and fairly treated. The three main types of investment companies are

1. Face-amount certificate companies
2. Unit investment trusts
3. Management companies (open-end and closed-end)

Face-amount certificate companies normally issue certificates at less than face value to investors, which are worth face value at maturity. Unit investment trusts are closed-end trusts that issue redeemable securities representing an undivided interest in the unit investment trust. Unit investment trusts have no management fee since they invest in a fixed portfolio of municipal or corporate bonds. The fund is operated by a board of trustees. Management companies manage a diversified portfolio of securities according to the investment objectives of the fund. Management companies are operated as either open-end funds or closed-end funds.

Investment companies must register with the Securities and Exchange Commission (SEC); however, the SEC does not approve or disapprove of the fund and does not supervise the management of the fund. For an investment company to change its investment objectives, the change must be approved by a majority of the outstanding securities. The Investment Company Act of 1940 also requires that an investment company have a minimum net worth of $100,000 before it can begin operations. No more than 60% of the board of directors of the fund can be officers, directors, or employees of the fund or its affiliated companies (interested directors). Therefore, 40% must be independent (noninterested) directors of the fund.

An investment company's prospectus under the 1940 Act must state its investment objectives and important practices and policies. The prospectus must state that the SEC has neither approved nor disapproved of the fund or its securities. The SEC does not pass on the adequacy or accuracy of the statements contained in the prospectus, which must make clear that there is no assurance that the fund will attain its investment objectives. Upon liquidation of the fund shares, the fund shareholder may receive more or less than his original amount invested. This fact must be made clear in the prospectus.

The prospectus contains information from the complete registration statement, which is of interest to the ordinary investor buying shares. The prospectus is the communication document used by issuers, underwriters, and dealers to offer the fund shares to prospective investors.

Investment companies must make payment for shares tendered to the fund or its principal underwriter within seven calendar days. Therefore, shares of mutual funds are liquid investments. Open-end investment companies may issue only common stock. They are allowed to borrow or lend money and can purchase call or put options. However, open-end investment companies cannot issue senior securities such as preferred stock or bonds. The fund's investment advisory contract under the Investment Company Act of 1940 must be approved by the fund shareholders and a majority of the board of directors. The custodian of the mutual fund is normally a commercial bank. The custodian holds the assets of the fund (cash and securities) for physical safekeeping. The transfer agent for an investment company

- Cancels shares redeemed by investors
- Issues new shares to investors
- Makes dividend and capital gains distributions to investors in the fund

The custodian bank and the transfer agent **do not**

- Perform any management, supervisory, or investment function
- Take any part in selling or distributing fund shares
- Offer any protection against the fund's assets depreciating (declining) in value

SALES CHARGES

A sales charge (load) is normally charged only when the fund is sold to the customer. It includes not only the commission to be retained by the dealer and the salesman, but also the underwriter's concession. It does not include the management fee—an operating expense of the fund. The sales charge is based on the ask price. For example, if the net asset value per share (NAVPS) of a fund was $14.49 (bid price) and the fund has a sales charge of 8%, the ask price (offering price) would be found by dividing the $14.49 by 0.92. The divisor is found by subtracting the percentage load from 100%. Note that the ask price could **not** be found by multiplying the bid price of 8% and adding the answer to the bid price. In the example used, the ask price would be

$$\text{Ask price} \quad = \quad \frac{14.49}{0.92} \quad = \quad \$15.75$$

Note the relationship between these amounts.

$15.75	Ask price	
−14.49	Bid price	The $1.26 sales charge is 8%
$ 1.26	Load	of the ask price of $15.75

The bid price is that at which the fund will buy back its own shares. Some funds, however, charge a redemption fee. This fee is usually based on the NAVPS of the shares being redeemed and is generally 1% or less. If, for example, a fund has a bid price of $20 and an ask price of $21.50 and a redemption fee of ¾ of 1%, an investor redeeming 1,000 shares would receive $19,850

$20 x 1,000 shares	=	$20,000
$20,000 x .0075	=	− 150
Proceeds to investor	=	$19,850

The method of calculating the public offering price must be described in the fund's registration statement and prospectus. Information concerning sales charge, redemption fee, or management fee can always be found in the prospectus. Prices quoted in the daily newspaper are bid and ask prices based on that day's closing price. A person deciding to invest the next day would not pay an amount related to either of these newspaper amounts since her price will be based on the net asset value next computed after the dealer receives her order on that day. The sales charge paid by an investor would be the same, whether the fund shares are purchased through a broker/dealer or wholesaler or from the fund itself. Broker/dealers and registered representatives (RRs) must be registered with the National Association of Securities Dealers (NASD) in order to sell mutual fund shares.

Mutual fund companies normally allow investors to swap funds for a nominal charge and avoid another sales charge. A mutual fund company may have a **family** of funds, such as growth, aggressive growth, growth and income, and income and money markets. An investor may sell an income fund and buy a growth fund. Even though the investor is avoiding a second sales charge, the transaction may have tax consequences. The Internal Revenue Service (IRS) considers a swap a sale of one security and a purchase of another security. If the customer realizes a capital gain on the sale of the income fund, he is subject to federal income tax on the gain. The customer, by immediately reinvesting in the growth fund, does not postpone the tax liability on the realized capital gain.

BREAKPOINTS

A **breakpoint** is the dollar amount required to qualify for a reduced sales charge on purchases of mutual fund shares. A breakpoint schedule might appear as follows:

Amount of purchase	Sales charge
$1,000–$9,999	8%
$10,000–$24,999	6%
$25,000–$99,999	4%
$100,000 and over	2%

The prospectus must include a table showing a sales charge for different breakpoints. The Investment Company Act of 1940 permits such reduced sales charges by any person making appropriate quantity purchases either in one lump sum, by accumulating the required sum with securities previously purchased, or through a letter of intent. Two terms require further elaboration. The Investment Company Act of 1940 defines *any person* as

- An individual
- An individual, spouse, and their children under the age of 21, purchasing securities for his or their account
- A pension plan, profit-sharing plan, or trust

An **investment club** is not eligible for a reduced sales charge. It is a group of individuals who pool their funds to follow a common investment program.

A **letter of intent** may be backdated as much as ninety days to enable the investor to take advantage of a recent large purchase. The total time covered by the letter of intent may not exceed thirteen months under federal securities laws.

Some of the shares purchased by the investors under a letter of intent may be held in escrow by the fund. If the investor does not meet the obligations of contributing the required dollar amounts within the thirteen-month period, the fund will send the investor a bill for the difference in the sales charge. If the investor does not pay the bill, shares held for the investor in escrow will be liquidated to cover the difference in the sales charge.

Assume a customer signs a letter of intent to invest $20,000 in a mutual fund. His original investment of $11,000 has increased to $15,000. What amount must the customer invest to maintain his original agreement and obtain the discounted sales charge? Capital appreciation is not considered in a letter of intent. The customer is obligated to invest an additional $9,000.

Rights of accumulation permit reduced sales charges on future purchases after the investor has reached a new breakpoint. For example, a customer invests $1,000 a month in the ABC Fund. ABC's sales charges are 8% on the first $10,000 and 6% from $10,000 to $25,000. For the first ten months the sales charges will be $80 each month (8% x $1,000); but on the eleventh month, as the 6% breakpoint is reached, the charge will be reduced and will stay at 6% until the next breakpoint is attained. This is different from the letter of intent, which applies the lower charges to the entire amount invested.

In rights of accumulation, capital appreciation is taken into consideration. Assume a customer invests $13,000 in a mutual fund. The investment appreciates in value to $17,500. The customer will now invest an additional $1,000. What will the sales charge be based on from the following information?

Amount invested	*Sales charge*
$1–$9,999	8½%
$10,000–$14,999	8¼%
$15,000–$19,999	8%
$20,000–$49,999	7¾%

The sales charge on the additional $1,000 investment by the customer would be 8%. Appreciation is taken into consideration when determining the sales charge in a rights of accumulation purchase. However, capital appreciation is not taken into consideration in a letter of intent.

ADVERTISING BY FUNDS

The SEC has, in recent years, taken a very close look at mutual fund advertising. As a result of their analysis, stock and bond mutual funds are required to use current standardized performance figures in their advertising. The funds must include the average annual total return, after expenses, for the most recent one-, five-, and ten-year periods. These figures must be printed on the prospectus in a typeface that is no smaller than other performance figures.

In addition to requiring uniform calculation of total return, the SEC requires that income funds use a uniformly calculated thirty-day figure in any advertising of their yield. Also, the SEC requires fund fee tables to illustrate every expense or fee, as well as how much these reduce a hypothetical $1,000 investment for one, three, five, and ten years. The fee table must appear in the beginning of all fund prospectuses. The purpose of these fee tables is to make it easier to compare the charges imposed by individual funds. The rules apply to front- and back-end loads and funds that levy 12b-1 fees.

Funds that levy 12b-1 fees are referred to as **12b-1 funds**. These fees are named after the SEC regulation that governs them. Both load and no-load 12b-1 funds are allowed to use a portion of the shareholders' assets to pay marketing and advertising costs.

In recent years, some funds have begun charging low loads instead of the normal load of approximately 8½%. Mutual funds are available today with different loads or sales charges.

- **Load fund**—normally charges over 3% up to 8½%

- **Low-load fund**—sales charge normally 2 to 3%
- **No-load fund**—no sales charge levied on a customer purchase

MUTUAL FUND SALES LITERATURE

Sales literature concerning mutual funds is broadly defined as any communication used to induce the purchase of investment company shares. Such statements may be oral or written. The important considerations are whether or not these statements are passed on to prospective purchasers or are designed for use in the sale of shares. A piece of sales literature shall be deemed materially misleading by reason of an implication, if such sales literature: (1) includes an untrue statement of a material fact or (2) omits to state a material fact necessary in order to make a statement made, in light of the circumstances of its use, not misleading.

This broad definition of sales literature is quite inclusive. It not only includes advertising material that would usually be considered to be sales literature, it includes the company's annual and quarterly reports.

Sales literature is considered to be **materially misleading** under NASD rules if it

- Represents or implies that the investor will receive a stable, continuous, dependable, liberal, or specified rate of return
- Discusses appreciation possibilities, without including an explanation of the market risks and the possibility of incurring a capital loss on redemption
- Refers to registration or regulation of any investment company under federal or state laws without explaining that this does not involve any supervision of a fund's investment policy
- Implies that the custodian bank protects the investor against loss or protects against unsuitable investment policies
- Makes extravagant claims concerning the ability or competency of the management such as stating that the fund's investment managers are the most competent in the industry
- Discusses any continuous investment plan without making it clear that such a plan does not assure a profit nor does it protect against a loss in a declining market

Sales literature relating to the securities of a particular investment company must be accompanied or preceded by a prospectus. Mutual funds are sold to investors by a prospectus and cannot be sold using only sales literature such as research reports or magazine articles.

DOLLAR COST AVERAGING

Dollar cost averaging is the investment of a specific sum in the same security or group of securities over a long period of time, without regard to the price level of that security. It may be referred to only as "dollar cost averaging" or "cost averaging," *not* "dollar averaging" or "averaging the dollar." The key to dollar cost averaging is the mathematical certainty that if the price of a security continually rises and falls, the average cost of the security will be less than its average price. The reason is that when the price is low, the investor will purchase more shares than when the price is high. An example will demonstrate this.

Months	Amount of purchase	Security price	Shares purchased
1	$100	$ 6	16.667
2	$100	$ 5	20,000
3	$100	$ 3	33.333
4	$100	$ 4	25.000
5	$100	$ 8	12.500
6	$100	$10	10.000
Totals	$600	$36	117.500

The average price is $6 ($36 ÷ 6), but the average cost is $5.11 ($600 ÷ 117.500). Dollar cost averaging does not ensure a profit to an investor.

NASD RULES CONCERNING INVESTMENT COMPANIES

Certain NASD rules apply to investment companies, including

- The lowest price at which an NASD underwriter may sell shares of an open-end investment company to another NASD member is the NAVPS. However, sales to public customers or nonmember broker/dealers must take place at the ask price.
- Open-end company shares may be purchased by the broker/dealer from the underwriter, for the sole purpose of covering customer's orders or for the broker/dealer's investment account. A broker/dealer is not

allowed to make a market in open-end investment company shares by trading them with other broker/dealers.

- Selling dividends is prohibited under NASD rules. This expression is used to describe the salesman's procedure to influence an investor to buy mutual funds just before a dividend is payable on the incorrect assumption that he will profit. Net assets of the fund decline after the dividend is paid and, therefore, the investor does not benefit. The dividend was already considered in the price.
- The rules concerning the public offering price of an investment company are as follows:

  - No member may purchase an open-end investment company security from an underwriter at a discount from the public offering price unless

    - The buying broker/dealer is also a member.
    - A sales agreement is in effect between the parties at the time of the sale.
    - The required contents of the sales agreement are specified in accordance with NASD rules.

  - No underwriter member shall participate in the offering or sale of any such security if the public offering price includes a gross selling commission or load that is unfair if all relevant circumstances are considered.
  - The net asset value on which the public offering price is based is the minimum price at which a member may purchase any such security from the issuer. (The rule then specifies the time of calculation of the net asset value to be used as the basis of the public offering price.)

    - "No member shall withhold placing customers orders for any such security so as to profit himself as a result of such withholding."
    - A member may purchase securities of an open-end investment company only to cover purchase orders already received or for investment.

  - "No member who is an underwriter shall accept a conditional order for the securities of an open-end investment company on any basis other than at a specified definite price."

- NASD rules cover "special deals" relating to the sale of investment company shares. This rule holds that giving or accepting anything of material value in addition to the discounts or concessions set forth in the prospectus is conduct inconsistent with just and equitable principles of trade. This applies to a principal underwriter or persons associated with or affiliated with him, members, registered representatives, or associated persons.

  Examples of items which constitute "anything of material value" are

  - Gifts of more than $100 per person per year. Therefore, gifts of $100 or less per person per year are not considered of material value and may be given.
  - Gifts of management company stock or other security or making such security available on a preferred basis.
  - Loans to a noncontrolled dealer or his associate.
  - Discounts from the offering price more than those set forth in the prospectus and regular selling group arrangement.
  - Wholesale overrides granted to a dealer on its own retail sales unless they are described in the prospectus.
  - Gifts or payments of any kind by a wholesale representative to a dealer firm employee except for

    - Occasional dinner or tickets to a sporting event or theater
    - Reception or cocktail party given for a group of registered representatives with a bona fide business meeting
    - Gifts or reminder advertising amounting to no more than $100 per person per year

- Compensation for sales of investment company shares must be reasonably related to the dealer's discount described in the latest prospectus and/or the agreement of the selling group. An RR may receive continuing commissions at retirement provided a bona fide contract exists between him and the employing broker/dealer.
- Members must forward promptly to the underwriter (or custodian) any funds received from customers in payment of shares. Payment must be made within ten business days after the date of the transaction; oth-

erwise, the underwriter must notify the dealer and the NASD office in the district covering the dealer's office. Such transactions are subject to Regulation T of the Federal Reserve.

- In order to avoid the increasing abuse of the withdrawal plan, the NASD prohibits members from suggesting or encouraging the use of the partial withdrawal and reinstatement privilege. This is usually included in single payment and periodic unit investment trusts. It permits withdrawals of up to 90% of the current value of the planholder's account in cash and return of the money later without a sales charge. Its purpose is to provide emergency funds for the planholder, but it was found that certain planholders were making withdrawals for short-term trades in speculative securities, hence the rule.
- No member is permitted to favor or disfavor the distribution of investment company shares on the basis of brokerage commissions received or expected. However, the **reciprocal brokerage rule** permits members who sell investment company shares to execute portfolio transactions for that investment company as long as such orders are not obtained on the basis of their sales of the investment company shares.
- On open-end investment company shares, the ex-dividend date is the date designated by the issuer or principal underwriter of the fund.
- Assume a mutual fund is quoted $11 bid $11.96 offering price. An NASD member must sell the funds to a public customer or a non-NASD member at $11.96, which is the public offering price or ask price. An NASD member can sell the fund to another NASD member at $11, the bid price.
- The sale of investment company shares in dollar amounts just below the point at which the sales charge is reduced on quantity transactions so as to obtain the higher sales charges applicable on sales below the breakpoint is contrary to just and equitable principles of trade. Furthermore, breakpoints should be fully explained to customers contemplating large purchases of the fund.
- A registered representative working for a firm that does not distribute a specific fund may, on the customer's instructions, sell the fund shares for the customer to the fund or underwriter at the net asset value and charge the customer a commission.

MUTUAL FUND SALES BY BANKS

In recent years, many banks have engaged in the business of selling mutual funds to bank customers. Individuals who purchase mutual funds through banks should understand the following points:

- Investing in mutual funds is not the same as depositing money into a bank account. Mutual funds are not bank deposits and therefore are not Federal Deposit Insurance Corporation (FDIC) insured. Mutual fund shares are not insured by any agency of the federal government.
- Mutual fund shares sold by banks are not obligations of the bank and are not guaranteed by the bank who sells the mutual funds.
- An investor who purchases mutual fund shares is taking an investment risk, including possible loss of principal. Investment return and the principal value of a mutual fund will fluctuate, and the value of an investor's shares, when redeemed, may be worth more or less than their original cost.
- An investor should purchase mutual funds to meet specific investment objectives such as capital growth, current income, nontaxable income, liquidity, and preservation of capital. Investments designed to meet a client's investment objectives are "suitable" investments for the client.
- Mutual funds are sold to investors by a prospectus. The prospectus contains certain information from the complete registration statement filed with the SEC. The prospectus contains information that would be of interest to the ordinary investor buying shares in the fund. The statement of additional information is not a prospectus, but may be read in conjunction with a fund's prospectus. The statement of additional information explains in detail the fund's investment policies and limitations, how portfolio transactions are executed, and the manner in which the portfolio is valued. All investors purchasing fund shares must be given a prospectus. All sales literature pertaining to mutual funds must be preceded or accompanied by a prospectus. The statement of additional information, under federal securities laws, must be given to investors who request it.
- Investors should understand the difference between bank products and investments. Bank products include checking accounts, money market accounts, and certificates of deposit. Mutual funds are investment products offered through the bank and normally include mutual funds, money market funds, income funds, and tax-exempt funds.

ADDITIONAL CONCEPTS

Mutual funds are subject to a variety of regulations.

- Open-end investment companies are allowed, under the Investment Company Act of 1940, to borrow or lend money or to purchase put or call options. However, the Investment Company Act of 1940 prohibits an open-end investment company from issuing senior securities (preferred stock or bonds). Open-end investment companies can issue only common stock.
- Investment companies are sold by use of a prospectus under federal securities laws. The prospectus contains information concerning the fund's investment objectives, sales charges, and refunds on the load relating to the fund. The prospectus for a mutual fund contains certain information from the registration statement, which is of interest to the ordinary investor buying shares. The prospectus is the communication used by a person to offer to sell securities of an investment company.
- Mutual funds issue annual reports that include a listing of income and expense items of the mutual fund. The annual report also lists all securities owned by the mutual fund and all assets and liabilities of the fund. If a fund wants to send its annual report to shareholders as sales literature, it must be approved by a principal of the firm prior to use and it must be preceded or accompanied by a prospectus.
- Registered representatives, under federal securities laws, are restricted concerning oral statements they can make to customers. For example, an RR is allowed to state that "our investment managers are determined to provide customers with the best service of which they are capable." However, the following statements made by an RR would be in violation of securities industry regulations:

  - "This fund will always yield at least 9%."
  - "Since this fund is an aggressive growth fund, it will increase faster than the stock market as a whole."
  - "Our fund managers are the most competent in the entire securities industry and this will be true forever."

- RRs, when selling a contractual plan to a customer, must make the following points clear relating to the sales charge:

  - How sales charges are deducted from payments made during the early years of the plan
  - The consequences to the customer of liquidating the plan in early years and the sales charge refund provisions applicable to the contractual plan
  - The total sales charges over the life of the contractual plan

- Only individuals who are licensed or registered with the NASD to sell mutual funds to the public can be paid a commission on their sale. Assume a local insurance agent wants to sell a mutual fund offered by your firm and split the commission with you. This arrangement is prohibited under securities industry regulations since the local insurance agent is not registered (licensed) with the NASD.
- RRs selling mutual funds to customers must act in the best interest of the customer. The following are probable violations of NASD rules relating to fair dealing with customers:

  - Encouraging customers to buy load funds before the ex-dividend date called selling dividends. This practice is not beneficial to a customer because the amount of the distribution is included in the price paid for the shares.
  - A pattern of short-term trading in load funds.
  - Switching customers from one load fund to another in discretionary accounts controlled by the broker/dealer (firm).
  - Recommending that a customer maintain a withdrawal plan and contribute to a mutual fund contractual plan at the same time.

- Customers who redeem mutual funds must be paid within seven calendar days of tender. Mutual funds are normally sold as long-term investments. However, no guarantee of principal protection exists when a customer buys mutual funds. A customer who sells shares of a mutual fund will receive a confirmation statement relating to the sale. When a mutual fund is redeemed by a customer, the amount received may be more or less than the amount invested.
- Some customers purchase mutual funds under a letter of intent. If the customer cannot continue to make the required investments, the fund will send a bill to the customer for the difference in the sales charges. Assume the customer does not send the payment in order to make up the difference. In this case, shares

owned by the investor held in escrow by the fund will be liquidated to cover the difference in the sales charges.

- XYZ Fund's prospectus states that shares are sold at net asset value plus a sales charge of 8%, which is 9.3% of the net amount invested. It is important for a customer to understand that the 8% is calculated on the offering price of the fund. Along with the prospectus for a fund, federal securities laws require that the statement of additional information be distributed to customers who request it. When a customer purchases investment company shares, he receives a form detailing the transaction, called a "customer's confirmation."

- Customers seeking capital appreciation would normally invest in a common stock fund. Customers interested in current income would normally invest in a money market fund or an income fund. Customers must be made aware of any breakpoints relating to a fund, if the amount of money invested falls just below the breakpoint.

- SEC Rule 12b-1 allows a mutual fund to spend money on advertising, printing, and mailing of sales literature to customers and for compensation to underwriters. The 12b-1 fees must be clearly stated in the fund's prospectus and are charged against the assets of the fund. The purpose of this rule is to allow mutual funds to be able to pay distribution expenses relating to the sale of fund shares. Any fund advertisements containing performance data are required, under SEC rules, to disclose the risk of loss of principal and the risk of fluctuation of income. Also, mutual fund sales literature, which contains a quotation of yield or equivalent yield, must contain the fund's total return information. Total return information must be provided for one year, five years, and ten years. Assume a mutual fund has been in business for twelve years. The mutual fund wants to provide only the one-year and five-year total return information. This is prohibited under SEC rules. The mutual fund, since it has been in business for more than ten years, must provide average annual returns for one year, five years, and ten years.

- An investor who purchases investment company shares could file suit to rescind a transaction or collect damages if

  - The prospectus omitted certain material facts.
  - He did not receive a prospectus at or before completion of the transaction.
  - A sales presentation given to the investor, which influenced his investment decision, contained an untrue statement of a material fact.

- Federal securities laws require that an investment advisory contract of an investment company be approved by the shareholders and a majority of the board of directors.

- The expense ratio for an open-end investment company is the cost of portfolio management plus operating costs divided by average net asset value. The expense ratio for an open-end investment company measures the fund's operating efficiency.

- Mutual fund shareholders must receive certain financial information at least semiannually from the fund. The financial information consists of a balance sheet, income statement, and a list of the securities in the portfolio.

- The maximum sales charge, under NASD rules, may not exceed 8.5% of the offering price. In order to charge the maximum of 8.5%, the fund must offer all three of the following benefits to customers:

  - Rights of accumulation
  - Quantity discounts on single purchases
  - Dividend reinvestment at net asset value

- Mutual funds may be diversified funds or nondiversified funds. For a mutual fund to be considered a **diversified fund,** it must meet the "75-5-10 rule." A diversified fund must have 75% of its assets invested so that

  - The fund does not have more than 5% of its total assets in any one security, and
  - The fund does not own more than 10% of the voting stock of any one security.

REVIEW QUESTIONS

1. When selling mutual fund shares, there is no objection to which of the following statements?

    I. "We are proud to announce that the XYZ Bank safeguards the cash you invest."
    II. "The XYZ Bank is custodian of the fund's cash and securities."
    III. "All cash and securities are held in custody of the XYZ Bank."
    IV. "You can have confidence in the fund because the XYZ Bank is our custodian."

    a. I only
    b. II and IV
    c. II and III
    d. I, III, and IV

2. When a registered representative is selling a contractual plan to a client, which of the following points should be made clear concerning the sales charge?

    I. The consequences to the customer of liquidating the plan in the early years and sales charge refund provisions applicable to the contractual plan
    II. The total sales charge over the life of the contractual plan
    III. How sales charges are deducted from payments made during early years of the plan

    a. I only
    b. I and II
    c. II and III
    d. All of the above

3. Mr. Kelly is considering exchanging one mutual fund for another. Which of the following considerations are important for Mr. Kelly?

    I. His desire for more current income
    II. The objective of the fund to which he is transferring
    III. The tax consequences relating to the exchange of the fund shares
    IV. Recent movements or changes in the stock market and economy

    a. I and II
    b. III and IV
    c. I, II, and IV
    d. All of the above

4. Mr. Williams is sixty-five years of age and wants to invest $20,000 in a mutual fund withdrawal plan. The withdrawal plan will pay Mr. Williams $400 per month. He should clearly understand which of the following?

    I. He is guaranteed to be paid $400 a month for life.
    II. Invested capital may be exhausted.
    III. Ownership of principal amount is given up when withdrawals begin.
    IV. More money may be withdrawn from the account than the present amount Mr. Williams provisioned for.

    a. I and II
    b. III and IV
    c. I and III
    d. II and IV

5. In open-end investment company sales literature, the phrase "dollar cost averaging" in connection with any continuous investment plan may not be used without making clear which of the following?
    a. That the investor must take into account his financial ability to continue such plan through periods of low price levels
    b. That the investor is investing his funds in securities subject to market fluctuations and that the method involves continuous investment in such shares at regular intervals regardless of price levels
    c. That the investor will incur a loss under such plan if he discontinues the plan when the market value of his shares is less than his cost
    d. All of the above

6. Mrs. Smith purchases open-end investment company shares and signs a letter of intent, which is accepted by the fund underwriter. The letter of intent covers purchases made within a period of not more than
    a. Two months from the date of the letter
    b. Three months from the date of the letter
    c. Twelve months from the date of the letter
    d. Thirteen months from the date of the letter

7. The custodian of a mutual fund, which is normally a commercial bank, holds the assets of the fund
    a. For physical safekeeping
    b. To protect investors against loss in the value of the shares
    c. To collateralize customer loans and handle margin transactions
    d. To guarantee return of the customer's principal plus interest

8. Fund advertisements containing performance data are required, under SEC rules, to do which of the following?

    I. Disclose the risk of fluctuation of income.
    II. Disclose the risk of loss of principal.
    III. Include purchase applications for the fund in the advertisement.

    a. I only
    b. II and III
    c. I and II
    d. All of the above

9. Which of the following statements are in violation of securities industry regulations?

    I. The custodian protects the investor against unsuitable investment policies.
    II. Dollar cost averaging ensures that the investor's account will fall below his cost basis.
    III. Regulation of investment companies does not involve supervision of the fund's investment policies.
    IV. Mutual funds can be redeemed, but on redemption the amount received by the investor may be more or less than the amount invested.

    a. I and II
    b. III and IV
    c. I and III
    d. II and IV

10. Securities industry regulations would allow which of the following statements to be made by a registered representatives involving investment companies?
    a. "This fund will always yield at least 10%, but that is probably low."
    b. "Our investment managers are the most competent in the securities industry and this will be true for all time."
    c. "Our managers' dedication is to provide you with the best service of which they are capable of providing."
    d. "This fund is a growth fund and will increase faster than the market as a whole and decrease less than the market as a whole."

11. Under securities industry regulations, a mutual fund's sales literature that contains a quotation of yield or equivalent yield must also contain
    a. The fund's total return information
    b. The names of all stockholders in the fund
    c. The fund's incorporation date
    d. The fund's taxpayer identification number

12. According to SEC Rule 12b-1, fund expenditures may be used for all of the following **except:**
    a. Advertising
    b. Compensation to underwriters
    c. Brokerage costs for portfolio transactions
    d. The cost of printing and mailing of sales literature to customers

13. Among the provisions of the Investment Company Act of 1940, designed to protect the interests of investors, is the provision that
    a. Any change in fundamental investment policy must be approved by a majority of the outstanding shares.
    b. Advertising and sales literature must be approved in advance of its use by the NASD.
    c. Selection of company investments must be approved by the SEC.
    d. Net asset value of a fund may not decline below 90% of the current market price of the fund portfolio.

14. Which of the following would normally be the custodian of an investment company?
  a. A full-service broker/dealer
  b. Member firm of the NASD
  c. Commercial bank
  d. An underwriting firm

15. A mutual fund's annual report includes all of the following information **except:**
  a. Income and expense items of the mutual fund
  b. A list of all securities owned by the mutual fund
  c. Income and expense items of the mutual fund's management company
  d. A list of the mutual fund's assets and liabilities

16. Mr. Foster is considering investing in XYZ Growth Fund. He must be made aware of the breakpoints relating to the fund
  a. Under no circumstances
  b. Only if they are detailed in the fund's prospectus
  c. Only if the customer specifically asks about the breakpoints
  d. If the amount of money invested falls just below the breakpoint

17. Your broker compares a withdrawal plan from a mutual fund to a savings account. He states that if you withdraw $500 a month from the withdrawal plan, which has a current market value of $50,000, your return will be 12%. This is much better than the present savings account rate of 3%. Which of the following statements is true concerning this comparison?
  a. This is a proper comparison in every way.
  b. This comparison is completely proper but the broker should advise you to leave the money in the account and continue to earn 12%.
  c. This is an unfair comparison and may be fraudulent.
  d. Federal securities laws do not cover comparisons such as this in any way.

18. An investor is considering two mutual funds with the same objective as potential investments. Which of the following nonperformance items should the investor consider for the two funds?

  I. Availability of a letter of intent
  II. Availability of withdrawal plans
  III. Availability of an exchange privilege
  IV. The price (net asset value or ask price) at which dividends may be reinvested in additional shares

  a. I and II
  b. III and IV
  c. I, II, and IV
  d. All of the above

A customer has $5,000 to invest and he makes the following purchases each year:

Amount invested	Share price	Number of shares purchased
$1,000	$11.76	85
$1,000	$10.00	100
$1,000	$8.13	123
$1,000	$5.00	200
$1,000	$4.00	250
$5,000		758

19. What is the customer's approximate average cost per share?
  a. $0.15
  b. $6.60
  c. $7.58
  d. $7.81

20. The statement of additional information, according to federal securities laws
  a. Must be sent to customers prior to sending the prospectus
  b. Must be given to investors who request it
  c. Must precede or accompany any sales literature sent to customers
  d. Is not available to investors under any circumstances

21. Customers who purchase mutual fund shares through a bank should clearly understand which of the following?

     I. That the mutual fund is not FDIC insured
    II. That the mutual fund is not guaranteed by the bank
   III. That the customer may receive more or less than the original amount invested upon liquidation

    a. I only
    b. II only
    c. III only
    d. All of the above

22. Assume the Western Fund, an open-end investment company, has a bid price of $18 and an ask price of $19.67. The Western Fund has no redemption fee. The amount the customer will receive on liquidation of 1,200 shares is
    a. $19,670
    b. $21,600
    c. $22,610
    d. $23,600

23. Under federal securities laws an investment advisory contract for an investment company must be approved by
    a. The custodian bank
    b. The transfer agent
    c. The shareholders and a majority of the board of directors
    d. The fund's underwriter

24. All of the following are permitted if given by a fund underwriter to a registered representative of a member firm **except:**
    a. Gifts of less than $100
    b. Tickets to a baseball game valued at $60
    c. Dinner for the registered representative and spouse
    d. An expense-paid trip for two to Paris, France

ANSWERS TO REVIEW QUESTIONS

1. c	5. d	9. a	13. a	17. c	21. d
2. d	6. d	10. c	14. c	18. d	22. b
3. d	7. a	11. a	15. c	19. b	23. c
4. d	8. c	12. c	16. d	20. b	24. d

5 VARIABLE ANNUITIES AND RETIREMENT PLANS

INTRODUCTION

In this chapter we will discuss variable annuity contracts, variable life contracts, and other types of retirement plans. The two main types of annuities are

1. Fixed Annuities
2. Variable Annuities

FIXED ANNUITIES

In a **fixed annuity contract,** the insurance company guarantees to pay the annuitant a fixed sum of money for the life of the annuitant. For example, a fixed annuity may pay an annuitant $500 a month for the life of the annuitant. The term *annuity* refers to a stream of payments. For a fixed annuity, the payment is guaranteed by the insurance company. Therefore, a fixed annuity is an insurance product and *not* a security. With a fixed annuity, the income remains level and the annuitant is exposed to the purchasing power risk. The purchasing power risk is the risk that the purchasing power of the dollar will decrease in the future. Premiums by annuitants into a fixed annuity are invested into the general account after expenses are deducted.

In a fixed annuity, the investment risk is assumed by the insurance company. The insurance company provides a guaranteed rate of return, income, and interest, and a guaranteed payment to a beneficiary, if the annuitant dies before annuity payments begin.

To summarize the main points concerning a fixed annuity contract

- During the distribution period an annuitant receives a fixed amount monthly for life.
- The insurance company guarantees the rate of return, income, interest, and payments to a named beneficiary, if the annuitant dies before the distribution period begins.
- A fixed annuity is *not* a security, since the contract is guaranteed by an insurance company. A fixed annuity is an annuity in which the payments are fixed.
- The annuitant takes the purchasing power risk (inflation risk).

VARIABLE ANNUITIES

Variable annuities are securities that attract investors seeking retirement income with inflation protection. However, the investment risk in a variable annuity belongs to the annuitant. Assume Mr. Jones, a single person, is forty-five years old and wants to provide for his retirement needs. He invests in a non-tax-qualified variable annuity. The term **non-tax-qualified** means that Mr. Jones will be investing after-tax dollars. There is no restriction on the amount Mr. Jones can invest in the variable annuity.

Assume Mr. Jones invests $100 a month in the variable annuity for twenty years. The twenty years he invests in the variable annuity is the **accumulation period**. The money purchases accumulation units in the variable annuity. The annuitant owns accumulation units in the separate account of securities. The earnings (interest, dividends, and capital gains) accrue on a tax-deferred basis in the separate account. No taxes are paid during the accumulation period. Over twenty years Mr. Jones will have invested $24,000 in the variable annuity. At the end of the accumulation period, Mr. Jones can take a lump-sum distribution or annuitize the principal. If Mr. Jones surrenders the variable annuity for a lump sum, he will realize ordinary income in excess of his basis (cost). Assume the value of the variable annuity has grown to $80,000. Mr. Jones will realize ordinary income of $56,000.

$80,000   Surrender value (sales proceeds)
− 24,000   Amount invested (cost)
$56,000   Ordinary income

Assume that instead of surrendering the annuity for a lump sum, Mr. Jones takes a life annuity. He gives up the rights to the principal of $80,000 and agrees to receive a monthly payment, which will vary according to the performance of the separate account. The payments Mr. Jones receives monthly will be partly taxable and partly a return of capital. The portion that is taxable represents the earnings. The portion of the monthly payment representing a return of capital is not taxable. Variable annuities invest in common stocks and equity mutual funds and are not susceptible to the purchasing power risk that affects fixed annuities. For a person who wants to receive income for life at retirement with inflation protection, a variable annuity is an excellent choice.

A particular variable annuity may have surrender charges for the first five years on a declining scale. Withdrawals prior to age 59½ may result in a 10% tax penalty to the annuitant. The penalty is assessed only on the earnings portion and not on the annuitant's return of capital. Assume Mr. Jones invested $12,000 in his variable annuity, which was cashed in for $40,000 after ten years, when Mr. Jones is fifty-five years old. Mr. Jones is in the 28% tax bracket. Mr. Jones' total tax is $10, 640.

$$
\begin{array}{lllll}
\$28,000 & \text{x} & 28\% & = & \$ \ 7,840 & \text{Regular Tax} \\
\$28,000 & \text{x} & 10\% & = & \$ \ \underline{2,800} & \text{Penalty Tax} \\
& & & & \$10,640 & \text{Total Tax}
\end{array}
$$

If Mr. Jones decided to take a lifetime income from the variable annuity, no penalty tax would be assessed even though he is fifty-five years old. He would be able to choose from certain annuity payment options, such as

- *Life annuity.* All payments would cease on the death of Mr. Jones. This payment option would give him the highest cash flow.
- *Joint and last survivor.* If Mr. Jones were married, he might choose this payment option. On the death of Mr. Jones, payments would continue for the life of his spouse.
- *Life annuity—period certain.* Assume Mr. Jones chooses a life annuity—twenty-year period certain. If Mr. Jones dies after eight years, his beneficiary will receive payments for the remaining twelve years or may elect a single payment.

When an annuitant decides to **annuitize** a variable annuity, accumulation units are converted into a fixed number of annuity units. The annuitant receives a monthly payment, which is the number of annuity units multiplied by the value of each annuity unit. The number of annuity units remains fixed during the annuity or distribution period. However, the value of the annuity unit varies with the investment performance of the separate account. Some insurance companies offer a combination fixed and variable annuity.

A variable annuity is considered to be a security under federal securities laws. The NASD requires that all persons selling variable annuities have a securities license. A variable annuity must be registered under the Securities Act of 1933 and the Investment Company Act of 1940, since it is both a security and an investment company.

Variable annuitants have the right to vote on any proposed change in investment policy and for the election of the portfolio managers. They must be sent proxies allowing them to vote without attending the annual meeting.

Owners of variable annuity contracts normally have the right to

- Vote on proposed changes in investment policy
- Vote on the choice of the portfolio manager
- Reduced sales charges on large purchases (sales charge breakpoints)

Investment return in the separate account of a variable annuity consists of dividend and interest income, realized capital gains and losses, and unrealized appreciation or depreciation. The earnings accrue on a tax-deferred basis during the accumulation period.

Since variable annuities are subject to the Securities Act of 1933, their sale must be preceded or accompanied by a copy of the variable annuity's current prospectus. The prospectus contains the investment objectives and investment policies of the separate account and other information of interest to the ordinary investor.

Different purchase methods apply to variable annuities. There are generally three methods from which to choose, depending on when the annuity payments to the annuitant are to begin. Variable annuities can be purchased by a lump-sum payment or by periodic payments. For example, a person could invest a lump sum now and receive payments at a later date or receive payments immediately. Another choice would be to invest periodically and receive payments at a later date. If payments are to be received at a later date, it is a **deferred annuity**. If the annuitant receives payments immediately after investing a lump sum, it is an **immediate annuity**.

Charges for services such as premium billing and collecting, recordkeeping, and communications are administrative fees for a variable annuity and described in the prospectus. For example, a variable annuity would normally have a charge for investment management expenses. Variable annuity contracts levy administrative fees, which are charges for premium billing and collecting, recordkeeping, and communications.

As with the purchasers of mutual funds, variable annuity contract holders may get reduced sales charges if their investments exceed the specified **breakpoints**. The amount of money invested in the variable annuity may permit the investor to obtain a reduced sales charge. Many variable annuities also offer purchasers rights of accumulation.

Mutual funds are valued on a per-share basis; variable annuities have unit values. During the accumulation period, the value of a variable annuity is expressed as an accumulation unit while valuation during the payout period is expressed as an annuity unit. The value of the units is determined by the value of the investment portfolio in the separate account, calculated once a day at the close of business of the securities markets.

The **accumulation unit** is an accounting measure that determines the contract owner's interest in the separate account. As stated in the prospectus, the units are revalued periodically to reflect changes in the market value of the portfolio's common stock and other investments. The value will change according to changes in market values, realized capital gains and losses, and investment income. Accumulation units are also adjusted daily for the charges and fees, such as mortality and expense. The net value divided by the number of units outstanding yields the value of one accumulation unit. The value of the contract holder's account is determined by multiplying the value of one unit by the number of units the contract holder owns.

The annuity unit is an accounting measure that determines the amount of each payment to the annuitant during the payout or annuity period. It is essential to realize that the number of units credited to the annuitant remains fixed. It is the changing value of each unit that results in a variable payout during the annuity period.

If an annuitant chooses to annuitize the contract, immediately before the payout period begins, the accumulation units are "converted" into annuity units. This period is known as the **annuity commencement date**.

The number of annuity units the annuitant will receive depends upon the

- Value of the accumulation units
- Age and sex of the annuitant
- Type of settlement option selected

If the actual earnings exceed the assumed interest rate (AIR), the value of the annuity unit will increase. The amount of the annuity payment received by the annuitant is found by multiplying the number of annuity units by the value of each unit for that valuation period. For example, if an annuitant had 150 units and each was valued at $8, he would receive a payment of $1,200 for that period. The more risk the annuitant assumes, the higher the payout received for a given sum of money. For example, a **life annuity** pays an annuitant a larger amount each month than a **joint and last survivor annuity**.

ADDITIONAL CONCEPTS—VARIABLE ANNUITIES

The following information is critical to understanding how variable annuities work:

- During the accumulation period of a variable annuity, the separate account earns interest and dividends and realizes capital gains. However, no taxes are due from the annuitant during the accumulation period. Taxes are paid by the annuitant during the annuity or distribution period.
- The separate account of a variable annuity contains investments that must be consistent with the variable annuity's investment policy described in the prospectus. Variable annuities normally have objectives of growth or growth and income (total return).
- A variable annuity invests mainly in equities and neither the principal nor the payout is guaranteed. Therefore, a variable annuity is an annuity in which the payments "vary."
- The surrender value of a deferred variable annuity contract is equal to the number of accumulation units multiplied by the value of an accumulation unit next computed after receipt of the request for surrender by the issuer.
- Variable annuities offer benefits such as deferral of taxes during the accumulation period, reinstatement provisions, and various settlement options.
- When the value of an accumulation unit in a variable annuity contract is calculated, components of the separate account include realized and unrealized capital gains and losses and investment income.
- Securities industry regulations require that an advertisement containing variable annuity total return performance show the disclosure of sales charges, an offer to provide a prospectus, and year-end average annual return.
- Assume Mr. Charles Dawson recently annuitized his variable annuity contract. The variable annuity has an assumed interest rate of 4%. Mr. Dawson's first payment was $600. In the second month, the separate account earned 7% and Mr. Dawson received $635. In the third month, the separate account earned 5%.

Mr. Dawson's payment in the third month will be an amount greater than $635. The comparison of the amount received each month is made to the previous month's payment. If the separate account earns more than the AIR, then the payment received by the annuitant will increase from the previous month's payment. If the separate account earns less than the AIR, then the payment received by the annuitant will decrease from the previous month's payment.

- Some insurance companies offer combination fixed and variable annuities, which offer a guaranteed fixed payment with a variable payment from a variable annuity.
- Variable annuities levy charges for premium billing and collecting, recordkeeping, and communications with annuitants. These charges are classified as administrative fees or expenses.
- A variable annuity would be an excellent choice for a middle-aged person investing for retirement, who is concerned about running out of money in later years.
- Variable annuities could be single-premium immediate, single-premium deferred, and a periodic payment deferred.
- If the owner of a variable annuity decides to annuitize the contract, the insurance company agrees to continue to pay the annuitant, even if the annuitant lives longer than normal life expectancy. This guarantee from the insurance company is referred to as the **mortality guarantee**.
- Variable annuity contracts also have an **expense guarantee** from the insurance company. Assume the owner of a variable annuity decides to annuitize the contract. The insurance company guarantees that the amount of the annuity payments will not be reduced by increased operating expenses of the insurance company (expense guarantee).

VARIABLE LIFE INSURANCE

The second type of variable contract, in addition to a variable annuity, is variable life insurance. **Variable life insurance** is an innovation in life insurance and allows policyholders an opportunity to earn capital gains on their insurance investment and still maintain death benefit coverage. Therefore, variable life insurance can be defined as a form of life insurance where the amount of the death benefit and the cash surrender value (benefit) can vary. The variations will occur as a result of the investment performance of the assets in the separate account. The assets in the separate account in a variable life insurance contract are primarily invested in common stock or equity mutual funds. However, a variable life insurance contract guarantees a minimum death benefit, regardless of the investment experience of the separate account.

Individuals may consider variable life insurance contracts attractive because the minimum death benefit is guaranteed and the policy offers the opportunity for an increase in the actual amount of the death benefit payable. The increase in the death benefit will depend on the results obtained by the separate account. The opportunity for an increase in the death benefit above its guaranteed amount is a potential hedge against inflation for the purchaser of a variable life insurance contract.

However, the cash surrender value of a variable life insurance contract is not guaranteed. There is no minimum cash surrender value. The cash surrender value will fluctuate according to the investment performance of the separate account. Most other standard policy provisions that apply to whole life insurance also apply to variable life insurance, including reinstatement provisions and changes in ownership and beneficiaries.

Variable life insurance contracts are considered securities and are subject to federal and state regulations. Variable life insurance contracts must be sold by use of a prospectus as required by the Securities Act of 1933. They are also considered investment companies and are also subject to antifraud provisions of the Securities Exchange Act of 1934.

The primary difference between variable life insurance and whole life insurance is that whole life insurance has a fixed, guaranteed death benefit while variable life insurance has a fixed minimum death benefit. The fixed minimum death benefit may increase depending on the performance of a separate account.

Fixed-benefit and guaranteed insurance company contracts are funded by a general investment account. The separate account is established to fund variable life contracts. The investment of these funds depends on an investment objective established in advance and may be in many types of investments, including money market instruments, stocks, and bonds.

Variable life and fixed-benefit whole life insurance may have many similarities. If required premiums are paid, the coverage is for the insured's lifetime. Both policies have a cash value. The cash value is available either by terminating the contract or through a policy loan provision. Both types of insurance have suicide clauses, nonforfeiture provisions, and incontestability periods. The major difference is in the death benefit.

Whole life has a fixed and predetermined guaranteed death benefit, while variable life has a death benefit that can increase based on investment performances of the separate account.

While both variable and whole life have a cash value, the cash value is determined differently. In whole life, premiums are invested in the company's general account and the cash value of the policy grows at a guaranteed rate. Some such policies are **participating**. In participating policies, part of the premium may be returned to the policyholder as a dividend if the issuer has a favorable mortality, expense, or investment experience.

In variable life contracts, the premium is invested in the separate account. The actual cash value depends on the performance of the separate account. It may increase or decrease, but not below zero. The cash value is not guaranteed, and there is no guaranteed rate of return. The cash value of a variable life insurance policy will be affected by fluctuating market values and loans taken by the policyholder.

In variable life contracts, the amount of the premium actually invested in the separate account is reduced by administrative fees. Administrative fees are charges for premium billing and collecting, recordkeeping, and communications with policyholders. The guaranteed minimum death benefit plus the variable insurance amount equals the death benefit payable. The death benefit must be calculated at least annually.

Variable life contracts permit borrowing against the cash value. At the time a loan is made, the amount borrowed is taken out of the separate account and placed in the insurance company's general account. There it will earn the assumed rate of interest. Taking this amount out of the separate account will reduce the value of the insured's funds in the separate account.

The insured must maintain a positive net cash value in the separate account. If at any time the amount of the loan is greater than the net cash value, the insurance company will notify the holder, who has thirty-one days to pay off enough of the loan to make the cash value positive, or the insurance company may terminate the contract.

Since there is a decrease in the amount in the separate account, there is a permanent effect on cash value and death benefits. The cash value and death benefit will not increase as rapidly if, during the period the loan is outstanding, the investment results in the separate account are favorable.

Since variable life insurance is a life insurance company product, state regulations concerning life insurance sales apply. These contracts are also defined as securities by the Securities and Exchange Commission (SEC) and, therefore, must meet the registration and reporting requirements of the Securities Act of 1933, the Securities Exchange Act of 1934, and the Investment Company Act of 1940. Annual statements must be sent to the policyholders showing the amount of the death benefit payable and the cash value. Annual and semiannual reports concerning the separate account must be provided to the policyholder and include a list of securities held in the separate account's portfolio.

To comply with the 1933 Act, investment risks must be fully disclosed and, prior to or during the solicitation of a sale, a prospectus must be delivered. The 1934 Act requires an individual involved in the solicitation of these policies to be registered as an agent with the state and federal regulatory agencies before the individual can sell variable life insurance. The company that issues the contract must also be registered.

MAIN POINTS—VARIABLE LIFE INSURANCE CONTRACTS

Variable life insurance contracts have benefits and risks.

- The cash value of a variable life insurance policy will be affected by fluctuating market values and loans taken by the policyholder.
- The cash value in a variable life policy is *not* guaranteed.
- Assume a variable life insurance policyholder surrenders the policy for cash and one year later decides to reinstate the policy. The insurance company issuing the contract would normally require evidence of insurability and the payment of unpaid past premiums.
- Variable life insurance policies are referred to as variable because the death benefit and surrender value vary based on the investment experience of the separate account. The variable life insurance policyholder bears the investment risk related to the contract. Prospective purchasers of variable life insurance contracts must be provided with a prospectus. However, the cash value of a variable life insurance policy is not guaranteed.
- Variable life insurance contracts allow policyholders to select different investment options. They provide a death benefit and cash value that can fluctuate based on investment performance. Variable life insurance contracts have expense charges for administrative expenses, sales expenses, and expenses charged for mortality premium taxes.

- The effect of policy loans on benefits under a variable life insurance contract include

  - The current death benefit will be reduced by the amount of the loan.
  - A maximum loan may increase the possibility of the policy lapsing.
  - The benefits will be affected even if the loan is repaid.

- A variable life insurance policy has cash value accumulation, and the death benefits rise and fall based on the performance of the underlying investments chosen by the policyholder. Variable annuities and variable life insurance policies are types of variable contracts.
- The two main types of variable contracts issued by insurance companies are variable annuities and variable life insurance. The primary reason a person would invest in a variable annuity is to provide for retirement. The primary reason a person would purchase a variable life insurance contract is for life insurance protection with investment choices.
- Variable life insurance refers to life insurance where the cash value and death benefit "vary."
- The death benefit on a variable life insurance policy must be calculated at least annually.
- The cash value on a variable life insurance policy must be calculated at least monthly.
- Variable life insurance policyholders can normally borrow up to 80% of the cash value in the policy. However, they are not allowed to borrow 100% of the cash value.
- Premium payments on variable life insurance contracts are normally paid in fixed amounts on fixed dates.
- The variable life insurance policyholder bears the risk that investment returns will be lower than initially anticipated.

EMPLOYEE RETIREMENT INCOME SECURITY ACT OF 1974

The Employee Retirement Income Security Act of 1974 (ERISA) is a major piece of legislation that governs the operation of private pension plans. ERISA eased pension eligibility rules for many participants. It also set up the **Pension Benefit Guaranty Corporation** and established rules and regulations relating to the management of private pension funds. Government pension plans are exempt from ERISA provisions.

ERISA was intended to protect employees whose pensions are covered under the Act, from imprudent investment decisions of their employers or trustees of the plan. ERISA requires fiduciaries (managers of the plan) to act with prudence when managing pension plan assets. Fiduciaries must act in the best interests of the participants of the plan and not in their own best interests.

Fiduciaries who engage in prohibited transactions are subject to penalty excise taxes. The Act specifically defines prohibited transactions. The purpose of prohibiting certain transactions is to prevent a fiduciary from gaining personal benefits at the expense of the plan participants. Non-tax-qualified deferred compensation plans do not have to comply with ERISA provisions. Participants in non-tax-qualified deferred compensation plans are generally creditors of the employer.

KEOGH PLANS

Keogh plans allow self-employed individuals to establish a retirement plan on a tax-deductible basis. Keogh plans are also referred to as **HR 10 plans**. The maximum deductible contribution allowed to a Keogh plan is 20% of earned income or $30,000, whichever is less.

In addition to the tax-deductible Keogh contributions, the Act also permits voluntary contributions (non-deductible) by an owner-employee of up to 10% of earned income. Voluntary contributions are available to owner-employees only if they are also available to their employees. Such contributions are not tax deductible. However, the earnings on the contributions will accumulate on a tax-deferred basis. Distributions from a Keogh plan may be subject to five-year averaging.

Keogh plans must cover full-time employees at least twenty-one years of age, with one year's work experience with that business. Full-time employees are persons who work 1,000 hours or more during a twelve-month period. If a person files a Schedule C (Profit or Loss from Business), that person can normally set up a Keogh plan.

INDIVIDUAL RETIREMENT ACCOUNTS

Beginning January 1, 1998, taxpayers were able to have a traditional or regular individual retirement account (IRA) or a **Roth IRA**. In a regular IRA, taxpayers who have earned income can deposit $2,000 into an IRA. A nonworking spouse can also deposit $2,000 into an IRA. Whether the contributions are tax deductible depends on whether the person is a participant in an employer-sponsored retirement plan and his or her adjusted growth income. The dividends, interest, and capital gains in a regular IRA are tax deferred until the money is withdrawn. If the money is withdrawn prior to age 59½, the amount withdrawn is subject to a 10% penalty tax and the entire amount withdrawn is taxed as ordinary income. The penalty tax does not apply in certain instances such as permanent disability, distributions over one's life expectancy, distributions used to purchase a first home, or for college expenses.

Distributions from a regular IRA must begin by April 1 following the year in which the person turned 70½. The distributions must be taken according to the person's life expectancy. Insufficient distributions are subject to a 50% penalty tax.

Since January 1, 1998, taxpayers with earned income can open a Roth IRA provided their income is below certain amounts. Contributions to a Roth IRA are *not* tax deductible for any taxpayers. A person can contribute up to $2,000 a year into a Roth IRA. If a person maintains a Roth IRA for at least five years and has reached age 59½, withdrawals from a Roth IRA are not taxed. Withdrawals are also tax-free if the distribution is used for a first-time home purchase. Therefore, the earnings on a Roth IRA will not be taxed to the taxpayer if the account has been opened five years and the taxpayer has reached age 59½ or the money is used for a first home purchase.

A taxpayer with adjusted gross income of less than $100,000 can transfer funds from a traditional IRA into a Roth IRA. However, a person must pay taxes on the before-tax contributions in the traditional IRA when transferred to a Roth IRA.

To summarize the main points concerning a traditional IRA and a Roth IRA

- The contribution limits to a traditional IRA or Roth IRA is $2,000 for a taxpayer.
- In a traditional IRA earnings and capital grow on a tax-deferred basis. However, taxes are paid at ordinary income tax rates on the earnings in a traditional IRA. In a Roth IRA, there are no taxes on earnings if the account has been open five years and the person has reached age 59½ or the distribution is used to purchase a first home.
- Contributions to a traditional IRA may be tax deductible if the person is not in an employer-sponsored retirement plan or has income below a certain level. Contributions to a Roth IRA are not tax deductible.
- Withdrawals prior to age 59½ are subject to a 10% penalty tax in a traditional IRA unless an exemption applies such as permanent disability, annuity distribution, first home purchase, or college expenses. No penalties apply to a distribution from a Roth IRA if the account has been open five years and the taxpayer is at least 59½ years old or the withdrawal is used to purchase a first home.
- Distributions from a traditional IRA must begin by April 1 following the year the person reaches age 70½. With a Roth IRA there is no requirement to begin distributions by age 70½.
- Funds can be transferred from a traditional IRA to a Roth IRA, but taxes will apply to before-tax contributions and earnings.
- The most a taxpayer can contribute to an IRA in any combination is $2,000. A taxpayer must choose whether a traditional IRA or a Roth IRA would be more beneficial.
- If a taxpayer does not qualify to deduct his IRA contribution because of his participation in a retirement plan and income level, he can still deposit money into an IRA on an after-tax-deferred basis. Taxes would be paid on the earnings when they are withdrawn from the IRA.
- IRA funds can be invested in gold or silver coins issued by the US government. However, IRA funds cannot be invested in other collectibles, such as diamonds, stamps, paintings, or rugs. Any amount invested in these collectibles will be treated as a distribution from the plan for tax purposes.
- Contributions to an IRA are entirely vested immediately and must be in cash.
- Contributions to an IRA may be made up to the due date of the taxpayer's federal tax return.
- The contribution to an IRA can exceed that stated limit of $2,000 in the case of a rollover. A rollover occurs when money is transferred from a qualified plan (Keogh, pension, or profit-sharing) into an IRA. A rollover is tax free if it is placed into an IRA rollover account within sixty days of the distribution. A partial rollover is permitted. The amount not rolled over is taxed as ordinary income.
- The law also allows a person to transfer from one kind of IRA investment to another, tax-free, once a year. If an individual wanted to transfer from an annuity to a savings account, he could do so without tax penalties. However, if a transfer is made more than once a year, the individual will be subject to income taxes on the amount withdrawn, and possibly a 10% penalty tax.

SIMPLIFIED EMPLOYEE PENSION PLAN

The Simplified Employee Pension Plan (SEP) allows employers to annually contribute to an employee's IRA. The employer contribution is deductible under federal tax law. Thus, an employer benefits from an SEP in much the same manner as a Keogh; however, there is usually less work involved in establishing and administering the plan. The employee must include the employer's contribution in his or her gross income. However, the employee can take a deduction for the amount of the employer contribution and for an additional deduction up to $2,000 if the employee is eligible for a deductible contribution to his or her IRA. The maximum contribution an employer can make on behalf of an employee is 15% of the employee's compensation or $30,000, whichever is less.

PENSION AND PROFIT-SHARING PLANS

The two main types of retirement plans offered by employers are

1. Defined contribution plans
2. Defined benefit plans

In a **defined contribution plan,** each participant has an individual account and benefits are paid to that participant based solely on the amount contributed to his individual account. Defined contribution plans include the following types of plans:

- Profit sharing
- Money purchase pension
- Target benefit
- Stock bonus

A **defined benefit plan** is a pension plan that provides for benefits that are definite and predeteminable. The employer calculates the benefit to be received by the employee and then determines the contributions necessary to provide that benefit level. Defined benefit plans favor high-salaried employees who are near retirement age. Benefits received from pension plans are taxable to the employee to the extent that they are not a return on capital.

Contributions by an employer are tax deductible to a pension plan. Assets in the plan accumulate on a tax-free basis. Benefits are taxable when received by the employee or beneficiary. Benefits are normally payable to the employee when he retires, dies, or becomes disabled. In certain cases, benefits may be paid to a person when he terminates employment.

A pension plan requires regular contributions by a company regardless of profits. Pension plans must meet IRS regulations concerning benefits, eligibility, and reporting. Pension plans are costly to administer and should be considered only if a company has a stable earnings record. All tax-qualified retirement plans have provisions called **eligibility requirement provisions** detailing which employees may participate in the plan.

Tax-qualified plans must also meet **funding and vesting requirements** under ERISA. Funding requirements are necessary to ensure that sufficient funds will be available to pay participants during their retirement years. In other words, the plan must be properly funded. Vesting requirements define when the portion of a participant's account in a pension or profit-sharing plan belongs to that person should he terminate employment.

A profit-sharing plan is a qualified retirement plan that offers the employer greater flexibility. A company makes contributions out of corporate profits and allocates the funds to employees participating in the plan according to a formula. The employee, at retirement, receives the balance in his account. A profit-sharing plan is a type of defined contribution plan. If a company loses money in a particular year, it may contribute nothing to the profit-sharing plan for that year.

401(k) PLANS

A **401(k) plan** is a voluntary program sponsored by an employer. It is often referred to as a **capital accumulation plan**. One reason for their popularity is that the employer does not have the usual pension plan obligation of guaranteeing benefits. They are also popular because they permit considerable growth of assets and allow employees to make tax-deferred contributions into their own programs.

The employee's contribution is made by deferring part of his salary into the plan. The employer may also make contributions. Under a 401(k) plan, employees actually reduce their own salaries. This is why the plan is sometimes referred to as a **salary-reduction plan**.

The basics of a 401(k) plan are

- A certain amount of pretax money may be deferred to the plan by an employee.
- An additional sum may be contributed by the employer for the employee without the employee's being taxed on the contribution.
- Until distributed, contributions are placed in a trust account for the employee and grow on a tax-deferred basis.

403(b) PLANS

The Internal Revenue Code allows employees of certain nonprofit organizations (hospitals, charities, state and local school systems, religious organizations) to invest in a tax-sheltered annuity. Therefore, 403(b) plans are retirement plans for employees of nonprofit organizations.

The following employees are eligible to participate in a tax-sheltered annuity under Section 403(b) of the Internal Revenue Code:

- Employees of local school systems (such as a teacher, librarian, or custodian)
- Employees of state colleges or universities, such as a professor
- Employees of nonprofit hospitals or charities
- Civilian employees of US military academies

REVIEW QUESTIONS

1. Which of the following is correct concerning variable annuities?
   a. Those selling variable annuities do not have to be registered with the NASD or SEC.
   b. The insurance company bears the investment risk as it does in a fixed annuity.
   c. The annuity unit is the accounting measure used to determine the amount of each payment to the annuitant.
   d. Future payments from a variable annuity maybe decreased because of an increase in the expense of administering the contract.

2. Concerning variable annuities, all of the following are correct **except:**
   a. The shares of other mutual funds may be held in the portfolio.
   b. The portfolio protects the annuitant against capital loss.
   c. The holders may vote to change the investment objectives of the variable annuity.
   d. They provide the annuitant with professional management of the portfolio.

3. Which of the following terms is associated with a variable annuity?
   a. Special account
   b. Investment account
   c. Separate account
   d. General account

4. The owner of a non-tax-qualified variable annuity withdraws funds prior to the contract's being annuitized. The owner would realize which of the following tax consequences?
   a. Any ordinary income is taxable, but losses are not allowed.
   b. Capital gains or losses.
   c. Tax-deferred income.
   d. Ordinary income in excess of his basis.

5. Owners of variable annuities normally have which of the following rights?

   I. Right to vote on proposed changes in investment policy
   II. Right to reduced sales charges for larger purchases
   III. Right to vote for the portfolio manager

   a. I only
   b. I and II
   c. II and III
   d. All of the above

6. Which of the following is true during the annuity period of a variable annuity?
   a. The number of accumulation units is fixed, and the value per unit is fixed.
   b. The value per annuity unit is fixed, and the number of annuity units varies.
   c. The AIR varies, and the number of annuity units varies.
   d. The value per annuity unit varies, and the number of annuity units is fixed.

7. Which of the following is used to determine the sales charge breakpoint on a variable annuity?
   a. The frequency of the purchases by the investor.
   b. The performance results of the variable annuity.
   c. The number of times the portfolio is turned over by the variable annuity.
   d. The amount invested in the variable annuity by the investor.

8. An individual gets annual pay of $25,000 from the employer. He is not covered under a qualified retirement plan. He also earns $18,000 pretax as a self-employed musician. He wants to open a Keogh plan and make the maximum allowable tax-deductible contribution. How much can he deposit?
   a. $1,500
   b. $3,600
   c. $5,000
   d. $7,500

9. A person is not an active participant in a retirement plan. What maximum deductible amount of his $10,000 can he contribute to a traditional IRA for himself and his nonworking spouse?
   a. $4,000
   b. $2,000
   c. $1,125
   d. $1,000

10. Which of the following represents the maximum age at which withdrawals must start from a traditional IRA before a penalty is assessed?
    a. 59½
    b. 60
    c. 65½
    d. 70½

11. A doctor plans to retire from his corporation and take his retirement plan in a lump sum. Under the IRA rollover rules, how long does he have to invest his benefit check in a new traditional IRA before incurring a tax liability?
    a. 30 days
    b. 60 days
    c. 90 days
    d. 1 year

12. Assuming a person is not permanently disabled, the minimum age at which withdrawals may normally begin from a traditional IRA without penalty is
    a. 59½
    b. 62
    c. 65
    d. 70½

13. All of the following are correct concerning variable annuities and mutual funds **except:**
    a. At death, shares not withdrawn from a retirement plan by a mutual fund holder become part of his estate.
    b. Variable annuity holders cannot determine the amount of monthly payments they will receive.
    c. Mutual funds and the separate accounts of non-tax-qualified variable annuities are registered under the Investment Company Act of 1940.
    d. Even though the variable annuity issuing company keeps all dividends, the contract holder must pay taxes on them in the current year.

14. All of the following are types of variable annuity payout options **except:**
    a. Invest a lump sum now, receive payments later.
    b. Invest a lump sum now, receive a lump sum later.
    c. Invest periodically, receive payments later.
    d. Receive payments now, invest a lump sum later.

15. A customer at 55 years of age began investing in a variable annuity. He is now 65 years old and makes a lump-sum distribution. The customer invested $40,000, and the value of the variable annuity is $65,000. What amount is taxable to the customer?
    a. $ 25,000
    b. $ 40,000
    c. $ 65,000
    d. $105,000

16. An individual is allowed to invest funds in a traditional IRA in all of the following **except:**
    a. Common stocks
    b. Money market funds
    c. Savings account
    d. Paintings

17. The major objective of a variable annuity is normally to
    a. Provide maximum growth of capital during the annuity period.
    b. Provide retirement benefits during the annuity period.
    c. Provide maximum current income during the accumulation period.
    d. Provide tax-free income during the annuity period.

18. Which of the following is an excellent prospect to purchase a variable annuity?
    a. A person with no cash reserves who is beginning his first job
    b. A middle-aged person with adequate cash reserves and life insurance who wants to provide for his retirement
    c. A person one year from retirement with very limited cash reserves and no life insurance
    d. None of the above

19. Which of the following are normally true of a variable annuity contract?

    I. Taxes are not paid by the contract holder until funds are withdrawn.
    II. The minimum death benefit during the accumulation period is the total amount deposited or the value of the account, whichever is greater.
    III. The annuity will increase in value if the actual return in the separate account is greater than the AIR.

    a. I only
    b. II and III
    c. I and III
    d. All of the above.

20. Since fixed annuity income remains level, the annuitant is exposed to
    a. Market or systematic risk
    b. Purchasing power risk or inflation risk
    c. Default risk
    d. Interest rate risk

21. The two main types of variable contracts are
    a. Variable annuities and variable life
    b. Fixed annuities and whole life
    c. Keogh plans and individual retirement accounts
    d. Defined benefit and defined contribution

22. Which of the following statements are true concerning variable annuities?

    I. A variable annuity provides greater protection of purchasing power than a fixed annuity.
    II. A person's cash flow would be greatest if he chooses a life annuity payout option.
    III. Companies issuing non-tax-qualified variable annuities must be registered with the SEC and the NASD.
    IV. The monthly payout varies.

    a. I and II
    b. III and IV
    c. I, III and IV
    d. All of the above

23. Which of the following statements are true of Keogh plans?

    I. They are retirement plans for self-employed individuals in which deposited funds grow on a tax-deferred basis.
    II. Keogh plans are also referred to as HR 10 plans.
    III. They must include all full-time employees.

    a. I only
    b. I and III
    c. II and III
    d. All of the above

24. Which of the following statements are true concerning variable annuities?

    I. The accumulation unit and the annuity unit changes in value in a manner that corresponds most closely to the value of the securities in the separate account.
    II. The accumulation unit is an accounting measure used to determine the contract owner's interest in the separate account.
    III. When accumulation units are converted into annuity units, the annuitant receives a fixed number of annuity units.

    a. I only
    b. I and III
    c. II and III
    d. All of the above.

25. All of the following statements concerning variable annuities are true **except:**
    a. A variable annuity guarantees lifetime payments based on a fluctuating dollar value of a fixed number of units each month.
    b. A variable annuity is funded by a separate account of securities.
    c. During a major business decline, the unit value of a variable annuity will probably decrease.
    d. Persons selling variable annuities only need to possess an insurance license.

26. All of the following are types of non tax-qualified variable annuities available to investors, **except:**
    a. Single-premium immediate
    b. 403(b) group annuity
    c. Periodic payment deferred
    d. Single-premium deferred

27. Miss Johnson is 49 years of age and has $90,000 to invest for her retirement. She is concerned about not having sufficient funds in her later years. Which of the following is probably the most suitable investment for Miss Johnson?
    a. Money market fund
    b. Limited partnership
    c. Variable annuity
    d. Precious metals

28. During the payout period, if the separate account continues to earn a rate of return in excess of the AIR, the monthly payments to the annuitant will
    a. Increase
    b. Decrease
    c. Decrease substantially
    d. Remain the same

29. Components of the separate account of a variable annuity include

    I. Investment income.
    II. Realized capital gains and losses.
    III. Unrealized capital gains and losses.

    a. I only
    b. II only
    c. III only
    d. All of the above

30. Under federal securities laws, which of the following statements are true concerning a prospectus for a variable annuity contract?

    I. It must be filed with the SEC under the 1933 Act.
    II. It must make full and fair disclosure.
    III. It must precede or accompany sales literature.

    a. I only
    b. II only
    c. I and III
    d. All of the above

ANSWERS TO REVIEW QUESTIONS

1. c	6. d	11. b	16. d	21. a	26. b
2. b	7. d	12. a	17. b	22. d	27. c
3. c	8. b	13. d	18. b	23. d	28. a
4. d	9. a	14. d	19. d	24. d	29. d
5. d	10. d	15. a	20. b	25. d	30. d

NASD RULES AND REGULATIONS

The passage of the Securities Exchange Act of 1934 by the Congress of the United States extended federal regulation to all areas of trading in listed securities. However, there was no effective federal regulation covering trading in the over-the-counter (OTC) securities market.

Congress felt that federal regulation should extend to the OTC market. Basically, they had two choices before them.

1. Expand the SEC staff to monitor the OTC market.
2. Permit a self-regulatory organization to monitor the OTC market.

Congress chose the second alternative. In 1938 they passed the Maloney Act, permitting national associations of broker/dealers, which became Section 15(A) of the Securities Exchange Act of 1934. The NASD is a national association of broker/dealers operating under the Maloney Act. Trading practices in the OTC market for corporate securities is subject to regulation by the NASD and the Securities and Exchange Commission (SEC). The NASD is still subject to review by the SEC. All disciplinary actions of the NASD are reviewed by the SEC. Broker/dealers that operate exclusively on a national securities exchange in listed securities do not have to register with the NASD.

CERTIFICATE OF INCORPORATION

In its certificate of incorporation, the purposes of the NASD are stated as follows:

- To promote just and equitable principles of trade
- To provide a medium through which the membership may consult and cooperate with governmental and other agencies in the solution of the problems affecting the industry
- To administer and enforce rules of fair practice and to prevent fraudulent and manipulative acts and practices
- To promote self-discipline among members, to adjudicate differences between members and the public

BYLAWS OF THE NASD

The bylaws of the NASD contain a number of articles dealing with membership requirements, qualification of registered personnel, administration of the NASD, and other areas. Some of the more important of the bylaws concern membership rules, branch offices, qualification of associated persons, and the NASD committees. The NASD Board of Governors receives its powers to prescribe regulations concerning associated persons from the NASD bylaws.

NASD membership or registration is not available to applicants except by an order of the SEC in the following situations:

- Where the broker/dealer has been suspended or expelled from a national securities exchange for violating just and equitable principles of trade
- Where the SEC or a stock exchange has an order revoking or denying the registration of the broker/dealer
- Where the individuals have been convicted in the last ten years of a felony or misdemeanor involving crimes such as embezzlement or misappropriation of funds
- Where the individuals do not meet the training and experience standards or other standards that the NASD Board of Governors may feel is necessary

The NASD requires that certain personnel in member organizations be registered with it and pass qualifying examinations. The four main classes of registration are

1. General securities principal
2. Financial and operations principal
3. General securities registered representative

4. Registered options principal, senior registered options principal, and compliance registered options principal

The NASD also has certain limited categories of registration for persons who intend to sell only certain investment products or engage in specific areas of activity. The limited categories of registration include

- Investment company and variable products representative
- Direct participation program representative

The NASD District Business Conduct Committee has original jurisdiction for hearing trade practice complaints against an NASD member. A decision of the NASD District Business Conduct Committee may be appealed to the Board of Governors of the NASD. If an NASD member wants to appeal a decision of the Board of Governors of the NASD, he can appeal it to the SEC.

For a rule violation, the NASD may impose the following penalties on a member firm or a person associated with a member:

- Fine
- Censure
- Suspension
- Expulsion

ADVERTISING RULES

A separate file of all advertisements, sales literature, and market letters, including the name(s) of the person(s) who prepared them and/or approve their use, must be maintained for a period of three years from the date of each use, the first two years in a place readily accessible to examination or spot checks. All advertising to be used by member firms must be submitted for review within five business days after initial use, unless the advertising has been approved by a stock exchange. Advertising material would generally include

- Material for use in a newspaper or magazine
- Radio or television advertising

Advertising literature does *not* include

- Tombstone ads
- In-house material
- Personal recommendations designed for one client

A **tombstone ad** is an ad that identifies only the member, security to be offered, and price of the security. No sales literature is contained in a tombstone ad.

It is a violation of the rules of fair practice to

- Publish any advertisement that contains untrue or misleading statements.
- Make statements in any advertisement that are exaggerated.
- Make promises of specific results in any advertisement.
- Give opinions in any advertisement that have no reasonable basis founded on inquiry by the member.

Statements in sales literature or in conversation with customers stating or implying a specific gain expected in the price of a security, a higher price after a split, or promises of a specific number of shares of a new issue if a client places an order for existing securities are examples of those violating securities industry regulations. All advertising and sales literature must be approved by an NASD principal prior to use.

In making recommendations, the member must have a reasonable basis for the recommendation and disclose

- Price at the time the original recommendation is made
- That the member usually makes a market in the issue, if this is true
- If applicable, that the member intends to buy or sell the securities recommended for the firm's own account, unless the ownership is merely nominal
- The ownership, if any, of options, rights, or warrants to purchase the security recommended, unless ownership is nominal

Sales literature used to solicit purchases of common stock under NASD rules must state

- The name of the member firm
- The date the material was originally published
- The price at the time the material was distributed

Sales literature, under NASD rules, does not have to disclose the member firm's inventory or investment position. The member must also provide or offer to furnish, on request, available investment information supporting the recommendations.

Material referring to past recommendations may be used if it sets forth all recommendations as to the same type, kind, grade, or classification of securities made by a member within the last year. Such references cannot imply that these recommendations would have been profitable to any person nor that they indicate the general quality of a member's recommendations. Longer periods of years may be covered if they are consecutive, include the most recent year, and contain the required information.

Testimonial material must make clear that such experience does not indicate future performance or results obtained by others. It must state whether any compensation was paid to the maker and, if it implies an experienced opinion, the qualifications of the maker.

BROKER/DEALERS

A broker/dealer is a financial institution registered with the SEC. Most broker/dealers are also members of the NASD, unless they operate exclusively in listed securities on a national securities exchange. A broker/dealer executes securities transactions for customers either as agent or as principal. When a broker/dealer charges a customer a commission on a securities transaction, it is acting as agent for the customer. A broker acts as agent for a customer and charges a commission. The broker/dealer, when acting as agent for the customer, buys the security from another broker/dealer for the account of the customer.

The broker/dealer can also act as principal or dealer in a securities transaction with a customer. When a broker/dealer sells securities to a customer from its own inventory, it is acting as dealer or principal. The term **broker/dealer** is derived from the fact that in some transactions the securities firm acts as a broker for customers. In other transactions, the securities firms acts as a dealer or principal and sells securities directly to customers. When a broker/dealer sells securities directly to a customer, it receives a markup instead of a commission. However, any commission, markup, or markdown charged to a customer must be fair and reasonable.

RECOMMENDATIONS MADE TO CUSTOMERS

It is the member's responsibility to see that all recommendations made to customers are suitable as far as the member knows the facts. Statements concerning a company's financial status and future can be made only if they have a reasonable basis founded on inquiry by the salesman. The member has the responsibility to obtain the facts on both the customer and the company recommended and to sell at a price related to the market.

Certain prices have been interpreted by the NASD to be violations of the NASD rules of fair practice. The following is a partial list:

- Recommending speculative low-priced securities to customers, without knowledge of the customer's financial situation
- Churning or excessive trading in a customer's account
- Short-term trading in mutual fund shares
- Establishment of fictitious accounts to hide certain transactions
- Transactions in discretionary accounts without prior written permission of the customer
- Unauthorized use of a customer's funds or securities
- Private transactions by a registered representative (RR) without the employer's knowledge
- Recommending a purchase beyond a customer's financial ability to meet the commitment

Assume a customer, Mr. Jones, has $30,000 to invest. Mr. Jones is young and well educated and fears the stock market. His RR, before selling any securities to Mr. Jones, should learn about the following:

- His net worth
- His income tax bracket
- His investment objectives
- His other investments

Assume Mrs. Wilson is living on a fixed income and worries about inflation. Mrs. Wilson is most exposed to the purchasing power risk (inflation risk).

PRIVATE SECURITIES TRANSACTIONS

NASD rules prohibit an associated person, such as an RR, from participating in a private securities transaction unless prior written notice is given to the broker/dealer. A private securities transaction is a securities transaction outside the regular course or scope of his employing broker/dealer business.

Assume an RR has been asked by a real estate agent to help sell condominium units that are not registered with the SEC. This is an example of a private securities transaction because it would be outside of the RR's regular scope of employment.

Under NASD rules, the RR must give the member firm prior written notice before engaging in a private securities transaction. The written notice must

- Describe in detail the proposed transaction and the person's proposed role.
- State whether the person has received or will receive selling compensation in connection with the transaction.

If the member firm approves the associated person's participation in the private securities transaction, then the transaction must be recorded on the books and records of the member firm. The member firm must supervise the associated person's participation in the private securities transaction as if the transaction were executed on behalf of the member. If the member firm disapproves the associated person's participation, then the associated person must not participate in the private securities transaction in any manner, directly or indirectly. In the case of a private securities transaction in which an associated person will not receive any compensation, the member firm must promptly provide the associated person with written acknowledgement of the notice. The member firm may, at its discretion, require the associated person to adhere to specified conditions in connection with his participation in the transaction.

PROMPT RECEIPT AND DELIVERY OF SECURITIES

A member may not accept a purchase order from a customer unless the member has determined that the customer placing the order, or his agent, agrees to receive securities against payment in an amount equal to any execution, even if the execution is only part of a larger order.

No member may mark a sell order received from a customer as a long sale unless one of the following conditions is present:

- The member has the security in its possession.
- The customer is long the security in his account with the member.
- Assurance is received from the customer that the security will be delivered in good deliverable form within three business days.
- The security is on deposit with another broker/dealer, bank, or depository, and instruction has been given to deliver the securities against payment.

PROXY MATERIAL

A member must forward to each beneficial owner of securities all proxy material, annual reports, and other material furnished to it by the issuer of the securities. This is necessary when customer securities are in street name. If the securities are registered in the name of a customer, the proxy material is sent directly to the customer. The person soliciting the proxies will reimburse the member for expenses. However, a member does not have to send proxy material to persons residing outside of the United States. Proxy costs are payable by the issuer of the securities.

NASD HOT-ISSUE RULES

An NASD member participating in the distribution of a new issue of securities to the public is required to make a bona fide public offering at the public offering price. Failure to make such a bona fide public offering at the public offering price is known as **free riding and withholding**.

This is especially important when a member is distributing a **hot issue,** which is an issue that, on the first day of trading, sells at a premium over the public offering price. For example, the issue may have been offered to the public at $10 per share and, on the first day of trading, rises in price to $11 per share.

Instances when underwriters or selling group members are free riding and withholding include

- Selling blocks to the accounts of partners or officers
- Maintaining positions by selling to members or their families

- Selling the securities to brokers and dealers outside the selling group who position the securities to sell later at a higher price

Can a member withhold any securities of a hot issue for its own account or the account of officers, directors, partners, or employees? The answer is "no." A member *cannot* withhold shares of a hot issue for its own account or sell shares of a hot issue to officers, directors, partners, employees, or members of their immediate families.

Under NASD rules, a member **cannot** sell any shares of a hot issue to

- An officer of the member firm
- A director of the member firm
- A partner of the member firm
- An employee of the member firm, whether registered or unregistered with the NASD
- Employees of other broker/dealers

An NASD member **can** sell shares to the following customers provided it is in accordance with their normal investment practice with the member and the aggregate of the securities so sold is insubstantial and not disproportionate in amount as compared to sales to members of the public and that the amount sold to any one of such persons is insubstantial:

- Senior officer of a bank, such as a bank president
- Senior officer of an insurance company
- Senior officer of an investment company
- A member of the immediate family of an officer of the distributing broker/dealer provided that the officer does not contribute directly or indirectly to the support of such member of the immediate family
- A finder of the issuer (an individual who brings together the issuer and the investment banking firm)
- Another NASD member for the account of a customer

The term *immediate family* under NASD Rules means parents, mother-in-law or father-in-law, husband or wife, brother or sister, brother-in-law or sister-in-law, children, or any other relative to whose support the member or person associated with the member contributes directly or indirectly. It does *not* include

- Aunts or uncles
- Grandmothers or grandfathers
- Nieces or nephews

Hot issues are issues that trade at an immediate premium from their offering price. A hot issue could be an equity security in a primary or secondary distribution, or could even be a debt issue.

CHARGES FOR SERVICES

Any charges for services performed by the member, including services such as safekeeping of securities, or transferring securities, shall be reasonable and not unfairly discriminatory between customers.

CONFIRMATIONS

A member must send a customer a written confirmation on or before the first business day following the trade date. A confirmation gives a customer the complete details concerning his trade. The confirmation statement contains information such as

- Name of the security purchased or sold
- Price per share at which the transaction was executed
- Number of shares or units purchased or sold
- Whether the broker/dealer acted as agent or principal
- Amount of commission charged if the broker/dealer acted as agent
- Trade date and settlement date

When a firm acts as broker, it must furnish or be prepared to furnish information as to the date and time of the transaction, the source and amount of the commission received by the member from all sources, and the identity of the purchaser or seller.

If a member acts as a broker for a customer in transactions in listed securities in the **third market,** at a price that is in line with the current price on the exchange plus or minus a differential, with the retail firm absorbing the differential, a legend should be used on the confirmation to the customer which explains these facts in order to insure adequate disclosure to the customer.

DISCRETIONARY ACCOUNTS

A **discretionary account** is an account in which the customer gives to the broker/dealer the right to purchase and sell securities for his account without securing prior customer consent for each transaction. No member or RR is allowed to exercise any discretionary power in a customer's account unless such customer has given prior written authorization and the account has been accepted in writing by the member. An RR cannot accept an order from one spouse (e.g., the husband) to execute a trade in the other spouse's account unless written instructions have been received from the other spouse (e.g., the wife) authorizing such orders.

All discretionary orders must be approved promptly and in writing by an NASD principal. They must be approved on the same day they are placed, but not prior to execution. All discretionary accounts must be reviewed at frequent intervals to detect and prevent transactions that are excessive in size or frequency.

What if a customer tells an RR to buy 100 shares of XYZ but to enter the order only when he believes the price is right? Would this be considered a discretionary order? The answer is "no." If a customer instructs an RR to purchase or sell a definite amount of a specified security, but gives discretion as to the price and time, this is not considered to be a discretionary transaction. However, if a client gives his RR a sum of money and instructs him to buy whatever security he thinks best, the order is discretionary and the RR would need prior written authorization before executing it.

If an RR handles a discretionary account, he must

- Obtain prior written authorization from the customer
- Designate each such order as discretionary
- Not make transactions that are excessive in size or frequency (churning)

DEALING WITH NONMEMBERS

A member cannot grant any nonmember broker/dealer any selling concession, discount, or allowance not allowed to members of the general public. A member cannot join with a nonmember broker/dealer in any distribution of an issue of securities to the public. The term *nonmember* includes suspended or expelled dealers or anyone not admitted to membership in the NASD.

OTHER PROVISIONS OF NASD RULES

NASD members are subject to many rules.

- No member may give anything of value to any person for the purpose of influencing or rewarding such person in connection with publishing or circulating information intended to influence the market price of a security.
- A member must disclose to a customer a situation in which the member is controlled by, controlling, or under common control with the issuer of a security that the customer intends to purchase. If the disclosure is not made in writing, it must be supplemented by the giving or sending of written disclosure at or before the completion of a transaction. Firms normally make the disclosure with a notation on the confirmation.
- No member shall guarantee a customer against loss in any securities account or securities transaction. Assume a new stock issue is sold to the public at $20 per share. One month after the offering, the stock is quoted 14⅜ bid 15 ask. A customer who purchased the new issue at $20 per share is unhappy that the price decreased. He wants his RR to buy back the shares at $20 per share. The RR is not allowed to do this under any circumstances since it is prohibited, under NASD rules and rules of other self-regulatory organizations, to guarantee a customer against loss.
- No member or person associated with a member shall share directly or indirectly in the profits or losses in any account of a customer, unless such member or person obtains prior written authorization from the member carrying the account. In addition, the member or person may share only in direct proportion to that amount invested in the account.
- A member must obtain certain information from customers when opening an account such as name, address, whether the customer is of legal age, signature of the RR, and signature of the partner, officer, or manager. Discretionary accounts require the customer's occupation as well as the signature of each person authorized to exercise discretion.

- Members must keep a separate file of all written complaints received from a customer. The separate file of written complaints must be kept for six years, the first two years in a readily accessible place.
- A member must make available to any bona fide customer, upon request, a copy of the firm's most recent balance sheet or statement of financial condition. The balance sheet or statement of financial condition must be made available to the customer immediately.
- The **reciprocal brokerage rule** states that sales of investment company shares shall not be a qualifying or disqualifying factor in the selection of a broker/dealer to execute portfolio transactions.
- An RR must notify his member firm if

  - He is convicted of securities fraud.
  - He is convicted of illegal gambling.
  - He files for bankruptcy.
  - He is accused of wrongfully taking property of another person.

- The sale of variable contracts of an insurance company by an NASD member is subject to the rules of fair practice. A member may not participate in the offering of variable contracts unless the sales load is fair, taking into consideration all relevant circumstances. No member who is a principal underwriter as defined in the Investment Company Act of 1940 may sell variable contracts through another broker/dealer unless (1) such broker/dealer is a member and (2) there is a sales agreement in effect between the parties.
- The NASD Outside Business Activities Rule prohibits RRs from engaging in any employment for compensation with any person or institution other than the employed member without giving notice to the employed member. Therefore, an RR must notify his employer if he takes a full-time or part-time job. If an RR is hired as a managing general partner in a limited partnership, he must notify his member firm. However, an RR would not have to notify his employing member firm.
- If an RR wants to open an account with another member firm to invest in securities, he must notify the executing firm in writing of his affiliation with his present member firm. This is true if the RR invests in any type of securities including a real estate limited partnership.
- Complaints against RRs, under NASD rules, can be brought by any of the following:

  - The NASD Board of Governors
  - A customer of the particular RR
  - Other broker/dealers

- An RR employed by an NASD member firm is required to submit to arbitration in a dispute submitted by

  - A public customer
  - His employing member firm
  - An RR employed by another member firm

- In order to become registered, a person must file a U-4 form with the NASD along with fingerprints. An individual, when signing the U-4 form, agrees to be bound by the NASD Code of Procedure concerning complaints and disciplinary proceedings. The individual also agrees to be bound by NASD arbitration proceedings. The difference between the Code of Procedure and the Code of Arbitration Procedure is a basic difference. The **Code of Procedure** handles complaints against individuals or member firms. The District Business Conduct Committee renders a decision on the complaint initially. A decision of the District Business Conduct Committee may be appealed to the Board of Governors of the NASD. A decision of the Board of Governors of the NASD may be appealed to the SEC.
- The **Code of Arbitration Procedure** handles disputes between RRs, public customers, and member firms. Decisions in an arbitration proceeding are final and cannot be appealed. In any proceeding relating to the Code of Procedure or Code of Arbitration Procedure, a public customer can bring an attorney, present evidence, and hear the charges levied against them. An NASD member firm cannot bring a complaint against one of its own employees. The member firm was responsible for supervising the activities of the RR. If an RR violates NASD rules, the NASD may bring a complaint against the RR or an NASD principal for failure to supervise the RR and the member firm itself.

NASD CODE OF PROCEDURE

The Code of Procedure of the NASD was established for the purpose of handling trade practice complaints relating to violations of the rules of fair practice. The NASD District Business Conduct Committee has original jurisdiction for hearing complaints against NASD members.

In certain complaints against NASD members, the facts are not in dispute and the respondent does not wish to have a hearing. In this case, a respondent may waive a hearing and accept a summary complaint procedure. A summary complaint procedure may be accepted by a member in a situation in which the facts are not in dispute and the member waives a hearing and accepts the summary complaint procedure.

If a member accepts a summary complaint procedure, the maximum penalty the District Business Conduct Committee can impose is censure and/or a fine of $2,500.

As mentioned earlier, a member may appeal any decision of the District Business Conduct Committee to the Board of Governors. If a member feels that the Board of Governors has not acted properly, it may appeal the decision to the SEC.

UNIFORM PRACTICE CODE

All OTC transactions in securities (except for transactions cleared through a registered clearing agency and exempt securities) are subject to the provisions of the Code. In trades between members, failure to deliver the securities sold or failure to pay for securities as delivered on or after settlement date does not effect a cancellation of the contract. The remedy of the buyer or seller is provided for according to the buy-in or sellout provisions of the Code unless the parties mutually consent to cancel the trade.

CONFIRMATIONS OR COMPARISONS

Each party to a transaction, other than a cash transaction, must send a uniform comparison or confirmation on or before the first business day following the date of the transaction. Comparisons or confirmations of cash transactions must be exchanged the day of the trade. Comparisons or confirmations must be compared upon receipt to determine whether any discrepancies exist.

If a broker/dealer receives a confirmation or comparison relating to a transaction that it does not have on its records, a DK notice should be sent to the contrabroker. This official NASD DK notice is used for unmatched trades and is always sent to the contrabroker (the other side of the trade). The DK notice is never sent to the customer or self-regulatory organizations such as the NASD or the New York Stock Exchange (NYSE).

GOOD DELIVERY OF SECURITIES

The term **good delivery** as it is used in the securities business means that a stock certificate is delivered by the selling broker to the buying broker in a form permitting ownership to be readily transferred. A registered stock certificate must be signed exactly as the name or names appear on the certificate. The signatures must be guaranteed by the broker/dealer.

TRADE DATE AND SETTLEMENT DATE

In the securities industry, a trade is considered settled when a customer pays for a securities purchase. Assume on Monday, June 12, 1995, a customer purchases 100 shares of Disney for a total purchase price of $5,400. Settlement date for the transaction is Thursday, June 15. The customer's funds are required to be at the broker/dealer's office by settlement date to **settle** the money owed on the purchase.

Regulation T of the Federal Reserve requires payment by the fifth business day after trade date. The Federal Reserve's Regulation T gives a two-day grace period past settlement before a broker/dealer must take action. If the customer has not paid by the close of business on the fifth business day after trade date, the broker/dealer must either

- Obtain an extension of time for payment from the appropriate regulatory agency, or
- Cancel or liquidate the unsettled portion of the transaction.

Prompt payment in the securities industry is necessary to maintain the financial integrity of the broker/dealers. The customer's payment is due by settlement date, because the 100 shares of Disney will be delivered by the selling broker/dealer on settlement date. Once a customer pays for a security purchase in full, the entire risk of the position is the customer's. If the customer did not pay the broker/dealer for the security purchase, the customer's broker/dealer would still have to pay for the 100 shares of Disney, when it is delivered by the selling broker/dealer.

When a securities transaction takes place, the two important dates are

1. **Trade date**—the date on which the transaction is executed in the marketplace.
2. **Settlement date**—the date on which payment is due from the customer on a security purchase or the securities are due from the customer on a sale. The customer must deposit funds on a purchase of securities or deliver securities on a sale in order to settle the transaction.

When a customer purchases a security, he is **long** the security. Long, in the securities industry, means ownership. A **long sale** occurs when a customer sells a security that he owns and the proceeds of the sale are credited to the customer's account on settlement date. A **short sale** occurs when a customer sells a security he does not own. A short sale requires a customer to deposit margin money to secure his promise to buy the stock back at some future date. A short sale must be done in a margin account and always represents risk to the broker/dealer.

If the securities transaction is for $1,000 or less, a broker/dealer would not have to obtain an extension of time and would not have to cancel or liquidate the transaction. US government securities and municipal securities are exempt from the provisions of Regulation T. The standard US securities settlement period is as follows:

- *Corporate securities*—the third business day following trade date (T + 3)
- *Municipal securities*—the third business day following trade date (T + 3)
- *Investment company securities*—the third business day following trade date (T + 3)
- *US government securities*—next business day following trade date (T + 1)
- *Options*—next business day following trade date (T + 1)

INVESTMENT COMPANIES AND THE NASD RULES OF FAIR PRACTICE

The rules of fair practice cover the sale of investment company shares. The following statements cover the important points contained in the rules of fair practice:

- The lowest price at which an underwriter may sell shares of an open-end investment company to a member is the net asset value per share (NAVPS).
- An NASD member may purchase shares of an open-end investment company from the underwriter only

  - For his own investment
  - To cover purchase orders already received (not to make a market in the security)

- A broker/dealer may purchase shares of an open-end investment company from an NASD member underwriter at a price other than the public offering price only if

  - The buying broker or dealer is also a member.
  - A written sales agreement is in effect between the parties at the time of the sale.

- An NASD member may not use an upcoming dividend or distribution to induce the purchase of investment company shares (called selling dividends).
- NASD members must promptly pay underwriters for sales of investment company shares. If the payment is not received within ten business days after the transaction date, the NASD must be notified.
- It is contrary to just and equitable principles of trade to sell just below the breakpoint. The breakpoint is the point at which the sales charge is reduced.
- In any transaction between dealers and customers, the public offering price must be maintained.
- The NASD standards concerning advertisements and sales literature by members apply to

  - Research reports
  - Form letters
  - Reprints of previously published articles

REVIEW QUESTIONS

1. Under NASD rules, an appeal of a decision of the NASD District Business Conduct Committee can be made to
    a. Securities Investor Protection Corporation (SIPC)
    b. Committee on Uniform Securities Procedures (CUSIP)
    c. Board of Governors of the NASD
    d. CBS

2. When an RR executes a long sale for a customer, the RR must, under securities industry regulations
    a. Be certain the trade was done on an up tick.
    b. Make certain that the trade was profitable for the customer.
    c. Determine the location of the securities.
    d. Pay out the proceeds to the customer on settlement date.

3. Decisions of the NASD District Business Conduct Committee may be appealed to the Board of Governors of the NASD. Decisions of the Board of Governors of the NASD
    a. Are final and may not be appealed
    b. May be appealed to the SEC
    c. May be appealed to the Municipal Securities Rulemaking Board (MSRB)
    d. May be appealed to the Federal Reserve

4. Which of the following are true of an official NASD DK notice?

    I. It is sent out to the customer.
    II. It is sent to the contrabroker.
    III. It is sent to the NASD and the NYSE.
    IV. It is used for unmatched trades.

    a. I and II
    b. III and IV
    c. I and III
    d. II and IV

5. All of the following are considered immediate family members under NASD free riding and withholding rules **except:**
    a. Sister
    b. Daughter-in-law
    c. Aunt
    d. Parents

6. A customer purchases 300 shares of ABC at $8 per share. The market price of ABC declines to 5½. The RR feels responsible and personally offers to buy the shares back at $8 per share. Which of the following statements is true?
    a. This is allowed because the customer benefits from the buyback.
    b. This is allowed because the RR is personally absorbing the loss.
    c. This is a violation because the RR is guaranteeing the customer against loss.
    d. This is allowed without restriction.

7. Under security industry regulations, customer confirmations must be sent out
    a. On trade date
    b. On the next business day following trade date
    c. On settlement date
    d. On the seventh business day following trade date

8. Which of the following are purposes of the NASD?

    I. To promote just and equitable principles of trade
    II. To administer and enforce the rules of fair practice
    III. To provide a means for arbitrating disputes among members
    IV. To cooperate with the SEC and other agencies to solve problems affecting the securities industry

    a. I and II
    b. III and IV
    c. I, III, and IV
    d. All of the above

9. Under NASD rules, if an RR is brought before the District Business Conduct Committee, he may do all of the following **except:**
   a. Hear charges levied against him.
   b. Go directly into the state court system in the state where the customer resides.
   c. Bring his attorney to the hearing.
   d. Present evidence on his behalf.

10. The NASD Outside Business Activities Rule prohibits an RR from
   a. Accepting reimbursement of expenses from the NASD except with written approval of the employment member
   b. Being a member of the National Guard without the consent of the employing member
   c. Owning OTC securities without the knowledge of his employer
   d. Engaging in any employment for compensation with any person other than the employed member without giving notice to such member

11. Under NASD rules, arbitration may be used to settle which of the following disputes?

   I. A dispute between two NASD member firms
   II. A dispute between two RRs employed by two different NASD member firms
   III. A dispute between an NASD member firm and a public customer

   a. I only
   b. II only
   c. III only
   d. All of the above

12. Advertising and sales literature under NASD rules must be approved by
   a. An NASD principal
   b. An outside director
   c. An RR
   d. A limited partner

13. Mr. Livingston, a major customer of yours, goes to Kenya on vacation. The stock market declines substantially and two large positions of Mr. Livingston are declining rapidly. Which of the following statements is true under securities industry regulations?
   a. Liquidate Mr. Livingston's entire portfolio immediately.
   b. Sell Mr. Livingston's largest position only.
   c. Wait until you hear from the customer even though he might be taking a loss.
   d. Attempt to reach Mr. Livingston and sell all of his positions if you cannot reach him.

14. Which of the following types of information is required under NASD rules to open a new customer's account?
   a. An indication whether the customer is of legal age
   b. An indication of the customer's desired rate of return, financial situation, temperament, needs, and investment objectives
   c. The name of the account's beneficiary and contingent beneficiary
   d. At least two credit references, but preferably six

15. An investor feels that an RR has recommended unsuitable investments, causing her to lose $250,000. Under securities industry regulations, the investor may
   a. Sue in state court.
   b. Submit a claim to SIPC for the loss.
   c. Take the matter to securities industry arbitration.
   d. Sue in federal court.

16. A broker/dealer is exempt from NASD membership if it deals exclusively in
   a. Securities listed on a national securities exchange
   b. Securities listed on NASDAQ
   c. Open-end investment companies
   d. Closed-end investment companies

17. Under NASD rules, an individual who accepts a summary complaint procedure offered by the NASD District Business Conduct Committee is subject to which two of the following?

    I. Suspension
    II. Expulsion
    III. Censure
    IV. Fine

    a.   I and II
    b.   III and IV
    c.   I and IV
    d.   II and III

18. If a broker/dealer sells securities to a customer from its own inventory, it is acting as a(n)
    a.   Underwriter
    b.   Agent
    c.   Principal
    d.   Broker

19. Under NASD rules, which of the following is a private securities transaction that requires written notification of your firm?
    a.   Securities transactions by the RR outside the scope of his broker/dealer business
    b.   The sale to private customers of less than 100 shares
    c.   The purchase of securities by an RR in his own account with another broker/dealer
    d.   The sale of securities at the home of the client or office of an RR

20. The NASD regulates member firms and associated persons in the OTC securities market. The NASD Board of Governors prescribes regulations for associated persons of member firms pursuant to its authority granted by the
    a.   State securities laws
    b.   SIPC
    c.   NYSE
    d.   NASD bylaws

21. Under securities industry regulations, RRs, in order to sell securities, must file Form U-4 and register with
    a.   SIPC
    b.   Federal Reserve Board (FRB)
    c.   Federal Deposit Insurance Corporation (FDIC)
    d.   NASD

22. An RR wishes to open an account with a member firm other than your employer to invest in corporate securities. Which of the following must he do under NASD rules?
    a.   Ensure that copies of all transactions are sent to the NASD and the SEC.
    b.   Nothing; NASD rules prohibit opening a securities account at a firm other than his employer.
    c.   Notify the executing firm in writing of his affiliation.
    d.   Update his U-4 filing to show dual affiliation.

23. NASD rules normally prohibit sales of hot issues to immediate family members. All of the following are defined as immediate family under the free riding and withholding rule **except:**
    a.   Sister
    b.   Father
    c.   In-laws
    d.   Grandfather

24. If a customer is charged a commission on a securities transaction, it would be a(n)
    a.   Risk less principal transaction
    b.   A transaction with a markup or markdown
    c.   Principal transaction
    d.   Agency transaction

25. Under NASD rules, all of the following gifts are allowed by a fund underwriter to a registered representative **except:**
    a.   A pocket calendar worth $15
    b.   A calculator valued at $110
    c.   A dinner for the RR and spouse
    d.   Two tickets to a professional football game

26. Ms. Gates has $80,000 to invest. She is young and well educated and has concerns about investing in the stock market. As an RR, before selling securities to Ms. Gates, you should learn more about which of the following?

    I. Her income tax bracket
    II. Her net worth
    III. Her investment objectives
    IV. Her other investments

    a.   I and II
    b.   III and IV
    c.   I, III, and IV
    d.   All of the above

27. DK notices for unreconciled trades are sent to the
    a.   NASD
    b.   Contrabroker
    c.   SEC
    d.   Customer

28. Under NASD rules, an RR is required to notify his employer in writing prior to all of the following **except:**
    a.   He takes a part-time job selling insurance.
    b.   He takes a full-time job as a window washer.
    c.   He invests as a passive partner in a gas station.
    d.   He takes a full-time job selling land.

29. A hot issue could be sold to which of the following relatives of an RR?
    a.   Sister-in-law
    b.   Son-in-law
    c.   Uncle
    d.   Brother

30. Under securities industry regulations, prospectus delivery requirements may be waived
    a.   With the consent of the broker/dealer
    b.   With the consent of the customer
    c.   Only if the customer is knowledgeable about financial matters
    d.   Under no circumstances

31. Under NASD rules, an RR of the distributing member firm can purchase shares of a hot issue
    a.   Without any restrictions of any kind
    b.   With permission from the branch manager
    c.   Only if it is 200 shares or less
    d.   Under no circumstances

32. The form that tells the customer the details of transactions in stocks or investment company shares is the
    a.   Customer confirmation
    b.   Contrabroker comparison
    c.   Broker's order ticket
    d.   DK notice

33. An RR employed by an NASD member firm is required to submit to arbitration in a dispute submitted for arbitration by

    I. A public customer
    II. An RR employed by another firm
    III. His employing member firm

    a.   I only
    b.   I and II
    c.   II and III
    d.   All of the above

34. An RR of an NASD member firm must notify the employing firm under which of the following circumstances?

    I. He is convicted of securities fraud.

   II. He files for bankruptcy.

  III. He is accused of wrongfully taking property.

  IV. He is convicted of illegal gambling.

    a.   I and II

    b.   III and IV

    c.   I, II, and IV

    d.   All of the above

35. Which of the following, under NASD rules, has the right to file a complaint against an RR for alleged violations of the rules?

    I. The NASD Board of Governors

   II. A public customer

  III. The member firm employing the RR

    a.   I only

    b.   II only

    c.   I and II

    d.   III only

ANSWERS TO REVIEW QUESTIONS

1. c	7. b	13. c	19. a	25. b	31. d
2. c	8. d	14. a	20. d	26. d	32. a
3. b	9. b	15. c	21. d	27. b	33. d
4. d	10. d	16. a	22. c	28. c	34. d
5. c	11. d	17. b	23. d	29. c	35. c
6. c	12. a	18. c	24. d	30. d	

7 FEDERAL AND STATE REGULATIONS

The public outcry arising from the great decline in stock prices between 1929 and 1933 motivated the passage of the major federal laws regulating the securities industry. During the late 1920s, many investors were speculating in the stock market. About 55% of all personal savings were used to purchase securities, and the public was severely affected when the Dow Jones Industrial Average fell 89% between 1929 and 1933.

During this period, security price manipulation was common, and adequate information concerning securities usually was not available. Regulation was badly needed in the industry. The basic federal acts were passed between 1933 and 1940. However, long before the enactment of legislation by the federal government, individual states had laws on their books concerning the sale of securities. In 1911, the state of Kansas was the first state to pass securities legislation. Today, almost all states have securities divisions regulating the sale of securities within their borders. This chapter will discuss the following industry acts and rules:

- Securities Act of 1933
- Securities Exchange Act of 1934
- SEC rules concerning market manipulation and financial responsibility
- Securities Investor Protection Act of 1970
- Trust Indenture Act of 1939
- Securities Acts Amendments of 1975
- State securities laws

SECURITIES ACT OF 1933

The Securities Act of 1933 is sometimes referred to as the **Truth in Securities Act**. Its basic purpose is to make certain that new securities offered to the public are fully and clearly described in the registration statement and prospectus. Under this law, the Securities and Exchange Commission (SEC) attempts to make certain that there is a full disclosure of all significant material facts concerning a security to be offered to the public on an interstate basis.

It should be noted that the SEC does not approve securities registered with it, does not pass on the investment merit of any security, and never guarantees the accuracy of statements in the registration statement and prospectus. The SEC merely attempts to make certain that all pertinent information is disclosed in the registration statement and prospectus by requiring that

- The issuer file a registration statement with the SEC before securities may be offered or sold in interstate commerce
- A prospectus that meets the requirements of the Act be provided to prospective buyers
- Penalties (civil, criminal, or administrative) be imposed for violations of this Act

Exempted Securities under the 1933 Act

The Securities Act of 1933 makes it unlawful to sell or deliver a security through any instrument of interstate commerce unless a registration statement is in effect. However, certain securities are exempted from the registration requirements of the Act. The following issues qualify as exempted securities:

- US government, federal agency, and municipal securities
- Commercial paper and bankers' acceptances with a maturity of nine months (270 days) or less
- Securities issued by nonprofit and religious organizations
- Securities issued by banks and savings and loans
- Sales of intrastate securities by locally incorporated organizations
- Regulation A offerings ($5 million or less)

Red-Herring Prospectus

A **red-herring prospectus** is a preliminary prospectus. It is given to prospective purchasers during the twenty-day waiting period between the filing date of the registration statement and the effective date. The red-herring does not contain information such as the public offering price or the underwriter's spread.

The purpose of issuing a red-herring prospectus is to acquaint potential investors with essential facts concerning the issue. A red-herring prospectus summarizes many of the important details contained in the registration statement. It can never be used to solicit orders, only indications of interest. These indications of interest are not binding commitments—they are not binding on the broker/dealer or the customer. A registered representative (RR) is not allowed to write comments or statements on a red-herring (preliminary) prospectus or mark it in any way.

Unless an exemption applies, it is unlawful for any person to use the mails or any other instrument of interstate commerce to offer a security for sale unless a registration statement has become effective. Therefore, a security can be offered for sale only after a registration statement is effective.

To summarize, during the period between the filing date and effective date of the registration statement

- No sales of the security may take place.
- Offers of the security may take place, but a written offer may be made only through a preliminary prospectus or a red-herring prospectus (tombstone advertising is permitted during this period).
- Brokers may answer unsolicited requests for information by sending out a preliminary prospectus and accept unsolicited orders for the security.
- Brokers cannot send out the company's research report or any report projecting the company's future sales and earnings.

Final Prospectus

A registration statement is normally a very long and complex document for an investor to read. The Act requires the preparation of a shorter document called a **prospectus**. The prospectus summarizes the information contained in the registration statement. It must contain all the material facts in the registration statement, but in shorter form. The prospectus must be given to every person solicited and to every person who purchases or indicates in interest in purchasing securities. The purpose of a prospectus is to provide the investor with adequate information to analyze the investment merits of the security. Even if an investor does not intend to read a prospectus, it still must be given to him. It is unlawful for a company to sell securities prior to the effective date of the registration statement. The **final prospectus** must contain a statement that the SEC neither approves nor disapproves of the security. The final prospectus must be dated.

Effective Date of Registration Statement

On the date a registration statement becomes effective, securities may be sold to the public by the investment bankers. The effective date of a registration statement is the twentieth calendar day after filing the registration statement with the SEC, provided the registration statement is in proper form. The twenty-day waiting period before the registration becomes effective is called the **cooling-off period**. The purpose of the cooling-off period is to allow the public sufficient time to study the information in the registration statement and prospectus. The SEC may accelerate the effective date of a registration statement if it finds that adequate information with respect to the issuer is available and it is in the public interest to do so.

A copy of the final prospectus must be delivered to each purchaser with a confirmation or with the delivery of a security, whichever occurs first. Additional sales literature may be used by the firm as long as the sales literature is preceded or accompanied by a prospectus. Funds may be accepted by the broker/dealer from customers at this time.

Liabilities under the 1933 Act

The Securities Act of 1933 provides penalties for false and misleading statements contained in the registration statement or prospectus. If misrepresentations were intentionally made, the individuals responsible are subject to criminal prosecution. The civil liabilities allow a purchaser of a security under a registration statement containing a false statement of material fact, or omission of a material fact, to sue

- Every person who signed the registration statement
- All directors of the issue
- Attorneys, accountants and underwriters

THE SECURITIES EXCHANGE ACT OF 1934

The Securities Act of 1933 was passed to make the sale of new issues to the public in interstate commerce subject to federal regulation. The Securities Exchange Act of 1934 extended this federal regulation to all phases of trading in existing securities. Its objective is to prevent unfair and unequitable practices and to bring trading on securities exchanges and over-the-counter (OTC) market under federal control.

This Act established the Securities and Exchange Commission. The SEC consists of five persons appointed by the president and administers all federal laws regulating the securities business, except those regulating the extension of credit. This Act also defines many terms, including *broker*, *dealer*, and *exchange*.

The Board of Governors of the Federal Reserve was authorized by the Act to establish regulations governing the use of credit for the purchase or carrying of securities. The Federal Reserve has issued Regulations T, U, and G governing this area.

Insider Transactions

SEC rules prohibit persons from trading securities based on inside information. This rule applies to all persons whether they are insiders in a corporation or members of the general public.

Insiders in a corporation are normally officers, directors, and principal stockholders (persons owning 10% or more of the outstanding shares). However, any person may be considered an insider if the person directly or indirectly has access to material inside information, and he uses this information in the marketplace for his own benefit.

Certain persons who are not officers, directors, or principal stockholders could obtain material inside information as a result of their employment. Examples include

- Attorneys
- Accountants
- Reporters for financial publications
- Research analysts for broker/dealers
- Laboratory technicians

These persons who possess the inside information must refrain from using it in the marketplace, from recommending the security, and from disclosing the information to the public. Disclosure to the public, in most cases, should come from the corporation. This would avoid potential liability that could accrue to a person who disclosed information that was later proven to be false.

The SEC and the National Association of Securities Dealers (NASD) use certain factors to determine whether an individual acted on inside information in a particular transaction. The first test is that the information must be material. It must be of sufficient importance to have an effect on the stock in the marketplace. If a reasonable man would consider the information important, then it is probably material information. Examples of information that, in most cases, is considered material are

- Earnings projections
- Dividend increases or decreases
- Merger or acquisition
- Major lawsuit
- Introduction of a new product
- Discovery of a valuable natural resource on company property

The second factor considered is whether or not the information was nonpublic. It is generally considered to be public information when it is released to the public by the news media. However, the general public should be given time to digest the news, especially when the news is complex. Therefore, officers and directors should not be placing buy or sell orders for their own account immediately after the news is released to the public because the SEC may still consider this acting on nonpublic information.

The third important factor is whether the information was a factor in the person's decision to buy or sell the stock. The SEC presumes that the information was an important factor in the purchase or sale decision. It would be up to the individual to prove that the information was not the reason the stock was purchased or sold at that time.

Assume Mr. Jones is an attorney engaged in mergers and acquisitions. Mr. Jones gives you nonpublic information that Ajax Corporation is about to be taken over by Ford Motor Company. Mr. Jones tells you to buy

Ajax Corporation stock. You purchase the stock and sell it three weeks later for a huge profit. In this example, both you and Mr. Jones violated federal securities laws which prohibit insider trading.

Officers, directors, or principal stockholders must file a report with the SEC showing the amount of shares they own. Any changes in ownership of the shares must be reported to the SEC.

Market Manipulation

The Securities Exchange Act of 1934 outlaws the use of any manipulative, deceptive or other fraudulent devices. The intent is to prevent any manipulation of securities markets. Some of the specified devices prohibited are listed below.

- **Churning** can be described as a broker/dealer effecting transactions in a discretionary account that are excessive in size or frequency in view of the financial resources and character of the account. This is sometimes referred to as **overtrading** and is prohibited.
- **Wash sales** are prohibited. A wash sale occurs when a customer enters a purchase order and a sale order at the same time through the same broker/dealer. This would, normally, be done to create an appearance of activity in a security. A wash sale for tax purposes is not related to this in any way. A wash sale for tax purposes occurs when a customer sells a security at a loss and repurchases it within thirty days after the sale.
- **Matched orders** are illegal under the Act. Matched orders occur when a customer enters a purchase order and a sale order at the same time, at the same price. In the case of matched orders, the customer places the orders through different broker/dealers. As is the case with wash sales, no change in ownership takes place as a result of the transaction.
- **Pegging, fixing,** and **stabilizing** are prohibited, except when specifically permitted by SEC rules. Such operations attempt to create a price level different from that which would result from the forces of demand and supply.

SECURITIES INVESTOR PROTECTION ACT OF 1970

In the period 1968–1970, the brokerage community was faced with a paperwork crunch as a result of unexpectedly high trading volume. A severe decline in stock prices also hit the industry at this time. Many brokerage firms were forced into mergers or went out of business. Many public customers lost money because the brokerage firms could not meet their obligations. Investor confidence in the securities markets was badly shaken.

In order to restore confidence in the securities markets, Congress created the **Securities Investor Protection Corporation (SIPC)**. SIPC is a nonprofit membership corporation. The members of SIPC are, with some exceptions, all persons who are members of a national securities exchange.

SIPC provides protection for customers of a SIPC member firm in liquidation up to $500,000 per separate customer, except that claims for cash are limited to $100,000 per separate account. Therefore, SIPC provides protection for investors against losses up to certain limits on money and securities which are left on deposit with a broker/dealer that becomes insolvent.

The definition of **separate account** for the purposes of protection under the Act requires further explanation. SIPC provides protection up to limits prescribed in the Act per separate customer, not per separate account. A customer having several different accounts must be acting in a bona fide separate capacity with respect to each account in order to obtain protection for each account.

Consider the following accounts on the books of a broker/dealer:

- Mr. John Jones
- John and Mary Jones
- John Jones, Custodian for Jimmy Jones, under the Uniform Gifts to Minors/Transfer to Minors Act of Massachusetts

Each of these accounts represents a separate customer under the Act and each is entitled to SIPC protection up to the maximum limits.

However, assume John and Mary Jones opened three accounts with the same broker/dealer. Common stocks were purchased in one account. The second account was used to purchase preferred stocks. In the third, corporate bonds were purchased. In this case, if the broker/dealer goes into an SIPC liquidation, the total of cash and securities in the three accounts would be added together. John and Mary Jones are one separate customer. They are acting in the same capacity in each account and, therefore, are not entitled to separate protection.

The following examples apply to claims remaining *after* the return to customers of securities registered in their names and *after* the pro rata distribution of **customer property** held by the firm.

- A remaining claim is for $350,000 in securities. The claim would be satisfied in full.
- A customer has a claim for $350,000 in securities in an individual account and for $400,000 in securities in a joint account with his or her spouse, as to which each has full authority. The spouse also has an individual account in which there is a claim for $300,000 in securities. All three claims would be fully covered.

STATE SECURITIES LAWS

State securities laws are called **blue-sky laws**. Blue-sky laws attempt to protect the public from the fraudulent sale of securities within a particular state. The Securities Act of 1933 does not prohibit any state from enacting laws governing the sale of securities within its borders. Therefore, an issuer that intends to offer securities for sale in several states must comply with the provisions of the Securities Act of 1933 and all securities laws of the appropriate states.

Most states require the registration or licensing of both resident and nonresident broker/dealers and their agents operating within the state. Certain states require broker/dealers to maintain a minimum amount of net capital in order to operate in the state. Some states also require broker/dealers to post bonds in order to do business in the state. A state securities division has the power to revoke the license of a broker/dealer or the license of any salesman for violations of its laws.

To summarize the main points to remember concerning state securities laws (blue-sky laws)

- The securities division of a state has the power to revoke a broker/dealer's and/or salesman's license if state laws are violated.
- An issuer who intends to offer securities for sale in various states must comply with the provisions of the Securities Act of 1933 as well as the securities laws within each appropriate state.
- State securities laws attempt to protect the public against the fraudulent sale of securities within a state.
- The Securities Act of 1933 does not establish standard provisions that must appear in every blue-sky law. The individual states set their own requirements that issuers, broker/dealers, and salesmen must meet in order to transact business within the particular state.

UNIFORM GIFTS TO MINORS ACT—UNIFORM TRANSFER TO MINORS ACT

This type of account will be discussed separately because it should be thoroughly understood by a registered representative. The Uniform Gifts to Minors Act has been amended in many states and is referred to as the Uniform Transfer to Minors Act. We will refer to the two statutes as **UGMA/UTMA**.

Since a minor cannot be bound by the terms of a contract, broker/dealers will not open accounts for them. Minors have a legal right to void contracts at their option, and this could result in losses to the broker/dealer. Therefore, broker/dealers prohibit minors from opening securities accounts in their own names unless they have a custodian.

States have adopted either UGMA or UTMA, which permits a donor to make a gift of securities to a minor by registering the securities in the name of the adult as custodian for the minor. The custodian of the account manages the account for the benefit of the minor. The custodian should manage the account in a prudent manner, seeking reasonable income and protection of principal. The custodian should not be investing in a very speculative security because of the risks involved. The custodian must not engage in speculative transactions such as

- Uncovered option writing
- Selling securities short
- Commodity futures trading

However, covered call writing is allowed since it is a conservative option strategy used to generate income.

It is important to remember that the donor gives up all rights to any property transferred to a minor under this statute. Any gift made under the UGMA/UTMA is irrevocable, and the donor may not take the gift back at a future date. Once the securities are registered in the name of the custodian for the minor's benefit, the gift is complete and the minor becomes the sole owner of the securities. When the minor reaches the age of majority, any cash and securities in the account are transferred by the custodian to the person who has just reached the age of majority.

The following is a summary of the important points to remember concerning the UGMA/UTMA:

- Only one custodian and one minor are allowed per UGMA/UTMA account.
- The minor's Social Security number must be obtained for the account.
- Checks in the custodian's own name can never be drawn on the account.
- Assume a thirteen-year old minor is the owner of an UGMA that generates $14,000 of investment income. The custodian of the account is the minor's uncle who is in the 33% tax bracket. The minor's mother is a widow and is in the 28% tax bracket. Under federal tax laws, the earnings will be taxed at the mother's tax bracket rate of 28%. Unearned income over $1,300 of a minor under fourteen years of age is subject to taxation at the parent's tax bracket.
- Securities in an UGMA/UTMA account must be registered to the custodian for the minor.
- Any gift under the Act is an irrevocable gift; the donor cannot revoke the gift.
- Margin accounts are prohibited under the Uniform Gifts to Minors Account. A margin account is a securities account in which borrowing is used to purchase securities.

REVIEW QUESTIONS

1. The Securities Act of 1933

   I. Covers the sale of new issues to the public
   II. Calls for full and fair disclosure
   III. Regulates trading on a national securities exchange

   a. I and II
   b. II and III
   c. I and III
   d. All of the above

2. All of the following are true under the Uniform Gifts to Minors Act **except:**
   a. Only an adult may make a gift under the Act.
   b. The original custodian may be the donor.
   c. Securities in a custodial account may be kept in a margin account.
   d. Custodial property may be used for the support of the minor.

3. When a custodian account is opened under the Uniform Gifts to Minors Act, the Social Security number that must be obtained is
   a. The donor's
   b. The custodian's
   c. The minor's
   d. The legal guardian's

4. An underwriter can get an indication of interest in a new underwriting by issuing a(n)
   a. Disclosure prospectus
   b. Effective prospectus
   c. Registration prospectus
   d. Red-herring prospectus

5. When a custodian account is opened under the Uniform Gifts to Minors Act, how many custodians and minors may there be per account?
   a. One custodian and unlimited minors
   b. One custodian and one minor
   c. Two custodians and two minors
   d. Two custodians and three minors

6. The Securities Act of 1933 is designed to
   a. Afford potential investors an adequate factual basis for judging the investment value of new securities offerings
   b. Reduce the potential of loss to investors
   c. Provide an objective review of the merits of new securities offerings
   d. All of the above

7. Which of the following, under certain circumstances, could be considered insiders?

   I. Corporate attorney.
   II. Laboratory technician.
   III. Financial news service employee.
   IV. Control person.
   V. Independent accountant

   a. I and IV
   b. II, III and V
   c. I, III, IV, and V
   d. All of the above

8. Which of the following is correct concerning the Uniform Gifts to Minors Act?
   a. Securities may be held in a margin account.
   b. The donor may serve as the original custodian.
   c. Parents may serve as joint custodians.
   d. A parent may be the custodian of an account shared in common by more than one child.

9. The number of custodians in an account under the Uniform Gifts to Minors Act must not exceed
   a.   Seven
   b.   Five
   c.   Two
   d.   One

10. After a registration statement has been reviewed by the SEC and has become effective, a securities salesman may tell his customers
   a.   That the statements in the prospectus have been approved by the SEC
   b.   That the SEC has passed on the accuracy of the statements contained in the prospectus
   c.   That the SEC has passed on the adequacy of the statements contained in the prospectus
   d.   None of the above

11. Under the Securities Investor Protection Act of 1970, customer claims for cash and securities in the event of the liquidation of an SIPC member are insured up to
   a. $100,000 per "separate customer"
   b. $100,000 per account
   c. $500,000 per account
   d. $500,000 per "separate customer"

12. A customer of a failed firm files a claim for $30,000 in securities and $15,000 in cash. What amount of this claim would be covered under SIPC rules?
   a. $15,000
   b. $30,000
   c. $45,000
   d. $50,000

13. State securities laws are also referred to as
   a.   Prudent man laws
   b.   The Truth in Securities Act
   c.   Insider securities laws
   d.   Blue-sky laws

14. Assume a twelve-year-old minor is the owner of an UGMA that generates $15,000 of investment income. The custodian of the account is the minor's aunt who is in the 33% tax bracket. The minor's mother is a widow and is in the 28% tax bracket. Under federal tax laws, at what tax bracket will the earnings be taxed?
   a.   33% at the aunt's bracket
   b.   28% at the mother's bracket
   c.   At the 60% bracket for unearned income
   d.   Zero—there is no tax on a minor's account

15. Mr. Smith is an attorney engaged in mergers and acquisitions. Mr. Smith gives nonpublic information that ABC Corporation is about to be taken over by Specific Motors Corporation. Mr. Smith tells you, his RR, to buy ABC Corporation's stock. Based on the inside information, you purchase the stock and sell it four weeks later for a huge profit. Which of the following statements is true?
   a.   No violation of any kind has taken place
   b.   Only Mr. Smith violated insider trading laws
   c.   Only you violated insider trading laws
   d.   Both you and Mr. Smith violated federal securities laws on insider trading

ANSWERS TO REVIEW QUESTIONS

1. a	4. d	7. d	10. d	13. d
2. c	5. b	8. b	11. d	14. b
3. c	6. a	9. d	12. c	15. d

SERIES 6 GLOSSARY

Accumulation unit. An accounting measure used to measure the contract owner's interest in the separate account for variable annuity contract. The investor buys accumulation units during the accumulation period when funds are invested in the variable annuity.

Advertising and sales literature. All advertising and sales literature used to sell investment company shares must be approved by an NASD principal. It must be maintained by the member firm for three years. Sales literature for an investment company must be preceded or accompanied by a prospectus.

Agency transaction. In an agency transaction, a security is bought for the account of a customer and the customer is charged a commission.

Annual report. An investment company's annual report includes information such as the fund's assets, liabilities, income, expenses and a list of securities owned by the fund. If an annual report is used as sales literature, it must be approved by an NASD principal and preceded or accompanied by a prospectus.

Annuity unit. An accounting measure used to determine the amount of each payment to the annuitant for a variable annuity contract. The number of annuity units multiplied by the value of each unit equals the monthly payment to the annuitant.

Arbitration. Securities industry–related disputes are settled by an arbitration process. Arbitration decisions are binding and cannot be appealed. Arbitration handles disputes between member firms and associated persons.

Ask price. For an open-end fund, the net asset value per share plus a sales charge. For a no-load fund, the bid price and the ask price are the same.

Asset allocation. The percentage of an investor's assets that are placed in stocks (mutual funds), bonds, and money market instruments. Normally, younger investors have a higher percentage in equity investments such as stocks or growth mutual funds. Older investors normally have a higher percentage of their investments in bonds (bond funds) or money market instruments (money market funds).

Assumed interest rate. In a variable annuity the rate of interest an insurance company uses to determine the monthly payout. If the assumed interest rate is 4% and the separate account earns more than 4%, the monthly payout will increase.

Bid price. Also referred to as net asset value per share. When an investor sells an open-end fund, he receives the bid price per share.

Breakpoint. The dollar amount where the sales charge is reduced on a mutual fund purchase. If the first breakpoint is $10,000, the customer will pay a lower sales charge by investing $10,000. The customer can receive a lower sales charge by investing the breakpoint at one time or by a series of smaller purchases.

Call features—bond issue. Call features allow the issuer to call the security in prior to maturity, which benefits the issuing corporation.

Call option. The buyer of a call option has the right to buy 100 shares of the underlying security at a fixed price.

Capital gains distribution. A distribution from an investment company's long-term capital gains. Capital gains distributions can only be made annually by a fund and are taxed as long-term capital gains.

Cash value—variable life contract. The cash value of a variable life insurance contract is not guaranteed. A policyholder can borrow from the cash value.

Class A shares. Shares of a mutual fund that normally impose a sales charge on the fund purchase.

Class B shares. Shares of a mutual fund that are subject to a contingent deferred sales charge.

Closed-end funds. Funds that have a fixed number of shares outstanding and are traded on a stock exchange or in the over-the-counter market. Closed-end funds can issue senior securities such as preferred stock or bonds. They can trade above, below, or at the net asset value per share.

Commercial paper. Short-term money market instrument issued by a corporation. It has a maximum maturity of 270 days and is the most frequently issued money market instrument by a corporation.

Continuing commissions. If a bona fide contract exists, a registered representative can receive continuing commissions after he ceases to be employed by a member firm.

Contractual plan. A plan in which a customer invests a certain amount of money over a certain period of time. The customer might invest $400 a month for ten years. A registered representative must make clear to the customer the total sales charge over the life of the plan, how sales charges are deducted during the early years, consequences of liquidating in the early years, and sales charge refund provisions.

Custodian. The custodian for an investment company is normally a commercial bank. The custodian safeguards the cash and securities of the fund. The custodian bank does not protect the investor against a decline in the value of the fund shares. The custodian bank does not get involved in management of the fund or selling fund shares.

Customer confirmation. When a shareholder purchases investment company shares, he receives a form detailing the transaction called a customer confirmation. It may also be referred to as a confirmation statement.

Debenture. An unsecured debt security. It is backed only by the full faith and credit of the issuing corporation.

Discretionary account. In a discretionary account the registered representative decides what securities will be bought or sold for the customer's account. Prior written authorization is necessary from the customer before a discretionary account can be opened.

Diversified fund. A fund that must meet the 75-5-10 rule. This means that 75% of its assets must be invested so that the fund does not invest more than 5% of its total assets in only one security and it does not own more than 10% of the voting stock of any one company.

DK notice. A notice sent by a broker/dealer to the contrabroker in an attempt to resolve an unreconciled trade. "DK" stands for "Don't Know." The broker/dealer is attempting to reconcile a trade it previously "did not know."

Dollar cost averaging. Occurs when a person invests the same amount of money ($500 a month) in the same security (XYZ Fund) at the same interval (monthly). Dollar cost averaging benefits an investor because more shares are purchased when prices are lower and fewer shares are purchased when prices are higher. This causes the average cost per share to be lower than the average price of the shares. Dollar cost averaging does not guarantee a profit to an investor.

Expense guarantee. If an investor annuitizes a variable annuity, the insurance company guarantees that the amount of the annuity payments made to the annuitant will not be reduced by an increase in operating expenses of the insurance company.

Expense ratio. The expense ratio for an open-end investment company is the cost of portfolio management plus operating costs divided by the average net asset value.

Firm-commitment underwriting. A type of securities underwriting wherein the underwriter buys the securities from the issuing company and resells them to the public. The underwriting firm takes the risk that the securities may not be sold promptly.

Fiscal policy. Congress controls fiscal policy, which refers to government spending and taxation policies. If Congress wanted to stimulate the economy, it would increase government spending and lower federal income taxes.

Fixed annuity. An annuity that pay a fixed amount of money to the annuitant each month. A person who receives a fixed annuity is subject to the purchasing power risk. A fixed annuity is not a security; it is an insurance contract.

403-B plans. Tax-qualified plans available to employees of certain tax-exempt organizations. Employees of educational institutions such as teachers, professors, custodians, and librarians, and civilian employees of military academies such as West Point or Annapolis are eligible to participate.

Front-end-load contractual plans. Plans that are sold as either 20% or 50% plans. Under a 20% plan or a 50% plan, if the customer cancels the plan within the first forty-five days, the investor receives the current value of his account plus all sales charges paid. After the first forty-five days, a customer who cancels a 20% plan will receive only the current value of his account. A customer who invests in a 50% plan has up to eighteen months to cancel and receive a portion of the sales charge as a refund.

Hot issue. A security issue that trades at an immediate premium over its public offering price. The initial public offering price might be $20 per share and the stock increase to $40 per share. Hot issues cannot be sold to employees of the broker/dealer or to employees of other broker/dealers.

Inside information. Trading on material nonpublic information, which is prohibited under federal securities laws. For example, a lawyer friend tells you about a takeover. You buy the stock and make a large profit. Both you and the lawyer have violated insider trading laws.

Investment advisor. An investment advisor is normally compensated by receiving a percentage of assets under management. A registered representative who gives investment advice as part of his normal employment does not have to be registered as an investment advisor. However, a registered representative who gives investment advice outside the scope of his normal employment and receives fee for such advice must be registered as an investment advisor.

Investment advisory contract. A contract between the mutual fund and its investment manager. The contract must be approved, under the Investment Company Act of 1940, by the shareholders and a majority of the board of directors.

Investment Company Act of 1940. The federal securities law that regulates the operation of investment companies. The purpose of the Act is to ensure that persons who invest in investment companies are fully informed and fairly treated.

Letter of intent. Allows a fund shareholder to obtain a reduced sales charge if the required dollar amount is invested over a thirteen-month period. The letter of intent is binding on the fund, but the fund shareholder could discontinue payments and sell the shares, if he chooses to do so. If an investor cannot make payments up to the required amounts under a letter of intent, either the fund will send the customer a bill for the difference in sales charges or shares held in escrow will be liquidated by the fund to cover the difference in sales charges.

Market timing. A person who uses market timing analysis bases his investment decisions on the analysis. Assume the person using market timing expects interest rates to fall and the economy to expand. The person would buy growth funds.

Monetary policy. The Federal Reserve controls monetary policy, which refers to the money supply and interest rates in the economy. The Federal Reserve increases interest rates in an attempt to slow down the economy and decreases interest rates in an attempt to stimulate the economy.

Mortality guarantee. In a variable annuity, the insurance company guarantees that when an annuitant annuitizes the variable annuity, payments will continue to be made to the annuitant even if he or she lives longer than normal life expectancy.

Municipal bonds. Bonds issued by states, cities, towns, counties, port authorities, turnpike authorities, and toll bridge authorities. Two main types of municipal bonds are general obligation bonds and revenue bonds. General obligation bonds are backed by the faith and credit of the issuer. Revenue bonds are backed by a municipal enterprise such as a port authority, turnpike authority, or toll bridge authority. The interest received on municipal bonds is exempt from federal income taxes.

Mutual fund. An open-end management company. The term does not apply to closed-end funds.

Mutual fund orders. These orders can be entered on a subscription basis or a wire order basis. Orders entered on a subscription basis occur when the broker/dealer sends in the customer check along with the new account information to the fund distributor. The customer receives the next computed price after the order is received by the fund distributor. On a wire order, the broker/dealer enters the order directly with the fund distributor. The broker/dealer must then obtain a check from the customer in payment of the purchase. The risk to the broker/dealer is due to the possibility that the customer may not pay for the purchase. The broker/dealer would still have to pay for the purchase to the fund distributor.

NASD Outside Business Activity Rule. Rule that prohibits a registered representative from engaging in any employment for compensation with any person other than the employed member, without giving notice to the member firm.

NASD principal. A person employed by an NASD broker/dealer in a supervisory capacity. NASD principals must approve all advertising and sales literature, all new accounts, all order tickets at the end of the day, and all discretionary accounts.

Net investment income. An investment company's net investment income is equal to: Dividend income + Interest income + Short-term capital gains – Operating expenses and the cost of portfolio management. Income distributions (income dividends) are paid from a fund's net investment income.

Nonqualified deferred compensation plan. A contractual agreement wherein an employee defers receipt of income to a later period. Income taxes are not paid by the employee until the funds are received. If the company goes bankrupt, the person may not receive payments.

Non-tax-qualified plans. Plans funded with after-tax dollars. Variable annuities, variable life insurance contracts, and nonqualified deferred compensation plans are examples of non-tax-qualified plans. When an investor receives funds from a nonqualified plan, taxes are paid only on the portion of the funds that has not been taxed.

Open account. Many fund shareholders choose an open account in which funds can be sent in at any time. Open accounts require a minimum investment to open the account. The shareholder decides whether to reinvest dividends and capital gains or receive them in cash. Fund shareholders send in dollar amounts that are invested in fund shares. The fund shares are full and fractional shares that are held in unissued form by the fund.

Participating preferred stock. Stock that has a provision for an extra dividend above its regular rate. The shareholder may receive an additional amount of dividends in a particular year if the corporation's earnings grow.

Payment options—variable annuities. An investor who annuitizes a variable annuity can choose a life annuity, joint and last survivor, or life annuity—period certain. With a life annuity, all annuity payments cease on the death of the annuitant. A joint and last survivor annuity would be appropriate for a husband and wife. If the husband dies, payments would continue for the life of the wife. A life annuity—period certain is best explained by an example. Assume a person chooses a life annuity—twenty-year period certain. The annuitant dies after five years. Payments would continue to the beneficiary for the remaining fifteen years.

Prospectus. A written communication used to offer to sell securities for an investment company. The prospectus is given by the issuing fund to underwriters and dealers, who give it to the prospective investor. The prospectus contains information that the ordinary investor would be interested in.

Purchasing power risk. The risk that inflation will decrease the real rate of return to a fixed income investor. A person who purchases a fixed annuity is subject to the purchasing power risk. The purchasing power risk is also called the inflationary risk.

Regulated investment company. An investment company that qualifies for special tax treatment by paying out 90% of its net investment income to shareholders. The investment company will not pay taxes on any income distributed to shareholders. Only the shareholders will pay the tax.

Regulation T. A regulation of the Federal Reserve, which defines when funds must be received by a broker/dealer on a customer security purchase. On a mutual fund purchase, settlement date is three business days following trade date (T + 3). Under Regulation-T, if a customer has not paid by the fifth business day after trade date, the broker/dealer must obtain an extension of time or cancel or liquidate the transaction. If the transaction is canceled or liquidated, the account must be frozen for ninety days.

Reinvestment—dividends and capital gains distributions. Fund shareholders can have dividends and capital gains distributions reinvested in additional shares. The fund shareholder must pay taxes on the dividend and capital gains distributions even if they are reinvested. Assume a fund shareholder invests $10,000 in the ABC Growth Fund. Assume $2,000 in dividend distributions and $3,000 in capital gains distributions are reinvested in additional shares of the fund. The customer sells the fund shares for $22,000. The capital gain realized by the fund shareholder is $7,000.

Sales charge. Refers to an open-end investment company or mutual fund. The sales charge is the difference between the amount the investor pays for the fund and the amount that is invested in the fund on behalf of the investor. Assume a mutual fund has a bid price of $17 and an ask price of $18.50. The sales charge is $1.50, which is the difference between the bid and ask prices. The investor paid $18.50 per share to purchase fund shares, but only $17 per share was invested in the fund on behalf of the investor.

SEC Rule 12b-1. Rule that allows investment companies to charge fees to fund shareholders to pay distribution expenses of the fund. These 12b-1 fees must be clearly stated in the prospectus and are charged against the assets of the fund. The 12b-1 fees collected by the fund may be used to pay advertising costs, compensation to underwriters, and the cost of printing and mailing of sales literature to customers.

Secondary distribution. A block of outstanding securities that are being redistributed. For example, the president of ABC Corporation sells 300,000 shares for his own account. He receives the proceeds from the sale of the shares.

Securities Investment Protection Corporation (SIPC). Protects public customers up to certain limits if the broker/dealer becomes insolvent.

Selling dividends. A practice that is prohibited under securities industry regulations. The customer is encouraged by the registered representative to buy fund shares just prior to the ex-dividend date.

Series EE bonds. Nonnegotiable US savings bonds. The yields on Series EE bonds are scaled down in the early years to encourage investors to hold them to maturity. Series EE bonds cannot be pledged as collateral for a loan.

Shareholders. Shareholders of a fund share proportionately in a fund's income, profits, and losses. If the net asset value of a fund increases from $15 to $28, the shareholder has an unrealized gain on the fund shares.

Statement of additional information. Statement that contains more detailed information about the fund's operations than the prospectus. It must be sent to investors who request it.

Suitability. An investment meets a customer's investment objectives, financial situation, and financial needs. For example, a registered representative may recommend a growth fund to a younger person, a municipal bond fund to a person seeking nontaxable income, and a money market fund to a retired person seeking current income and protection of principal.

Surety bond. Bond that protects a broker/dealer up to the amount of the bond against fraud, theft, misappropriation of funds, or other related crimes or offenses. A surety bond is also referred to as an insurance bond or a broker's blanket bond.

Surrender value—variable annuity. The surrender value of a variable annuity is the total amount received when the variable annuity is surrendered or liquidated. Assume a person invests $40,000 in a variable annuity and receives $75,000 when the variable annuity is surrendered. The person has a $35,000 gain, which is taxed as ordinary income.

Tax-qualified plans. Plans that allow businesses or individuals to take an immediate tax deduction for money deposited with the plan. Pension plans, profit-sharing plans, Keogh plans, and IRAs are examples of tax-qualified plans.

Taxes. Shareholders pay taxes on distributions from investment companies. Income distributions are taxed as ordinary income. Capital gains distributions are taxed as long-term capital gains.

Total return information. If a mutual fund's sales literature contains a quotation or yield, it must contain the fund's total return information for one year, five years, and ten years. If a variable annuity advertisement contains total return performance, it must disclose sales charges, offer to provide a prospectus, and contain unqualified year-end average annual returns.

Transfer agent. Agent for an investment company who would normally perform functions such as issuing new shares to investors, canceling shares redeemed, and making dividend and capital gains distributions to investors.

Types of investment companies. Some of the main types of investment companies are growth funds, income funds, balanced funds, municipal bond funds, and money market funds.

Unrealized capital gains. An unrealized capital gain is a gain on a security position which has not been sold. Assume an investor buys 100 shares of ABC at $20 per share, which increases in price to $50 per share. This is an unrealized capital gain since the shares have not been sold. No taxes are due on unrealized capital gains. When the shares are sold, it is a realized capital gain and taxable.

UGMA/UTMA. This Act allows gifts of securities and cash to minors without using a trust. The gift is irrevocable. The donor appoints the custodian and the custodian manages the account for the benefit of the minor.

Variable annuities. Variable annuities are both securities and investment companies. Earnings in a variable annuity accumulate on a tax-deferred basis until they are withdrawn. No taxes are due during the accumulation period. Variable annuity income fluctuates during the payout period.

Variable contracts. The two types of variable contracts available to investors are variable annuities and variable life insurance contracts.

Variable life insurance contracts. Contract that combines the tax-deferred accumulation of earnings with life insurance securities in the separate account.

Warrants. Long-term options to buy stock at a fixed price from the issuing corporation. The fixed purchase price is set above the current market price of the stock.

Wash sale rule. Under federal tax laws, an investor who sells a security, such as a mutual fund, at a loss must wait more than thirty days to buy back the security. If the investor buys the security back within thirty days, it is a wash sale and the loss cannot be deducted for tax purposes.

Withdrawal plans. A fund shareholder under a withdrawal plan receives a certain amount of money each month from the fund. The customer should clearly understand that if the withdrawals are greater than the income generated in the account, invested capital may be exhausted.

Zero coupon bonds. Bonds that pay all of the interest to bondholders in one payment at maturity. However, with zero coupon bonds, an investor may have to pay taxes on income he does not receive. This is the reason that most investors purchase zero coupon bonds in a tax-sheltered plan.

SERIES 6 FINAL EXAMINATION

1. The custodian of a mutual fund, which is normally a commercial bank, holds the assets of the fund
    a. For physical safekeeping
    b. To protect investors against loss in the value of the shares
    c. To collateralize customer loans made on margin accounts
    d. To guarantee return of the customer's principal plus interest

2. Mutual fund shareholders are not taxed on
    a. Dividends reinvested in additional fund shares
    b. Capital gains reinvested in additional fund shares
    c. Unrealized capital gains
    d. Dividends representing net investment income from interest-bearing debt obligations

3. Municipal bonds can be issued by

    I. Counties
    II. Cities and towns
    III. Port authorities
    IV. Turnpike authorities

    a. I and II
    b. III and IV
    c. II, III, and IV
    d. All of the above

4. XYZ Corporation wants to issue a money market instrument. Which of the following money market instruments is most commonly issued by corporations such as XYZ?
    a. Treasury bills
    b. Commercial paper
    c. Bankers' acceptances
    d. Certificates of deposit

5. Mrs. Johnson has $40,000 to invest. She is young and well educated and fears the stock market. Before selling any securities to Mrs. Johnson, you, as her registered representative, should learn more about which of the following?

    I. Her investment objectives
    II. Her income tax bracket
    III. Her net worth
    IV. Her other investments

    a. I and II
    b. III and IV
    c. I, II, and IV
    d. All of the above

6. When an investor tenders mutual fund shares for redemption, the investment company or its agent must make payment to the investor, under normal business conditions, not later than
    a. The day the shares are accepted from the investor
    b. Five days after acceptance of the shares
    c. Seven days after acceptance of the shares
    d. Thirty days after acceptance of the shares

7. Mrs. Truman states that her investment objectives are current income, stability of principal, and high liquidity. Which of the following types of mutual funds should be offered to Mrs. Truman?
    a. Specialized growth fund
    b. Money market fund
    c. Blue-chip growth fund
    d. Balanced fund

8. An open-end investment company is prohibited from
    a. Purchasing call or put options
    b. Borrowing money
    c. Lending money
    d. Issuing senior securities (preferred stock or bonds)

9. Mrs. Clinton is about to retire and wants to redeem shares in ABC Growth Fund and purchase shares in ABC Income Fund under different management. All of the following are true concerning the exchange **except:**
    a.   The investor will probably obtain a higher yield from the income fund.
    b.   The investor will obtain greater diversification in the income fund.
    c.   A sales charge may be incurred when Mrs. Clinton buys the income fund.
    d.   Mrs. Clinton will realize a capital gain on any unrealized appreciation of the growth fund shares.

10. When an account is opened under the Uniform Gifts/Transfer to Minors Act, whose Social Security number should be given?
    a.   The registered representative handling the account
    b.   The minor's
    c.   The custodian's
    d.   The special tax ID number assigned to the custodian account

11. Mrs. Duncan has adjusted gross income of $30,000. She is eligible for an IRA and wants to make the maximum deductible contribution for herself and her nonworking spouse. She may do this in which of the following ways?
    a.   Contribute $4,000 to a joint IRA
    b.   Contribute $2,000 to her IRA and $2,000 to her spouse's IRA
    c.   Contribute a total of $2,250 to their IRA accounts
    d.   Contribute $2,000 to her IRA only; her spouse is not eligible to have any money set aside on his behalf

12. An open-end investment company prospectus would normally contain information on all of the following **except:**
    a.   Investment objectives of the investment company
    b.   Refunds on the load
    c.   Sales charges applicable to a purchase
    d.   Individual portfolio changes

13. A registered representative employed by an NASD member firm is required to submit to arbitration in a dispute submitted for arbitration by

    I. His employing member firm
    II. A registered representative employed by another member firm
    III. A public customer

    a.   I only
    b.   I and II
    c.   II and III
    d.   All of the above

14. NASD rules require that written notification be given to his employing firm by a registered representative concerning a private securities transaction. Which of the following would be considered a private securities transaction under NASD rules?
    a.   When a registered representative sells a fund to a customer in the customer's private residence
    b.   The sale to a private customer of an odd lot (less than 100 shares)
    c.   Securities transactions by registered representatives outside the scope of their employing broker/dealer's business
    d.   The sale of an exempt security to a customer

15. Assume Mr. Dole is a purchaser of investment company shares. Securities industry regulations would allow Mr. Dole to file suit to rescind a transaction or to collect damages in which of the following instances?

    I. The prospectus given to Mr. Dole omitted certain material facts.
    II. Mr. Dole did not receive a prospectus at or before completion of the transaction.
    III. A sales presentation to Mr. Dole that influenced his investment decision contained an untrue statement of a material fact.

    a.   I only
    b.   II and III
    c.   I and III
    d.   All of the above

16. Shareholders in a mutual fund
    a.   Share proportionately in the fund's income profits and losses
    b.   Work with management to select investments for the fund
    c.   Own certain securities in the fund's portfolio directly
    d.   Will not realize a loss if they hold the shares long-term

17. Which of the following are probable violations of NASD rules relating to fair dealing with customers?

    I. A pattern of short-term trading in load funds by customers
    II. Recommending that a customer maintain a withdrawal plan and contribute to a mutual fund contractual plan at the same time
    III. Switching customers from one load fund to another in discretionary accounts controlled by the firm
    IV. Encouraging customers to buy load funds before the ex-dividend date

    a. I and II
    b. III and IV
    c. I, II, and IV
    d. All of the above

18. Tax-qualified retirement plans have provisions detailing which employees may participate in the plan and are called

    a. Distribution provisions
    b. Eligibility requirement provisions
    c. Vesting provisions
    d. Funding provisions

19. The NASD issues standards concerning advertisements and sales literature by members. Which of the following must conform to NASD standards relating to mutual fund sales literature?

    I. Reprints of previously published articles
    II. Form letters
    III. Research reports

    a. I only
    b. II only
    c. I and III
    d. All of the above

20. Mr. Buffett is sixty-five years old and wants to invest $20,000 in a mutual fund withdrawal plan. The withdrawal plan will pay Mr. Buffett $400 per month. Mr. Buffett should clearly understand which of the following?

    I. He is guaranteed to be paid $400 a month for life.
    II. Invested capital may be exhausted.
    III. Ownership of the principal amount is given up when withdrawals begin.
    IV. More money may be withdrawn from the account than the present amount Mr. Buffett provisioned for.

    a. I and II
    b. III and IV
    c. I and III
    d. II and IV

21. Under securities industry regulations, a mutual fund's sales literature that contains a quotation of yield or equivalent yield must also contain

    a. The fund's total return information
    b. The names of all stockholders in the fund
    c. The fund's incorporation date
    d. The fund's taxpayer identification number

22. Which of the following, under NASD rules, has the right to file a complaint against an RR for alleged violations of rules?

    I. Any customer of the particular registered representative
    II. The NASD Board of Governors
    III. The member firm employing the registered representative

    a. I only
    b. I and II
    c. II and III
    d. I and III

23. John Perry is a registered representative with ABC Broker/Dealer and he wants to open an account with another member firm to invest in corporate securities. Which of the following is required of Mr. Perry?

    a. He must update his U-4 form to show his affiliation with another member firm.

    b. Notify the executing firm in writing of his affiliation with ABC.

    c. Require duplicate copies of all transactions be sent to the SEC and NASD.

    d. None of the above. The account may be opened without restriction.

24. Assume an investor cannot make investments up to the required amounts under a letter of intent. Which of the following will occur?

    I. The fund will send a bill to the investor for the difference in the sales charges.

    II. Shares owned by the investor held in escrow by the fund will be liquidated to cover the differences in sales charges.

    III. The shareholder is subject to penalty fees and interest charges.

    IV. The shareholder will be required to pay the maximum sales charge stated in the prospectus, without regard to the amount invested in the fund.

    a. Either I or II

    b. III only

    c. IV only

    d. II and III

25. The net asset value of the Superb Fund, an open-end investment company, has increased from $14.86 to $15.91 over a five-month period. Which of the following statements is true concerning this increase in the value of the shares?

    a. There has been an increase in the demand for Superb Fund's shares.

    b. It is as a result of an increase in the value of the portfolio of Superb.

    c. It is as a result of management's decision to raise prices of Superb shares.

    d. The increase happened since more shareholders bought shares in the fund than those who sold shares.

26. XYZ Fund's prospectus states that shares are sold at the net asset value plus a sales charge of 8%, which is 9.3% of the net amount invested. It is important for a client to understand that the 8% is calculated on the

    a. Net asset value only

    b. Offering price

    c. The fund's closing bid price

    d. Average price of the net asset value and the offering price

27. Which of the following statements is true if a corporate bond is selling at a premium over par value?

    a. The current yield is less than the nominal yield.

    b. Its yield to maturity is greater than the nominal yield.

    c. Its current yield is greater than the nominal yield.

    d. None of the above

28. All of the following are ownership rights of common stock **except:**

    a. To vote for the directors of the corporation

    b. To receive their share of residual assets upon dissolution of the corporation

    c. To subscribe to new issues of stock in proportion to their percentage ownership

    d. To receive a fixed proportion of the company's earnings in the form of dividends

29. If an investor is told to buy a mutual fund just prior to a dividend payment to increase his return and benefit him financially, this practice is called "selling dividends." The practice of selling dividends is not beneficial to an investor because

    a. The fund's directors may decide not to pay the dividend.

    b. Dividends are paid only to shareholders who have owned the shares more than twelve months.

    c. The amount of the distribution is included in the price paid for the shares.

    d. A higher sales charge is paid by the investor prior to the dividend payment.

30. Which of the following statements are true concerning variable life insurance policies?

   I. They can be sold without a prospectus in every case.
   II. They provide a death benefit and cash value which can fluctuate based on the investment performance.
   III. Policyholders can select different investment opinions.
   IV. They can have expense charges for administrative expenses, sales expenses and expenses charged for mortality premium taxes.

   a. I and II
   b. III and IV
   c. I, II, and III
   d. II, III, and IV

31. All of the following statements are true concerning the redeeming of investment company shares **except:**
   a. The redemption price may be more or less than the cost to the investor.
   b. The redemption price is the last net asset value computed before the receipt of the request for redemption by the broker/dealer or registered representative.
   c. The transfer agent may require a stock power and signature guarantee for redemption for shares he is holding.
   d. If the shareholder has the certificates, the transfer agent will require a properly signed certificate and a signature guarantee to accompany the redemption request.

32. Which of the following is true under federal securities laws concerning the statement of additional information?

   a. It is given only to individuals who request it.
   b. It is contained in the annual report.
   c. It must be distributed with a prospectus.
   d. It is the same as a proxy.

33. If there is an increase in current yields on outstanding bonds, it is normally a result of which two of the following?

   I. An increase in market prices of currently traded bonds
   II. A decrease in market prices of currently traded bonds
   III. An increase in general interest rate levels
   IV. A decrease in general interest rate levels

   a. I and IV
   b. II and III
   c. I and III
   d. II and IV

34. The surrender value of a deferred variable annuity contract is equal to
   a. The number of accumulation units multiplied by the value of an accumulation unit next computed after receipt of the request for surrender by the issuer
   b. The number of annuity units multiplied by the value of an annuity unit computed at the end of the previous month
   c. The closing price of the annuity unit on the New York Stock Exchange multiplied by the number of annuity units owned
   d. The value of an annuity unit set by the insurance company once a week multiplied by the number of annuity units owned

35. Under NASD rules, registered representatives who have only a Series 6 license may sell which of the following?
   a. Shares of a closed-end investment company on an initial offering
   b. Shares in a real estate investment trust
   c. Shares in a closed-end fund currently traded on the New York Stock Exchange
   d. Exempt limited partnership interests

36. Summit Corporation decides to give its purchasers an opportunity to obtain shares of Summit at a fixed price for five years, the subscription price somewhat above the current market price. The corporation would be issuing
   a. Warrants
   b. Commercial paper
   c. Rights
   d. Call options

37. A secondary distribution is best defined as
    a. A new issue of previously unregistered shares.
    b. A private transaction between an underwriter and an investor.
    c. A block of outstanding securities that are being redistributed.
    d. A sale of authorized but unissued shares to company management.

38. All of the following functions may be performed by the transfer agent of an investment company **except:**
    a. Issuing new shares to investors.
    b. Canceling shares redeemed by investors.
    c. Making dividend and capital gains distributions to investors.
    d. Safekeeping the physical assets of the investment company.

39. Which of the following types of information is required under NASD rules to open a new customer's account?
    a. The name of the account's beneficiary and contingent beneficiary
    b. At least two credit references, but preferably four
    c. An indication whether the customer is of legal age
    d. An indication of the customer's desired rate of return, financial situation, temperament, needs, and investment objectives

40. Securities industry regulations would allow which of the following statements to be made by a registered representative involving investment companies?
    a. "This fund will always yield at least 8%."
    b. "Our investment managers are the most competent in the securities industry and this will always be true."
    c. "Our managers' dedication is to provide you with the best service of which they are capable."
    d. "This fund is a growth fund and will increase faster than the market as a whole."

41. In a variable life policy, the cash value in the policy is
    a. Not guaranteed
    b. Fully guaranteed
    c. Always equal to the death benefit
    d. Equal to the minimum death benefit plus a normal rate of return

42. All of the following statements are true concerning variable life insurance policies **except:**
    a. The policyholder of the contract bears the investment risk.
    b. Prospective purchasers must be provided with a prospectus.
    c. The policy is referred to as variable because the death benefit and surrender value will vary based on the investment experience of the separate account.
    d. The cash value in the policy is always guaranteed.

43. Open-end investment company shares differ from closed-end shares because the shares bought by individual investors are normally
    a. Newly issued shares of the fund
    b. Shares listed on a national securities exchange
    c. Shares sold by a broker/dealer from its inventory account
    d. Shares purchased from another individual investor

44. Which two of the following describe types of variable contracts?

    I. An annuity that invests mainly in equities and neither the principal nor the payout is guaranteed
    II. A fixed annuity that allows annuitants to contribute variable amounts
    III. A withdrawal plan in a mutual fund primarily invested in bonds
    IV. A life insurance policy that has a cash value accumulation and the death benefits can rise or fall based on the performance of the underlying investments that are chosen by the policyholder

    a. I and II
    b. III and IV
    c. II and III
    d. I and IV

45. A local insurance agent in Orlando, Florida, is not licensed with the NASD. The agent wants to sell a mutual fund offered by your firm. He wants to split the commission on the sale of the mutual fund with you. Which of the following statements is true concerning this proposed transaction?
    a. This transaction can be done without any restrictions.
    b. This transaction can be done provided a prospectus is delivered to the agent.
    c. This transaction is unacceptable because the insurance agent is not registered with the NASD.
    d. This is allowed only on a onetime basis.

46. During the accumulation period of a tax-qualified variable annuity, the separate account will earn interest, dividends, and capital gains. Who is responsible for paying federal income taxes on the interest, dividends, and capital gains?
   a. The life insurance company that issued the contract pays all taxes.
   b. The employer making the contributions pays all taxes due.
   c. No taxes are due during the accumulation period.
   d. The employee pays all taxes due during the accumulation period.

47. When a registered representative is selling a contractual plan to a client, which of the following points should be made clear concerning the sales charge?

   I. The consequences to the customer of liquidating the plan in the early years and sales charge refund provisions applicable to the contractual plan
   II. The total sales charges over the life of the contractual plan
   III. How sales charges are deducted from payments made during the early years of the plan

   a. I only
   b. I and II
   c. II and III
   d. All of the above

48. Mr. Nevers purchases 100 shares of ABC at $60 per share. Payment is not received by the fifth business day after trade date. A request for an extension of time is denied. The broker/dealer is required to do which of the following under the provisions of Regulation T?
   a. Immediately sue the customer to collect the money due.
   b. Loan the customer the funds to cover the purchase.
   c. Cancel or liquidate the transaction.
   d. Extend the settlement date for two additional weeks.

49. Mutual funds may require minimum initial investments for

   I. Contractual plans
   II. Open accounts
   III. Withdrawal accounts (plans)

   a. I only
   b. II only
   c. I and III
   d. All of the above

50. Assume that dividend payments to common stockholders decrease, but the price of the common stock does not change. Which of the following is true concerning the yield on the common stock?
   a. It will increase.
   b. It will decrease.
   c. It will remain exactly the same.
   d. It will increase substantially and then decrease.

51. All of the following features or benefits could appear in an individual variable annuity contract **except:**
   a. Reinstatement provisions
   b. Deferral of taxes
   c. Various settlement options
   d. Guaranteed cash values

52. Mrs. White is living on fixed income and worries to a great extent about inflation. Which of the following risks is Mrs. White most exposed to?
   a. Market or systematic risk
   b. Purchasing power risk
   c. Economic risk
   d. Interest rate isk

53. Normally, fluctuations in corporate earnings will have the greatest effect on the price of a corporation's
   a. First mortgage bonds
   b. Commercial paper
   c. Preferred stock
   d. Common stock

54. A variable annuity contract holder begins receiving funds during the payout period. The initial payout was $400 based on a 4% net investment rate. In the second month, a net investment rate of 8% is earned by the separate account. In this case, the contract holder will receive a payout of
   a. An amount substantially less than $400
   b. An amount greater than $400
   c. An amount slightly less than $400
   d. Exactly $400

55. A client realizes a loss on the sale of 100 shares of Spartan Growth Fund. Twenty-eight days later he buys 100 shares of the same fund. Which of the following statements is true concerning the tax consequences of these transactions?
   a. The client cannot take a loss for tax purposes.
   b. The loss is deductible in full in that tax year.
   c. This is a wash sale, and therefore the customer is allowed to deduct 50% of the loss.
   d. This is an unrealized loss and can only be subtracted from unrealized gains in the same tax year.

56. An advertisement containing variable annuity total return performance is required under securities industry regulations to contain

   I. The disclosure of sales charges
   II. A complete description of every investment option
   III. An offer to provide the prospectus
   IV. Unqualified year-end average annual return

   a. I only
   b. II and III
   c. I, III, and IV
   d. II, III, and IV

57. All of the following statements are true about the effect of policy loans on benefits under a variable life insurance policy **except:**
   a. The benefits will be affected even if the loan is paid.
   b. The amount borrowed ceases to earn any interest.
   c. The current death benefit will be reduced by the amount of the loan.
   d. A maximum loan may increase the possibility of the policy's lapsing.

58. In calculating the value of an accumulation unit in a variable annuity contract, which of the following are components of the separate account?

   I. Realized capital gains and losses
   II. Unrealized capital gains and losses
   III. Investment income

   a. I only
   b. II only
   c. I and II
   d. All of the above

59. The Performance Investment Company wants to use its annual report to shareholders as sales literature. Which of the following statements are true?

   I. It must be approved by a principal of the firm prior to use.
   II. It is considered sales literature by the NASD.
   III. It must be preceded or accompanied by a prospectus.
   IV. It must compare the fund's performance with the Dow Jones Averages, Standard & Poor's 500 Stock Index, and the Value Line Index.

   a. I only
   b. II and III
   c. I, II, and III
   d. II, III, and IV

60. The US dollar is said to be "cheap" when
   a. The exchange rate allows more dollars to be purchased for a given amount of foreign currency.
   b. The price of gold drops sharply in London.
   c. New York Stock Exchange securities are falling dramatically.
   d. The United States is in a period of deflation.

61. All of the following would normally be eligible to participate in a tax-deferred annuity according to Section 403-B of the federal tax laws **except:**
   a.   A librarian who works at a middle school
   b.   A tenured professor at a state college
   c.   A custodian at a municipal high school
   d.   A full-time student at a college that receives federal funds

62. Your friend Mr. Bailey, who is an attorney engaged in mergers and acquisitions, gives you nonpublic information that the Comet Corporation is about to be taken over by General Motors. He tells you to buy Comet stock. You do and sell the stock two weeks later for a huge profit. Which of the following statements is true?
   a.   No violation of federal securities laws has taken place.
   b.   Mr. Bailey violated insider trading rules.
   c.   You violated federal securities laws since you engaged in the securities transaction.
   d.   Both you and Mr. Bailey violated federal securities laws which prohibit insider trading.

63. The cash value of a variable life insurance policy will be affected by

   I.   Deferred sales charges
   II.   Changes in the death benefit
   III.   Loans taken by the policyholder
   IV.   Fluctuating market values

   a.   I and II
   b.   III and IV
   c.   I, II, and III
   d.   II, III, and IV

64. Which of the following would normally be the custodian of an investment company?
   a.   Full-service broker/dealer
   b.   Member firm of the NASD
   c.   Commercial bank
   d.   Underwriting firm

65. Mr. Reagan purchases a fixed life annuity to provide himself with retirement income. Which of the following risks is assumed by Mr. Reagan, the annuitant?
   a.   The investment risk relating to the contract.
   b.   Payments might end prior to the death of the annuitant.
   c.   The purchasing power of the dollar will decrease in the future.
   d.   The amount of retirement income will fluctuate each month.

66. In a rising stock market, you would expect the market appreciation to be shown by a(n)
   a.   Money market fund
   b.   Balanced fund
   c.   Income fund
   d.   Common stock fund

67. Mr. Adams is considering investing in XYZ Growth Fund. He must be made aware of the breakpoints relating to the fund under which of the following circumstances?
   a.   Under no circumstances
   b.   Only if they are detailed in the fund's prospectus
   c.   Only if the customer specifically asks about the breakpoints
   d.   If the amount of money invested falls just below the breakpoint

68. According to SEC Rule 12b-1, fund expenditures may be used for all of the following **except:**
   a.   Advertising
   b.   Compensation to underwriters
   c.   Brokerage costs for portfolio transactions
   d.   The cost of printing and mailing of sales literature to customers

69. All of the following statements are true concerning SEC Rule 12b-1 **except:**
   a.   The fees must be clearly stated in the fund's prospectus.
   b.   The fees may be used to pay distribution expenses.
   c.   The fees cannot exceed 8% of the cost of the transactions.
   d.   The fees are expenses charged against the assets of the fund.

70. It would be considered misleading under securities industry regulations relating to investment company sales literature dealing with redemption features to discuss
    a.   How soon the investor will be paid after a redemption
    b.   The benefits of holding the shares as a long-term investment
    c.   The administrative procedures for redeeming the shares
    d.   The redemption features as a way of providing a guarantee of principal protection for the shareholder

71. Mrs. Barnett is considering exchanging one mutual fund for another mutual fund. Which of the following considerations are important for Mrs. Barnett?

    I. Mrs. Barnett's desire for more current income
    II. The objective of the fund to which Mrs. Barnett is transferring
    III. The tax consequences relating to the exchange
    IV. Recent movements or changes in the stock market and economy

    a.   I and II
    b.   III and IV
    c.   I, II, and IV
    d.   All of the above

72. All of the following are characteristics of mutual fund open accounts **except:**
    a.   A customer must invest a minimum amount to open the account.
    b.   The customer may elect to take dividends in cash.
    c.   A customer normally purchases a certain amount of shares (share amounts).
    d.   Depending on the fund, reinvested dividends may or may not be subject to sales charges.

73. When a customer receives a notice in writing indicating whether the broker/dealer acted as agent or principal, the date of the transaction, and the price per share, this notice is best described as a
    a.   Full disclosure statement
    b.   Ledger statement
    c.   Financial statement
    d.   Confirmation statement

74. Which of the following gives the NASD Board of Governors powers to prescribe regulations concerning associated persons of member firms?
    a.   Securities Investor Protection Act of 1970
    b.   NASD Bylaws
    c.   Securities Act of 1933
    d.   Securities and Exchange Commission

75. Mrs. Thompson has not provided a tax certification form to the mutual fund holding her account. Mrs. Thompson may be subject to
    a.   Surcharges
    b.   Tax withholding
    c.   Alternative minimum tax
    d.   A special noncertification tax

76. NASD adopted the Outside Business Activities Rule which prohibits an RR from
    a.   Owning any securities without prior permission of his employer
    b.   Being a member of the Army Reserve without prior permission of employer
    c.   Engaging in any employment for compensation with any person or institution other than the employed member without giving notice to the employed member
    d.   Volunteering in any nonprofit activity such as Boy Scouts or Little League without giving notice to his employing member

77. Which of the following is true concerning a US government Series EE bond?
    a.   Interest is paid on the bond once a year.
    b.   Any interest received is subject to state income taxes, but exempt from federal income taxes.
    c.   Yields are scaled down in the early years to encourage purchasers to hold them to maturity.
    d.   It provides variable rates of return and is an excellent security to own for inflation protection.

78. If a variable life insurance policyholder surrenders the policy for cash and one year later decides to reinstate the policy, which of the following is true concerning reinstatement?
    a.   The policy cannot be reinstated under any circumstances
    b.   A premium of 150% of the amount required to keep the reinstated policy in force must be paid.
    c.   Normally, evidence of insurability and the payment of unpaid past premiums would be required.
    d.   The policyholder must pay an amount equal to the investment return on the separate account.

79. Mr. Morrison's investment objective is current nontaxable income. Which of the following would be most suitable for Mr. Morrison?
    a.   An aggressive growth fund
    b.   Any fund about to go ex-dividend within the next thirty days
    c.   Municipal bond fund
    d.   Money market fund that invests only in US government securities

80. Fund advertisements containing performance data are required, under SEC rules, to

    I.   Disclose the risk of fluctuation of income.
    II.   Disclose the risk of loss of principal.
    III.   Include purchase applications for the fund in the advertisement.

    a.   I only
    b.   II and III
    c.   I and II
    d.   All of the above

81. Which of the following statements are in violation of securities industry regulations?

    I.   The custodian protects the investor against unsuitable investment policies.
    II.   Dollar cost averaging ensures that the investor's account will fall below his cost basis.
    III.   Regulation of investment companies does not involve supervision of the fund's investment policies.
    IV.   Mutual funds can be redeemed, but on redemption the amount received by the investor may be more or less than the amount invested.

    a.   I and II
    b.   III and IV
    c.   I and III
    d.   II and IV

82. A fixed annuity and a variable annuity differ in which of the following ways?
    a.   Variable annuity income is guaranteed for life, while fixed annuity income is guaranteed for one year.
    b.   Variable annuity income can be guaranteed for only up to five years, while fixed annuity income can be guaranteed for up to ten years.
    c.   Variable annuity income fluctuates, while fixed annuity income remains level.
    d.   Variable annuity income cannot be continued for as long a period as fixed annuity income.

83. Mr. Carroll wants to avoid a taxable event when switching from one fund to another. Which of the following statements is true?
    a.   It is not a taxable event if the switch occurs within the same family of funds.
    b.   It is not a taxable event in every case.
    c.   It is not a taxable event if a sales charge was levied on the purchase.
    d.   None of the above statements are true—the switch is always a taxable event.

84. The best definition of a communication used by a person to offer to sell securities of any investment company to prospective investors is a(n)
    a.   Official statement
    b.   Internal memo
    c.   Prospectus
    d.   Sales literature

85. All of the following are normally eligible investments for a 403-B tax-deferred annuity **except:**
    a.   Variable annuity
    b.   Fixed annuity
    c.   Contributions to mutual funds by a custodian
    d.   Limited partnership

86. The best definition of the "expense ratio" of an open-end investment company is
    a.   Expenses minus income for the fund
    b.   The costs of portfolio management plus operating costs divided by average net asset value
    c.   The cost of buying one share of stock in the fund
    d.   The cost of distributing the fund divided by the offering price

87. A preferred stock issue containing a provision for an extra dividend above its regular rate is referred to as
    a.   Callable preferred
    b.   Participating preferred
    c.   Cumulative preferred
    d.   Prior preferred

88. A mutual fund's annual report will include all of the following information **except:**
    a.   Income and expense items of the mutual fund
    b.   A list of all securities owned by the mutual fund
    c.   Income and expense items of the mutual fund's management company
    d.   A list of the mutual fund's assets and liabilities

89. Federal tax laws require that distributions from an IRA or Keogh (HR-10) plan must begin no later than April 1 of the year following the year in which the person turns
    a.   55½
    b.   59½
    c.   65½
    d.   70½

90. The Securities Investor Protection Corporation (SIPC) provides protection for an investor against
    a.   Losses up to certain limits on money and securities which are left on deposit with a broker/dealer that becomes insolvent
    b.   Losses from declines in their stock portfolio
    c.   Losses from defaults on junk bonds
    d.   Losses from unauthorized transactions by registered representatives

91. All of the following concerning nonqualified deferred compensation plans are true **except:**
    a.   Nonqualified deferred compensation plans can be discriminatory.
    b.   Internal Revenue Service (IRS) approval is not required.
    c.   Participants in the plan are generally creditors of the employer.
    d.   The plan must comply with all of the provisions of ERISA.

92. Which of the following statements concerning a separate account is correct?
    a.   Any investments made in the separate account must be consistent with the variable annuity's investment policy described in the prospectus.
    b.   The separate account can invest only in common stocks.
    c.   The separate account can invest only in bonds.
    d.   The separate account contains the reserves necessary to pay its fixed annuity obligations.

93. An investment advisory contract of an investment company must, under the Investment Company Act of 1940, be approved by:
    a.   The underwriting manager
    b.   The shareholders and a majority of the board of directors
    c.   The NASD
    d.   The SEC

94. A customer purchases investment company shares and receives a form detailing the transaction is best described as a
    a.   Broker's commission
    b.   Broker's order ticket
    c.   Customer's confirmation
    d.   Customer's order ticket

95. All of the following are characteristics of a money market mutual fund **except:**
    a.   It may illustrate the effective annualized yield.
    b.   It invests mainly in financial instruments with maturities in twelve months or less.
    c.   It guarantees an investor against loss of capital in every case.
    d.   It uses a standardized method to calculate its yields.

96. A closed-end fund's ask price is based on
   a. Market demand
   b. The amount of the underwriter's concession
   c. Net asset value plus a sales charge
   d. The number of stock orders executed by the investment company with a broker/dealer

97. An investor considering the purchase of open-end investment company shares is given a prospectus. The prospectus
   a. Is guaranteed as to its accuracy by the SEC and the NASD
   b. Contains all of the information that is also contained in the registration statement that is filed with the SEC
   c. Must be sent to the NASD, and it will be reviewed to determine compliance with its advertising rules
   d. Contains certain information from the complete registration statement, which would be of interest to the ordinary investor buying shares

98. Which of the following determines the value of the conversion privilege relating to convertible bonds?
   a. The market value of the bonds
   b. The face amount of the bond
   c. The market value of the shares of the underlying common stock
   d. The par value of the shares of the underlying common stock

99. A customer invests in a municipal bond unit investment trust that invests only in high-quality bonds with long-term maturities. If there is a substantial change in general interest rates, the portfolio will exhibit which of the following characteristics?
   a. Investment income will fluctuate substantially and the market value will remain the same.
   b. The market value will fluctuate substantially and investment income will remain relatively stable.
   c. Both investment income and market value will fluctuate substantially.
   d. Neither investment income nor market value will fluctuate.

100. A twelve-year-old minor is the owner of an UGMA account that generates $12,000 of investment income. The custodian of the account is the minor's uncle, who is in the 33% tax bracket. The minor's mother is a widow and is in the 28% tax bracket. Under federal tax laws, at what tax bracket will the earnings be taxed?
   a. 28% at the mother's bracket
   b. 33% at the uncle's bracket
   c. At the 50% bracket for unearned income
   d. At the 30.5% bracket, which is the average of the mother and uncle's tax brackets

ANSWERS TO SERIES 6 FINAL EXAMINATION

1. a	21. a	41. a	61. d	81. a
2. c	22. b	42. d	62. d	82. c
3. d	23. b	43. a	63. b	83. d
4. b	24. a	44. d	64. c	84. c
5. d	25. b	45. c	65. c	85. d
6. c	26. b	46. c	66. d	86. b
7. b	27. a	47. d	67. d	87. b
8. d	28. d	48. c	68. c	88. c
9. b	29. c	49. d	69. c	89. d
10. b	30. d	50. b	70. d	90. a
11. b	31. b	51. d	71. d	91. d
12. d	32. a	52. b	72. c	92. a
13. d	33. b	53. d	73. d	93. b
14. c	34. a	54. b	74. b	94. c
15. d	35. a	55. a	75. b	95. c
16. a	36. a	56. c	76. c	96. a
17. d	37. c	57. b	77. c	97. d
18. b	38. d	58. d	78. c	98. b
19. d	39. c	59. c	79. c	99. b
20. d	40. c	60. a	80. c	100. a

ADDITIONAL PRACTICE QUESTIONS 1

1. Registration of open-end investment company shares with the SEC implies that
   a. The SEC approves the issue in every way.
   b. The SEC guarantees the accuracy of the disclosure in the registration statement.
   c. The prospectus contains the significant facts about the issue.
   d. The shares have investment merit and should be purchased by all investors.

2. The term registered investment company refers to an investment company that
   a. Qualifies under the Internal Revenue Code for special tax treatment
   b. Is supervised by the SEC
   c. Is under control of the federal courts due to financial irregularities
   d. Has less than $500,000 in net assets

3. The amount that the market value of an open-end investment company fund portfolio exceeds its cost is known as
   a. Appreciation
   b. Asset value
   c. Depreciation
   d. Capital loss

4. An investment company that is not a unit investment trust or a face-amount certificate company, would be a
   a. Mutual fund
   b. Management company
   c. Open-end company
   d. Closed-end company

5. Commercial paper normally has a maximum maturity of
   a. 7 days
   b. 30 days
   c. 60 days
   d. 270 days

6. A customer owns a corporate bond with a 9% interest rate and a $1,000 par value. The bond is quoted at 102. What is the current yield on the bond?
   a. 8.8%
   b. 9.0%
   c. 10.2%
   d. 11.3 %

7. All of the following are types of non-tax-qualified variable annuities **except:**
   a. Group annuity
   b. Single-premium deferred
   c. Single-premium immediate
   d. Periodic payment deferred

8. Under federal securities laws, prospectus delivery requirements can be waived
   a. By agreement with the investor
   b. At the option of the broker/dealer
   c. Only for established customers
   d. Under no circumstances

9. Under NASD rules, a DK notice for an unreconciled trade is given to the
   a. NYSE
   b. NASD
   c. Contra-broker
   d. Customer

10. All of the following are assets to an individual investor **except:**
    a. Common stock
    b. Mutual fund
    c. Cash value of life insurance
    d. Available line of credit

11. General obligation municipal bonds are
    a.   Unsecured
    b.   Backed by the full faith and credit of the issuer
    c.   Backed by a particular municipal enterprise
    d.   Backed by a private corporation

12. A registered representative, under NASD rules, may purchase shares of a hot issue his firm is distributing
    a.   Without any restrictions of any kind
    b.   Only if it is a small amount
    c.   Only if it is in accordance with his normal investment practice
    d.   Under no circumstances

13. A customer redeems 500 shares of the ABC Fund, which has a net asset value of $16 and an ask price of $17.39. The redemption fee for the fund is 1%. What dollar amount will the investor receive?
    a. $7,920
    b. $8,000
    c. $8,608
    d. $8,695

14. A customer invests $10,000 in a mutual fund and invests all dividend distributions. He sells the shares five years later for $17,000. What is the taxable gain?
    a. $ 7,000
    b. $10,000
    c. $17,000
    d.   The difference between the sales proceeds of $17,000 and the $10,000 invested plus the amount of dividends reinvested

15. A customer at 55 years of age began investing in a variable annuity. He is now 65 years old and makes a lump-sum distribution. The customer invested $10,000, and the value of the variable annuity is $19,000. What amount is taxable to the customer?
    a. $ 9,000
    b. $10,000
    c. $19,000
    d. $29,000

16. A main purpose of a nonqualified deferred compensation plan is to
    a.   Provide immediate tax deductions for the employer.
    b.   Provide a nondiscriminatory retirement arrangement for all employees.
    c.   Defer income to a later period.
    d.   Provide for highly compensated employees by setting up an IRS-approved and ERISA-covered plan.

17. The conversion privilege offered by some groups of open-end investment companies permits investors to
    a.   Exchange individually owned general securities for shares of the investment company.
    b.   Delay payments of taxes on appreciated securities.
    c.   Exchange shares of one open-end investment company for those of another on a net asset value basis.
    d.   Purchase additional fund shares from dividends paid by the fund.

18. A voluntary plan for the purchase of shares of an open-end investment company usually
    a.   Requires as a condition of participation, a minimum investment of $5,000 each year
    b.   Involves a sales charge on each purchase as made
    c.   Applies a 50% sales charge to each purchase of shares after the first such purchase
    d.   Involves a transaction fee that is fixed irrespective of the dollar amount of the purchase

19. Ms. Whitman wants to invest $18,000 in four different growth funds. Each fund has its portfolio managed by a different investment management firm. Which of the following is most important for her to understand thoroughly?
    a.   Automatic reinvestment plans available from these bonds
    b.   Conversion privilege
    c.   Sales charge breakpoints
    d.   Withdrawal program offered

20. Which of the following is nonnegotiable?
  a. Treasury bills
  b. Commercial paper
  c. Series EE bonds
  d. Bankers' acceptances

21. An RR of an NASD member firm must notify the employing firm under which of the following circumstances?
  I. He is convicted of securities fraud.
  II. He files for bankruptcy.
  III. He is accused of wrongfully taking property.
  IV. He is convicted of illegal gambling.

  a. I and II
  b. III and IV
  c. I, II, and IV
  d. All of the above

22. Under NASD rules, an RR must notify his employer in writing prior to all of the following actions **except:**
  a. He takes a full-time job selling real estate.
  b. He takes a part-time job selling real estate.
  c. He invests in a real estate limited partnership.
  d. He is hired as a managing general partner in a real estate limited partnership.

23. A corporate bond is quoted at 103¾. This represents a dollar price of
  a. $ 103.38
  b. $ 1,030.80
  c. $ 1,037.50
  d. $10,337.50

24. A college graduate wants to purchase stock. He is 24 years old and has $1,500 in a savings account and $3,500 in student loans. Which of the following is probably the best advice to give the customer?
  a. Defer stock purchases until he builds a stronger capital base.
  b. Since he is young, he can afford to take large risks in stocks.
  c. Invest in a load fund for income.
  d. Borrow money to invest in stocks.

25. Call features relating to a bond issue are most advantageous to the
  a. Issuer
  b. Trustee
  c. Transfer agent
  d. Bondholder

ANSWERS TO ADDITIONAL PRACTICE QUESTIONS 1

1. c	6. a	11. b	16. c	21. d
2. a	7. a	12. d	17. c	22. c
3. a	8. d	13. a	18. b	23. c
4. b	9. c	14. d	19. c	24. a
5. d	10. d	15. a	20. c	25. a

ADDITIONAL PRACTICE QUESTIONS 2

1. All of the following are correct concerning the fund custodian and would not violate SEC Regulations, **except:**
   a. The Surety Bank holds the cash and securities of the Nukely Fund, in which capacity it acts as custodian.
   b. The fund custodian is responsible for the safekeeping of the fund's cash and securities.
   c. The fund custodian can also be the transfer agent, registrar or dividend disbursing agent.
   d. The fund custodian protects the investors against loss on the fund shares.

2. An elderly person with $80,000 to invest is seeking preservation of capital and current income. Which of the following is the best choice for this person?
   a. Long-term bond fund
   b. Money market fund
   c. Municipal bond fund
   d. Speculative growth fund

3. ABC Fund has an $18 bid price and a $16 ask price. The ABC Fund is a(n)
   a. Open-end fund
   b. Closed-end fund
   c. Unit investment trust
   d. Face-amount certificate company

4. XYZ Corporation has common stock outstanding selling at $74 per share and a $1,000 face value bond quoted at 103. Which of the following statements is true?
   a. The bond is selling at a discount.
   b. The bond is selling at a premium.
   c. The bond is selling at par value.
   d. The bond is selling at parity to the common stock.

5. It is considered materially misleading to do which of the following concerning an open-end investment company?
   a. Assure an investor of a continuous, dependable, or liberal rate of return.
   b. Represent that an investor will receive a specified rate of return.
   c. Imply that an investor will receive a stable return.
   d. All of the above

6. Open-end investment companies normally levy sales charges
   a. When mutual fund shares are sold to the customer and when they are redeemed.
   b. When mutual fund shares are sold to the customer, but not at the time of redemption.
   c. Only if the customer redeems his shares within six months.
   d. When mutual fund shares are redeemed from the customer, but not when they are sold to him.

7. Under NASD rules, if an RR is brought before the District Business Conduct Committee, he may do all of the following **except:**
   a. Bring his attorney to the hearing.
   b. Present evidence on his behalf.
   c. Hear charges levied against him.
   d. Go directly to federal court.

8. Which of the following best describes an underwriting of securities, where the underwriter buys the entire issue and takes all of the risk?
   a. Best efforts
   b. All or none
   c. Firm commitment
   d. Standby

9. If a customer is charged a commission on a securities transaction, it would be a(n)
   a. Principal transaction
   b. Risk less principal transaction
   c. Transaction with a markup or markdown
   d. Agency transaction

10. All of the following are prohibited under securities industry regulations **except:**
    a. Paying commissions to a nonregistered accountant
    b. Guaranteeing a customer against a loss on a securities transaction
    c. Converting customer funds for the benefit of a registered representative
    d. Splitting commissions with another registered representative in your firm

11. The Securities Investor Protection Corporation (SIPC) provides protection for public customers in which of the following instances?
    a. When securities purchased by customers have declined in value
    b. When a matter is submitted for arbitration
    c. When a broker/dealer becomes insolvent
    d. When a customer loses a stock certificate from his safety-deposit box

12. As an RR you receive inside information from the president of Macrosoft, Inc. that the company will be taken over by Orange Computer, Inc. You, as an RR, can engage in which of the following transactions?

    I.   Buy Macrosoft.
    II. Sell Macrosoft.
    III. Buy Orange Computer.
    IV. Sell Orange Computer.

    a. I and II
    b. III and IV
    c. I and III
    d. None of the above

13. Which of the following is an unsecured debt instrument?
    a. First mortgage bond
    b. Equipment trust obligation
    c. Debenture
    d. Collateral trust security

14. Distributions from a company's 403(b) tax-deferred annuity is
    a. Tax-exempt
    b. 100% taxed as ordinary income
    c. Taxed as a long-term capital gain
    d. Tax deferred until the investor reaches age seventy-five

15. A capital gain realized by a municipal bond fund and distributed to shareholders is
    a. Tax-exempt to the shareholders
    b. Taxable to the shareholders
    c. Taxable at the state level, but not at the federal level
    d. Considered a return of capital and is partly taxable

16. In order to obtain an extension of time for payment on a securities transaction for a customer
    a. The broker/dealer must file for it with a regulatory organization.
    b. The customer files for it with the broker/dealer who can grant it directly.
    c. The customer files for it directly with the regulatory organization.
    d. The customer files for it with the broker/dealer and the broker/dealer files for it with the SEC.

17. Which of the following can make a fully deductible contribution to the IRA?
    a. All individuals
    b. An individual with income below a certain level
    c. An individual who is a participant in a tax-qualified plan, regardless of income
    d. Only an individual with a Keogh plan

18. All of the following statements are true concerning taxation on mutual funds **except:**
    a. An investor should keep copies of statements of dividends and capital gains to calculate cost basis.
    b. The tax treatment may be different between federal and state.
    c. If an investor reinvests dividends and capital gains distributions in additional fund shares, he escapes taxes on the reinvested amount.
    d. Capital gains distributions are taxed as long-term capital gains, while income distributions are taxed as ordinary income.

19. An investor who would purchase class B shares in a mutual fund would probably be subject to which of the following?
    a. An initial sales charge on the purchase
    b. Contingent deferred sales charge
    c. An initial sales charge and a deferred sales charge
    d. No sales charge of any kind

20. According to the Investment Company Act of 1940, an investor redeeming his shares must be paid by the fund within
    a. 2 calendar days
    b. 7 calendar days
    c. 10 calendar days
    d. 30 calendar days

21. All of the following statements are true concerning a unit investment trust **except:**
    a. They have a fixed portfolio.
    b. They redeem shares.
    c. They continuously sell new shares.
    d. They are organized under a trust indenture.

22. A customer is doing market timing to decide when to switch between money market funds and growth funds. The customer's investment timing model forecasts at the present time a peak in interest rates and the beginning of an expansion. The customer should
    a. Buy money market funds.
    b. Buy growth funds.
    c. Sell growth funds.
    d. Sell growth funds and buy money market funds.

23. Which of the following statements is true concerning a variable life insurance contract?
    a. The cash value is guaranteed.
    b. The contract has a fixed minimum death benefit.
    c. They can be sold without a prospectus since they are not considered securities or investment companies.
    d. They have no charges of any kind for expenses since the issuing company absorbs all costs relating to sales and administration.

24. A senior citizen has $200,000 to invest for retirement. She also wants her two children to inherit as much of her money as possible. Which of the following is most important when considering investment options for this customer?
    a. Speculative growth.
    b. Preservation of capital
    c. Maximum current income only
    d. Growth and income

25. In a variable contract, charges for premium billing and collecting, recordkeeping, and communications with owners are described as
    a. Sales load expenses
    b. Deferred sales load expenses
    c. Management fee (expense)
    d. Administrative fee (expense)

ANSWERS TO ADDITIONAL PRACTICE QUESTIONS 2

1. d	6. b	11. c	16. a	21. c
2. b	7. d	12. d	17. b	22. b
3. b	8. c	13. c	18. c	23. b
4. b	9. d	14. b	19. b	24. b
5. d	10. d	15. b	20. b	25. d

ADDITIONAL PRACTICE QUESTIONS 3

1. A single person, 45 years old, has $55,000 to invest for retirement. He is concerned about running out of money in later years. Which of the following is probably the best investment for this person?
    a. Speculative growth fund
    b. Money market fund
    c. Common stocks in computer companies
    d. Variable annuity

2. XYZ Fund has a $16 ask price and a 6% sales charge (load). The bid price is
    a. $15.04
    b. $15.96
    c. $16.06
    d. Cannot be determined with the information given.

3. When selling mutual fund shares, there is no objection to which of the following statements?
    a. "We are proud to announce that the XYZ Bank safeguards the cash you invest."
    b. "The XYZ Bank is custodian of the fund's cash and securities."
    c. "All cash and securities are guaranteed by XYZ Bank."
    d. "You can have confidence in the fund because the XYZ Bank is our custodian."

4. An investor is seeking investment information to compare the performance of various funds. Which of the following normally would be the best source of information for the investor?
    a. The prospectus for one of the funds
    b. A basic textbook on investments
    c. A listing of the funds' expenses and sales charges
    d. Industry comparative sources

5. An investor with an investment objective of conservative growth should invest in a(n)
    a. Aggressive growth fund
    b. Growth fund
    c. Income fund
    d. Money market fund

6. An investor, Mr. Weld, is considering two mutual funds with the same objective as potential investments. Which of the following nonperformance items should the investor consider for the two funds?

    I. Availability of a letter of intent
    II. Availability of withdrawal plans
    III. Availability of an exchange privilege
    IV. The price (NAV or ask price) at which dividends may be reinvested in additional shares

    a. I and II
    b. III and IV
    c. I, II, and IV
    d. All of the above

7. Among the provisions of the Investment Company Act of 1940 designed to protect the interest of investors is the provision that
    a. Any change in fundamental investment policy must be approved by stockholders.
    b. Advertising and sales literature must be approved in advance of its use by the NASD.
    c. Selection of company investments must be approved by the SEC.
    d. Net asset value of a fund may not decline below 90% of the current market price of the fund portfolio.

8. Typically, bonds are denominated in which of the following amounts?
    a. $ 10
    b. $ 100
    c. $ 1,000
    d. $10,000

9. John Wilson and his brother Tom Wilson have a tenants-in-common account. Each owns 50% of the account. John Wilson dies. Which of the following statements is true?
   a. John Wilson's interest in the account passes to Tom Wilson.
   b. John Wilson's interest in the account passes to his estate.
   c. John Wilson's interest in the account is frozen indefinitely.
   d. The account is liquidated immediately and the proceeds are paid to Tom Wilson.

10. John Smith is forty-two years old and inherits an IRA from his brother, Eddie Smith. The IRA has a value of $52,000. John Smith withdraws the entire amount in a lump sum. Which of the following is true concerning tax consequence?
    a. Eddie Smith's estate pays the tax on the withdrawal.
    b. John Smith pays the tax on the withdrawal.
    c. Eddie Smith's estate pays the penalty tax on the withdrawal.
    d. The withdrawal is tax-free.

11. Joe Margin, your broker, compares a withdrawal plan from a mutual fund to a savings account. He states that if you withdraw $500 a month from the withdrawal plan, which has a current market value of $50,000, your return will be 12%. This is much better than the present savings account rate of 3%. Which of the following statements is true concerning this comparison?
    a. This is a proper comparison in every way.
    b. This comparison is completely proper but the broker should advise you to leave the money in the account and continue to earn 12%.
    c. This is an unfair comparison and may be fraudulent.
    d. Federal securities laws do not cover comparisons such as this, in any way.

12. A customer has $80,000 to invest and he needs the money in four months to pay college expenses for his daughter. Which of the following is the best investment for the customer?
    a. A diversified portfolio of blue-chip stocks
    b. 90-day Treasury bills
    c. A bond fund
    d. A speculative growth fund

13. A customer purchases 100 shares of ABC at $90 per share on Monday, May 6. On settlement date the customer states he cannot pay for the purchase. The broker/dealer sells out the customer. Which of the following statements is true under Regulation T?
    a. The account must be frozen for 30 days.
    b. The account must be frozen for 45 days.
    c. The account must be frozen for 90 days.
    d. The account can continue as before—it never has to be frozen.

14. Under securities industry regulations, an RR, when comparing mutual funds to bank products for a prospective investor, must disclose all of the following **except:**
    a. That mutual funds involve investment risks and possible loss of principal.
    b. That mutual funds are not guaranteed by the bank.
    c. That mutual funds are not FDIC insured.
    d. That bank products may be FDIC insured.

15. All of the following statements are true concerning a qualified plan under IRS rules **except:**
    a. The plan must be in writing.
    b. Every participant in the plan must receive equal benefits.
    c. The plan must meet minimum vesting and funding requirements.
    d. The plan must be nondiscriminatory.

16. Assume a person inherits securities as a beneficiary. How are the shares valued for tax purposes?
    a. The market value of the shares when they are delivered
    b. At the date of death of the decedent
    c. The original purchase price paid by the decedent
    d. At the average market price of the shares during the year of the death of the decedent

17. Ms. Wynn is in the 28% tax bracket. She purchases a municipal bond with a current yield of 3.7%. Her after-tax yield on the municipal bond is
    a. 2.8%
    b. 3.7%
    c. 5.1%
    d. 5.6%

18. Open-end investment company shares differ from closed-end shares because the shares bought by individual investors are normally
    a. Newly issued shares of the fund
    b. Shares listed on a national securities exchange
    c. Shares sold by a broker/dealer from its inventory account
    d. Shares purchased from another individual investor

19. All of the following are money market securities **except:**
    a. Commercial paper
    b. Treasury bills
    c. Common stocks
    d. Bankers' acceptances

20. A young person with $30,000 to invest for capital growth would find all of the following suitable **except:**
    a. Growth fund
    b. Money market fund
    c. Aggressive growth fund
    d. International equity fund

ANSWERS TO ADDITIONAL PRACTICE QUESTIONS 3

1. d	6. d	11. c	16. b
2. a	7. a	12. b	17. c
3. b	8. c	13. c	18. a
4. d	9. b	14. d	19. c
5. b	10. b	15. b	20. b

SERIES 63 TEST PREPARATION

INTRODUCTION

Most states have enacted some form of legislation designed to protect investors by preventing the sale of fraudulent securities. Such legislation intends to exercise control over those selling securities and over the securities themselves. The term **blue-sky laws** is often used when referring to such state laws. The term itself originated in a Kansas law of 1911 wherein it was apparent that farmers had been exploited by promoters who sold the farmers securities of companies having as assets only the "blue sky."

The **Uniform Securities Act,** also referred to as the **Uniform Practice Code** or the "Act," has been adopted in most states. Prior to its adoption in the late 1950s there were 47 individual state laws—each different. These presented a horrendous problem to those persons or companies wishing to sell, issue, or underwrite securities nationally.

The Uniform Securities Agent State Law Examination is prepared by the North American Securities Administrators Association (NASAA) in cooperation with securities industry representatives. The examination consists of fifty multiple-choice questions. The passing score is 70% (35 correct answers). One hour is allotted for the examination. The relative importance given in the examination to particular sections of the Uniform Securities Act is as follows:

20%	Definitions of Terms
15%	Licensing or Registration Requirements for Broker/Dealers, Agents, and Investment Advisors
10%	Registration of Securities; Exempt Securities and Exempt Transactions
45%	Fraudulent and Other Prohibited Practices
10%	Regulatory Oversight, Criminal Penalties, Civil Liabilities, Scope of the Act, and General Provisions

The purpose of the Uniform Securities Act is to protect the public against fraudulent transactions within a state. In order for an agent to solicit business within a state, both the agent and the broker/dealer must be registered in that state or exempt from registration.

An **issuer** who sells securities to the public must make certain disclosures in the form of registration. The **purchaser** of a security can read the available information on the issue, such as a registration statement and prospectus, and decide whether to purchase the security.

The purpose of the Uniform Securities Act is to regulate securities transactions within a particular state. The individual states regulate the sales of securities within the state. They also regulate the activities of broker/ dealers and their agents and investment advisors and investment advisor representatives. The purpose of the Uniform Securities Act and state regulation is to prevent fraudulent or unethical business activities within the state. For an issuer to sell securities to the public, the issuer's securities must either be registered in the state or qualify for an exemption from registration (exempt security). An issuer of securities is the corporation selling the securities such as Coca-Cola, Johnson & Johnson, or XYZ Manufacturing Company. If the securities must be registered in the state, certain information must be filed with the administrator. The administrator is the state official who enforces the provisions of the Uniform Securities Act on behalf of the state. It is a violation of the Uniform Securities Act to "offer to sell" or "sell" unregistered nonexempt securities in a particular state.

The same rules apply to broker/dealers and their agents. The broker/dealer is the business entity such as Merrill Lynch or Paine Webber. The broker/dealer employs agents who are also referred to as registered representatives or brokers. Both the broker/dealer and the agents must be registered to solicit business within a state, unless they qualify for an exemption from registration. The burden of proving any exemption is on the issuer, broker/dealer, agent, or any other person claiming an exemption under the Act.

Investment advisors and investment advisor representatives must be registered to do business within the state, unless they qualify for an exemption from registration. The investment advisor is a business entity, and an investment advisor representative is an individual. The broker/dealers and investment advisors are responsible for the activities of their agents and investment advisor representatives. The term *person* under the Uniform Securities Act refers to a **legal person** as well as a natural or human person. Therefore, under the Uniform Securities Act the term *person* includes a corporation, partnership, sole proprietorship, business trust, government, political subdivision of a government such as a city or town, joint-stock company, an unincorporated association, a trust wherein the beneficial interests are evidenced by a security, and a natural person.

When a broker/dealer, investment advisor, agent, or investment advisor representative is initially registered in a state, two forms must be completed. One form is a registration application, and the second form is a consent to service of process. The **consent to service of process** allows the administrator to receive service of process (notice of a lawsuit or legal proceeding) on behalf of the entity or person being sued in a noncriminal suit. The administrator notifies the entity or individual of the legal proceeding. The consent to service of process allows a public customer to deliver notice of a lawsuit to the administrator against an out-of-state broker/dealer or investment advisor. The out-of-state broker/dealer or investment advisor must defend the lawsuit within the public customer's state. Therefore, assume a public customer in Vermont filed a lawsuit against a Montana broker/dealer doing business in Vermont. The public customer delivers the legal documents to the administrator in Vermont. The Vermont administrator notifies the Montana broker/dealer of the lawsuit. The Montana broker/dealer must defend the lawsuit in Vermont.

The US Congress in 1996 passed a federal law entitled **The National Securities Markets Improvement Act of 1996.** The purpose of the Improvement Act of 1996 was to allocate regulatory responsibility between the Securities and Exchange Commission (SEC) and the state securities administrators.

A security defined as a **federal covered security** (covered security) is exempt from state regulation and will be regulated by the SEC. A federal covered security is defined as

- Securities listed on the New York Stock Exchange (NYSE), American Stock Exchange, or NASDAQ National Market Securities
- Securities issued by investment companies registered under the Investment Company Act of 1940.
- Sales to qualified purchasers which are individuals or businesses with assets at certain levels.
- Certain offerings and transactions exempt from the Securities Act of 1933.

However, the individual states will be able to collect fees and require notice filings. The individual states will still be able to enforce antifraud provisions of the Uniform Securities Act against entities or individuals, even if they are exempt from state regulation.

Investment advisors managing $25 million or more in client assets or who advise a mutual fund must be registered with the SEC. Investment advisors managing less than $25 million in client assets will register only with the state in which the advisor maintains its principal place of business.

The SEC regulates all investment advisors not registered in any state, such as a large foreign investment advisor doing business in the United States. Therefore, investment advisors with assets of $25 million or more are registered only with the SEC. Investment advisors with assets of less than $25 million register only with the state. The Improvement Act also created a national standard for investment advisor registration outside of the home state. An investment advisor would not have to register in a particular state if it

- Has no place of business in the particular state, and
- During the preceding twelve-month period has had fewer than six clients who are residents of the particular state.

The SEC can deny registration to an investment advisor or investment advisor representative or other person who has been convicted of a felony within the previous ten years. The SEC denies registrations to persons who have served jail sentences of one year or more.

Investment companies, as a result of the Improvement Act, are subject to SEC regulation only and are not subject to state regulation. Broker/dealers are exempt from state registration and regulation if the customer has less than thirty days' temporary residency in a state.

IMPORTANT TERMS

The Uniform Securities Act defines the following terms as they relate to the purchase or sale of securities within a state:

- Administrator
- Agent
- Broker/dealer
- Guaranteed
- Investment advisor
- Issuer
- Person
- Sell or offer to sell
- Security

The **administrator** is the top state official who is given the power to enforce the provisions of the Uniform Securities Act for the protection of the public. The administrator and his officers and employees may make public or private investigations within his own state or even outside of his own state. For example, the administrator in the state of Idaho could conduct an investigation in Idaho or in another state.

The administrator can require persons to give oral or written statements or affidavits under oath relating to an investigation. The administrator can subpoena books, records, papers, and correspondence relevant to a matter under inquiry. The administrator can subpoena witnesses who live within or outside of the state. The administrator is allowed, under the Uniform Securities Act, to begin an investigation if he feels a violation will occur, even if it has not yet occurred. The administrator may have jurisdiction for a violation of the Uniform Securities Act, provided the transaction occurred in the state, regardless of where the customer or agent resides.

The administrator is given the power to summarily suspend or revoke the registration of an agent, broker/dealer, or investment advisor. However, the person whose registration is suspended or revoked must receive notification of the order and receives the right to a hearing. The administrator may deny or suspend a registration based on factors such as

- The public interest
- Training
- Knowledge of the securities business
- Experience

The administrator is not allowed to deny or suspend a registration *solely* on the basis of lack of experience, provided the applicant or registrant is qualified by training, knowledge of the securities business, or both. An applicant or registrant is never allowed to state that a security registered with the SEC or a state securities administrator has been approved by virtue of such registration. This type of statement is misleading and prohibited under the Uniform Securities Act (Uniform Securities Code).

The administrator registers a security, but never passes on the accuracy or adequacy of the prospectus, never approves the security, and never states that the registration statement or prospectus is true and complete.

If a person feels that a state securities administrator has ruled incorrectly concerning a matter, the administrator's order may be appealed. The person may file for review of the order with the appropriate court within sixty days after the entry of the order.

The term **agent** under the Act means any individual, other than a broker/dealer, who represents a broker/dealer or issuer in effecting or attempting to effect purchases or sales of securities. This includes an individual, such as the secretary of a salesman, who is authorized to accept orders. The secretary must be registered as an agent under the Act to accept orders and transact business with customers.

The term *agent* does not include an individual who represents an issuer in effecting transactions in a security that is classified as exempt by the Act or in effecting transactions that are themselves considered by the Act to be exempt transactions. A person is also not considered to be an agent if he effects transactions with employees, partners, or directors of the issuer, if no commission or remuneration is given for soliciting any person in the state. If an individual is not considered to be an agent under the Act, registration as an agent is not necessary.

The term *agent* under the Uniform Securities Act normally includes

- A person who sells registered securities to the general public
- A secretary of a salesman who is authorized to accept orders
- A person who sells securities such as common stock in a Canadian mining company or one-year commercial paper
- A person who engages in any transaction for the benefit of the issuer of the securities

The term *agent* under the Uniform Securities Act does *not* include

- A person who represents an issuer in an exempt transaction
- A bank, savings institution, or trust company
- An officer of a broker/dealer who does not effect or attempt to effect purchases or sales of securities
- A clerical person with no authority to accept orders
- A secretary to an officer of a broker/dealer
- A person who represents an issuer in effecting transactions in which no commissions are paid

- An officer selling his own company's stock to his employees and no commission is paid to the officer for soliciting purchasers
- A person who represents an issuer in transactions with an underwriter

If an agent violates the Uniform Securities Act, the agent could be subject to

- A criminal penalty
- A civil penalty
- Suspension or revocation of his license
- Disgorgement of commissions or profits

The term *agent* under the Uniform Securities Act is synonymous with broker or salesman. When a person is acting as an agent, he is purchasing securities for the account of a customer and earning a commission on the transaction.

The term **broker/dealer** means any person engaged in the business of effecting transactions in securities for the account of others or for his own account. The term does not include an agent, issuer, bank, savings institution, or trust company. The term *broker/dealer* also does not include a person who has no place of business in a particular state if

- He effects transactions in the state exclusively with or through

  - The issuers of the securities involved in the transactions
  - Other broker/dealers
  - Banks, savings institutions, trust companies, insurance companies, investment companies, pension or profit-sharing trusts, or other financial institutions or institutional buyers, or

- During any twelve-month period he does not direct more than fifteen offers to sell or buy into this state to persons other than issuers, broker/dealers, or institutional buyers.

Assume Montvale Securities Corporation is a broker/dealer registered in Arkansas with its only office in Little Rock. Montvale Securities has three bank customers in Texas and during a twelve-month period directs four offers to sell to individuals living in Texas. For purposes of the Uniform Securities Act, Montvale Securities is not required to be registered in the state of Texas.

Therefore, under the Uniform Securities Act, the following are considered to be broker/dealers:

- Any person engaged in the business of executing or effecting transactions for the account of others or for his own account.
- A broker/dealer who has a place of business in a particular state even if its only clients are financial institutions.

However, under the Uniform Securities Act, the following are **not** considered broker/dealers

- An agent
- An issuer
- A commercial bank
- A savings bank
- A person with no place of business in the state that does not direct more than fifteen offers to sell or buy into this state in any twelve-consecutive-month period

The word **guaranteed** under the Act means guaranteed as to the payment of principal, interest, or dividends. For example, a parent corporation could guarantee the payment of principal and interest on bonds issued by a subsidiary corporation. This action by the parent corporation would make the bonds more marketable and give the purchaser a higher-quality security.

The term **investment advisor,** under the Uniform Securities Act, includes any person who, for compensation

- Engages in the business of advising others, either directly or through publications or writings, as to the value of securities or as to the advisability of investing in, purchasing, or selling securities, or
- As part of a regular business, issues analyses or reports concerning securities.

Therefore, an investment advisor *advises others on securities for compensation*. The investment advisor must advise others either orally or in writing. The advice must be on securities. Securities are not insurance contracts, residential real estate, collectibles, or commodity futures contracts. The advice must be for compensation, either direct compensation or indirect compensation.

The term *investment advisor* does *not* include

- Bank, savings institution, or trust company
- Lawyer, accountant, engineer, or teacher whose performance of these services is solely incidental to the practice of his profession and he receives no special compensation for the advice
- Broker/dealer whose performance of these services is solely incidental to the conduct of his business, if he receives no special compensation for them
- Publisher of any bona fide newspaper, newsmagazine, or business or financial publication of general, regular, and paid circulation
- Persons whose advice, analyses, or reports relate only to securities exempted by the Act
- Persons who have no place of business in this state if

  - Their only clients in the state are other investment advisors, broker/dealers, banks, savings institutions, trust companies, insurance companies, investment companies, or other financial institutions or institutional buyers, or
  - During any twelve-month period they solicit less than six clients.

- Persons whom the administrator designates as not within the definition of an investment advisor

This definition of investment advisor is modeled after that used in the Investment Advisors Act. It recognizes the fact that broker/dealers commonly give a certain amount of advice to their customers as part of their regular business and that this should not bring them under the Investment Advisors Act. However, if the broker/dealer is specially compensated for such advice he would be subject to the Act. The important distinction concerns why the compensation was paid. Was the compensation paid for the advice itself or for other services to which the advice is merely incidental?

In the description of **publisher,** it should be noted that "paid" circulation is an integral part of the definition. A person who distributes a "hot-tip" sheet to attract clients would not, for example, be considered a publisher. The publishers of *US News & World Report* are not considered to be investment advisors, but anyone selling subscriptions to a market letter providing investment advice is considered an investment advisor under the Uniform Securities Act.

Investment advisors under the Act cannot take or have custody of any securities or funds of any client if

- The administrator, by rule, prohibits the investment advisor from taking custody, or
- The investment advisor fails to notify the administrator that he has custody of the securities or funds.

An investment advisor's compensation under the Act may be based on the average value of funds managed over a period of time. The investment advisor's compensation cannot be based on a percentage of the capital gains or losses generated in a client's account except for private investment companies.

The term *issuer* under the Act means any person who issues or proposes to issue any security. The term nonissuer transaction refers to a transaction not directly or indirectly for the benefit of the issuer. For example, an isolated nonissuer transaction is exempt from the registration requirements of the Uniform Securities Act. Assume John Jones sells 100 shares of XYZ to his brother. This is an isolated nonissuer transaction and not subject to the registration requirements of the Act since it is an exempt transaction.

The term *person* under the Uniform Securities Act refers to an individual, a corporation, a partnership, an association, a joint-stock company, a trust wherein the interests of the beneficiaries are evidenced by a security, an unincorporated organization, a government, or a political subdivision of a government. The term *person* refers to both a natural person and a legal person (business entity).

The terms *sale* or *sell* include every contract of sale of, contract to sell, or disposition of a security or interest in a security for value. In other words, the definition includes any disposition of a security for consideration.

The terms *offer* or *offer to sell* include every attempt or offer to dispose of, or solicitation of an offer to buy, a security or interest in a security for value.

The terms *sale, sell, offer,* and *offer to sell* include

- A security given or delivered with, or as a bonus on account of, any purchase of securities. Such securities are considered to constitute part of the subject of the purchase and to have been offered and sold for value.

- A purported gift of assessable stock is considered to involve an offer and sale under the Act. A gift of nonassessable stock is not considered a sale under the Act.
- The sale or offer of a warrant or right to purchase or subscribe to another security or a security convertible into another security is considered to include an offer of the other security.

The terms *sale*, *sell*, and *offer to sell* do *not* include

- A bona fide pledge or loan
- Stock dividend, if nothing of value is given by stockholders for the dividend
- Mergers, consolidations, reclassification of securities, or sale of corporate assets in consideration of the issuance of securities of another corporation

The term *security* under the Uniform Securities Act means but is not limited to any

- Note, stock, treasury stock, bond, debenture, or evidence of indebtedness
- Certificate of interest or participation in any profit-sharing agreement
- Collateral trust agreement, certificate of deposit for a security or transferable share
- Preorganization certificate or subscription
- Investment contract, voting trust certificate, or interest in farmlands or animals
- Certificate of interest or participation in an oil, gas, or mining lease
- Oil and gas drilling programs, real estate condominiums, and cooperatives
- Commodity option contracts, whiskey warehouse receipts
- Multilevel distributorship arrangements or merchandise marketing schemes
- Listed stock options
- Interest in a real estate investment trust
- Limited partnership interests
- Interest in a unit investment trust

In general, the term *security* applies to any interest or instrument commonly known as a security, or any certificate of interest or participation in, temporary or interim certificate for, receipt for, guarantee of, or warrant or right to subscribe to or purchase, any of the foregoing.

Investment contracts may be considered securities under certain circumstances. The federal courts have determined that the basic test to be used to determine whether an investment is a security concerns the following two questions:

1. Is the investment in a common enterprise?
2. Is the investor led to expect profits because of the managerial efforts of a third party, such as a promoter?

Investments that are considered securities, since they affirmatively answer these two questions, include commodity option contracts, whiskey warehouse receipts, oil and gas drilling programs, real estate condominiums, cattle programs, equipment-leasing programs, multilevel distributorship arrangements, and merchandising marketing schemes.

The term *security* does not include any insurance or endowment policy or annuity contract under which an insurance company promises to pay a fixed sum of money, either in a lump sum or periodically for life, or some other specified period. Therefore, a fixed annuity is not considered a security under the Act but a variable annuity is a security. The term *security* would include items previously mentioned such as listed stock options, limited partnership interests, an interest in a real estate investment trust, a certificate of interest in an oil well lease, an investment contract, and an interest in a unit investment trust. It would not, however, include Keogh plans, individual retirement accounts, or fixed annuity contracts. The term *security* under the Act would not include collectibles such as paintings, rugs, antiques, or precious stones and would not include real estate bought for residential use.

A **private placement** under the Uniform Securities Act is defined as any transaction pursuant to an offer directed to not more than ten persons in the state during any period of twelve consecutive months. The private placement exemption under the Uniform Securities Act is narrower in scope than the federal securities exemption. A private placement is an exempt transaction provided the provisions of the Act are complied with.

LICENSING/REGISTRATION REQUIREMENTS

It is unlawful for any person, broker/dealer, or issuer under the Uniform Securities Act to

- Transact business in a state as an agent unless that person is registered as an agent under the Act or exempt from registration. An agent cannot sell securities based on a pending application in a state. The application must be approved before the agent can transact any business in the state. This is true even if the agent has passed the Series 63 examination. No business can be conducted until the application is effective.
- Transact business in a state as a broker/dealer unless he is registered as a broker/dealer under the Act or exempt from registration.
- Employ an agent unless the agent is registered or exempt from registration

  - An agent's registration is not effective during any period when he is not associated with a registered broker/dealer or an issuer. If a broker/dealer's license is suspended, the licenses of all of the agents are not effective. The agents would have to transfer to a properly registered broker/dealer in order to effect transactions.
  - When an agent begins or terminates a connection with a broker/dealer or issuer, or begins or terminates those activities that make him an agent, the agent and the broker/dealer or issuer must promptly notify the administrator. The requirement to notify the administrator is placed on both the broker/dealer and agent concerning a change in registration.

- Transact business in a state as an investment advisor unless

  - He is registered as an investment advisor or exempt from registration.
  - He is registered as a broker/dealer.
  - He has client assets of $25 million or more (federal registered only).

The Uniform Securities Act permits the same person to exercise both broker/dealer and investment advisory functions without dual registration. It authorizes the administrator to condition a particular applicant's registration as a broker/dealer upon his not acting as an investment advisor, if the administrator finds he is not qualified to act as an investment advisor.

Every registration of a broker/dealer, agent, or investment advisor expires December 31 unless renewed. An initial or renewal registration may be obtained by filing an application with the administrator together with a **consent to service of process** for an initial registration.

In some states, applicants for initial registration are required to publish an announcement of their application in specified newspapers. If there is no denial order or pertinent pending proceeding, a registration of a broker/dealer, agent, or investment advisor becomes effective on the thirtieth day after the application is filed. Of course, the administrator may specify an earlier effective date. He may also defer the effective date until the thirtieth day after the filing of any amendment.

Registration of a broker/dealer or investment advisor automatically constitutes registration of any agent who is a partner, officer, or other person of similar status or similar functions. Every applicant must pay a filing fee specifically established for that applicant's category (broker/dealer, agent, or investment advisor). If the application is denied or withdrawn, the administrator retains the fee.

CAPITAL REQUIREMENTS

The administrator may require a minimum capital for registered broker/dealers and investment advisors. The administrator may also require registered broker/dealers, agents, and investment advisors to post surety bonds and may determine their conditions.

A **surety bond** is a contract issued by an insurance company whereby the insurance company agrees to make good the default or the debt of the insured party. For example, if money is stolen from a broker/dealer by an employee, a surety bond will normally cover the loss up to certain limits.

Surety bonds must provide for suit thereon by any person having a cause for action arising under the civil liabilities sections of the Act and, if the administrator requires, by any person who has a cause of action not arising under the Act. The surety bond shall also provide that no suit may be maintained to enforce any liability on the bond unless the suit is brought within two years after the sale or other act on which the suit is based.

RECORDKEEPING

Registered broker/dealers and investment advisors are required to make and keep such accounts, correspondence, memoranda, papers, books, and other records as the administrator prescribes. Such records must be preserved for three years unless the administrator prescribes otherwise. They must also file any financial reports required under the Act.

If information in any document filed becomes inaccurate or incomplete in any material respect, the registrant must promptly file a correcting amendment unless notification of the correction has been properly made under the rules. All required records are subject at any time to such reasonable periodic, special, or other examinations by representatives of the administrator as the administrator deems necessary or appropriate in the public interest, or for the protection of investors. To avoid unnecessary duplication of examinations, the administrator may cooperate with the securities administrators of other states, the SEC, and any national securities exchange or national securities association registered under the Securities Exchange Act of 1934. The SEC and state administrators can engage in joint examinations, rulemaking, investigations, hearings, and proceedings and can share personnel and have a central records depository.

ADMINISTRATIVE SANCTIONS

The administrator has the authority to deny, suspend, or revoke any registration of a broker/dealer, agent, or investment advisor, if he finds that the order is in the public interest and that the applicant or registrant

- Has filed an application for registration that contains an untrue statement of a material fact.
- Has willfully violated or failed to comply with any provision of the Uniform Securities Act.
- Has been convicted, within the past ten years, of any misdemeanor involving a security, or any aspect of the securities business, or any felony. A person would not be denied a registration if he has been **charged** with a felony but not convicted.
- Is permanently or temporarily enjoined by a court of competent jurisdiction from engaging in the securities business.
- Is the subject of an order of the administrator denying, suspending, or revoking his registration.
- Is the subject of an order entered within the past five years by the securities administrator of another state or the SEC denying or revoking registration or is the subject of an order of the SEC, or a national securities association registered under the Securities Exchange Act of 1934, or is the subject of a US Post Office fraud order.
- Has engaged in dishonest or unethical practices in the securities business.
- Is insolvent, either in that his liabilities exceed his assets or in that he cannot meet his obligations as they mature. Such an order entered against a broker/dealer or investment advisor would require a finding of insolvency.
- Is not qualified on the basis of factors such as training, experience, and knowledge of the securities business.
- Has failed reasonably to supervise agents if he is a broker/dealer or employees if he is an investment advisor.
- Has failed to pay the proper filing fee. The registration will be denied until the fee is paid.

The administrator may not institute a suspension or revocation proceeding on the basis of a fact or transaction of which he is aware when registration becomes effective, unless the proceeding is instituted within the next thirty days.

In applying the rules concerning denial or revocation, other pertinent provisions include

- The administrator may not enter an order
  - Against a broker/dealer on the basis of the lack of qualification of anyone other than the broker/dealer (if he is an individual) or an agent of the broker/dealer.
  - Against an investment advisor on the basis of the lack of qualification of any person other than the investment advisor himself (if he is an individual) or any person representing the investment advisor in actions making him an investment advisor.
  - Solely on the basis of lack of experience if the applicant or registrant is qualified by training, knowledge, or both.
- The administrator shall consider that
  - An agent who will work under the supervision of a registered broker/dealer does not need to have the same qualifications as the broker/dealer.
  - An investment advisor is not necessarily qualified solely on the basis of experience as a broker/dealer or agent. If he finds that an applicant for registration as a broker/dealer is not qualified as an investment advisor, he may condition the registration as a broker/dealer on his not doing business in the state as an investment advisor.

- The administrator may provide for an examination, written, oral, or both, to be taken by persons representing an investment advisor.

The administrator may summarily postpone or suspend registration pending the final determination of any proceedings. In this case, the administrator shall promptly notify the applicant or registrant as well as the employer or prospective employer that such order has been entered, the reasons for the order, and that within fifteen days after the receipt of a written request the matter will be set down for a hearing. If a hearing is not requested or ordered, the order remains in effect until modified or vacated by the administrator. The administrator may cancel the registration or application if he finds that a registrant or applicant is no longer in existence; has ceased to do business; is subject to an adjudication of mental incompetence or control of a committee, conservator, or guardian; or cannot be located after a reasonable search.

Withdrawal of a registration becomes effective thirty days after receipt of an application (or shorter period as determined by the administrator) unless a revocation or suspension proceeding is pending or a proceeding to revoke or suspend or to impose conditions on the withdrawal is instituted within thirty days after the application is filed. The administrator may institute a revocation or suspension proceeding within one year after the withdrawal became effective and enter a revocation or suspension order as of the last date on which the registration was effective.

For the administrator to enter an order related to denial or revocation of an application, there must be

- Appropriate prior notice to the registrant or applicant
- Opportunity for a hearing
- Written findings of fact and conclusions of law

The administrator is given broad powers to enforce the Uniform Securities Act. To summarize, the administrator, under the Act, may

- Subpoena witnesses, books, records, papers, and correspondence relating to a securities investigation.
- Require affidavits to be filed by persons relating to a particular investigation.
- Cancel a registration if a registrant or applicant is no longer in existence or has ceased doing business as a broker/dealer or agent.
- Deny, suspend, or revoke a registration if he finds that an applicant or registrant has violated any provisions of the Act, engaged in dishonest practices, or has been convicted within the past ten years of a felony or misdemeanor relating to securities.
- Subpoena witnesses whether they live within or outside the state.
- Begin an investigation if he feels a violation will occur even if it has not yet occurred.
- Summarily suspend the registration of an agent, broker/dealer, or investment advisor. However, the person suspended will receive notification of the order and must be given the opportunity to have a hearing on the matter. Hearings are public unless both parties request that it be private. The administrator can grant the request that the hearing be private.

REGISTRATION OF SECURITIES

Notification (Filing)

It is unlawful for a person to offer or sell a security in any state unless it is either registered or exempt from registration. There are different methods of registering a security—by notification, coordination, or qualification. Registration by notification is also called **registration by filing**. To qualify for registration by notification or filing, the issuer must meet certain tests concerning earnings and must not have had a default in the payment of principal, interest, or dividends in the past three years. Generally, high-quality securities registering in one state would registered by notification or filing.

If there is no stop order in effect and no proceeding pending under the Act, a registration by notification becomes effective at 3 P.M. Eastern time on the second full business day after filing, or at an earlier time if the administrator so determines.

Coordination

If a registration statement has been filed under the Securities Act of 1933 concerning an offering, a security may be registered by coordination. If the security is to be registered by coordination, copies of the registration statement and prospectus are filed with the administrator.

The registration statement must provide any information specified in the Act including a "consent to service of process." The registration statement automatically becomes effective when the federal registration statement becomes effective, if no stop order is in effect or no proceeding is pending.

Qualification

Any security may be registered by qualification. In this case, the registration statement must contain certain information concerning officers, directors, and the capital structure of the issuer.

If a security is registered by qualification, the registration statement becomes effective when the administrator so orders. The administrator may require that a prospectus be sent to specified persons participating in the distribution. A newly formed company registering securities for the first time in a state would have to register its securities by qualification.

Registration Provisions

A registration statement may be filed under the Uniform Securities Act by

- The issuer
- Any other person on whose behalf the offering is to be made
- A registered broker/dealer

The person filing must pay a filing fee. If the registration statement is withdrawn before the effective date or a preeffective stop order is entered, the administrator shall retain part or all of the fee.

So long as the registration statement is effective, the administrator may require the person filing to file reports, not more than quarterly, to keep the information in the statement reasonably current and to disclose the progress of the offering.

Denial of Registration

The administrator may issue a stop order denying effectiveness to, or suspending or revoking the effectiveness of, any registration statement if it is found

- That the order is in the public interest, or
- Material facts are misleading or provisions of the Uniform Securities Act have been violated.

The administrator may not institute a stop order proceeding against an effective registration statement on the basis of a fact or transaction known to him when the statement became effective, unless the proceeding is instituted within the next thirty days.

The administrator may postpone or suspend the effectiveness of the registration statement pending final determination of any proceeding. In such case, the appropriate persons must be notified that the order has been entered and the reasons for entering the order, and that within fifteen days after receipt of a written request, there will be a hearing. If no hearing is requested or ordered, the administrator, after notice of and opportunity for hearing to each person, may modify, vacate, or extend the order until final determination.

Except in the preceding case related to the final determination of a proceeding, no stop order may be entered by the administrator without

- Appropriate prior notice to the applicant or registrant, the issuer, and the person on whose behalf the securities are to be or have been offered
- An opportunity for a hearing
- Written findings of fact and conclusions of law

The administrator may vacate or modify a stop order, if he finds that the conditions prompting its entry have changed, or that it is otherwise in the public interest to do so.

EXEMPT SECURITIES

Securities exempt from registration and advertising filing requirements of the Uniform Securities Act, but not its antifraud provisions, include

- US government, federal agencies, and securities issued by any state or political subdivision of a state.
- Securities issued by the government of Canada or any other foreign government with which the United States currently maintains diplomatic relations.
- Securities issued by banks, savings institutions, and credit unions organized in the United States.

- Securities issued by insurance companies, not including variable annuities, organized in the United States.
- Securities issued or guaranteed by any common carrier, public utility, or holding company which is subject to jurisdiction of the Interstate Commerce Commission.
- Securities listed on national securities exchanges such as the NYSE, American Stock Exchange, and regional stock exchanges.
- Securities issued by nonprofit organizations. The administrator under the Act has the power to revoke this particular exemption if he feels it is in the public interest to do so.
- Commercial paper maturing within nine months of the date of issuance.
- Any investment contract issued in connection with an employee's stock purchase, savings, pension, profit-sharing, or similar benefit plan so long as required notice is given to the administrator.
- A federal covered security (covered security).

A **federal covered security** is exempt from state regulation as a result of the National Securities Markets Improvement Act of 1996. Federal covered securities are defined as

- Securities listed on the NYSE or American Stock Exchange.
- NASDAQ National Market securities.
- Securities issued by an investment company registered under the Investment Company Act of 1940.
- Securities sold to qualified purchasers. Qualified purchasers are individuals, married couples, family-owned businesses that have at least $5 million in investments, or a business or trust with $25 million in investments.
- Certain securities exempt under the Securities Act of 1933, including securities issued by the US government, federal or state banks; savings and loans and cooperatives; common carriers; employee pension, profit-sharing, and stock purchase plans; municipal securities outside of the home state of the issuer; private placements; secondary market transactions; fixed annuity contracts and other insurance contracts; and commercial paper with a maturity of nine months or less. However, the following securities are *not* defined as federal covered securities:

  - Securities issued by nonprofit organizations
  - Intrastate offerings, which are offerings sold exclusively in one state
  - Municipal securities offered within the issuer's home state

An **exempt security** is exempt from the registration requirements and the advertising requirements of the Uniform Securities Act. However, no security is exempt from the antifraud provisions of the Uniform Securities Act. Therefore, if a person commits fraud with a US government security, common stock, municipal bond, oil and gas drilling partnership, corporate bond, or any other security, he is subject to criminal, civil, or administrative penalties.

EXEMPT TRANSACTIONS

Transactions exempt from registration and advertising filing requirements of the Uniform Securities Act, but not its antifraud provisions, include

- Any isolated nonissuer transaction, such as one individual selling stock to another individual. For example, John Jones sells 100 shares of stock to his sister. This is an isolated nonissuer transaction.
- Any nonissuer distribution of an outstanding security if

  - A recognized securities manual contains specified information.
  - The security has a fixed maturity or a fixed interest or dividend provision and there has been no default during the current or preceding three fiscal years in the payment of principal, interest, or dividends.

- Any nonissuer transaction by or through a registered broker/dealer pursuant to an unsolicited order or offer to buy (the administrator may require that the customer acknowledge in a specified manner that the sale was unsolicited).
- Any transaction between the issuer and an underwriter or among underwriters. For example, XYZ Corporation sells stock to ABC Broker/Dealer relating to an underwriting. This is an exempt transaction.
- Any transaction secured by a real or chattel mortgage or deed of trust.

- Any transaction by a court supervised person such as an executor, administrator, sheriff, marshal, receiver in bankruptcy, guardian, or conservator.
- Any transaction executed by a bond fide pledgee without any purpose of evading the Uniform Securities Act.
- Any offer or sale to a bank, savings institution, trust company, insurance company, investment company, pension or profit-sharing trust, or other financial institution or institutional buyer or to a broker/dealer. To be considered an institutional buyer, no specific level of assets is necessary for the bank, insurance company, or other institutional buyer.
- Any transaction pursuant to an offer directed to not more than ten persons (other than institutional buyers) in the state during any twelve consecutive months if

  - The seller reasonably believes that all the buyers in the state are purchasing for investment other than institutional buyers.
  - No commission or other remuneration is paid or given for soliciting any buyer. This is the definition of the private placement exemption under the Uniform Securities Act.

- Any offer or sale of a preorganization certificate or subscription if

  - No commission or other remuneration is given for soliciting any prospective subscriber.
  - The number of subscribers is ten or less.
  - No payment is made by the subscriber.

- Any transaction pursuant to an offer to existing security holders of the issuer if no commission is paid for soliciting any stockholders in that state and the administration does not disallow the exemption.
- Any offer (but not sale) of a security for which registration statements have been filed under the Act and the Securities Act of 1933, if no stop order or refusal order is in effect and no public proceeding looking toward such an order is pending.
- Any transaction exempted by the National Securities Markets Improvement Act of 1996.

Upon specified conditions, an administrator may deny or revoke certain exemptions. The burden of proving an exemption or exception from any definition is on the person claiming it. As previously mentioned, no security is exempt from antifraud provisions of the Act.

FRAUDULENT AND OTHER PROHIBITED PRACTICES

It is unlawful under the Uniform Securities Act for any person, in connection with a securities transaction, to

- Employ any device or scheme to defraud any person
- Make any untrue statement of a material fact or omit stating a material fact necessary to make statements made not misleading
- Engage in any act, practice, or course of business that operates or would operate as a fraud or deceit on any person

It is unlawful for an investment advisor to enter into or to be a party to an investment advisory contract unless it provides in writing that

- The investment advisor shall not be compensated on the basis of a share of the capital gains or capital appreciation on the client's funds with an exception for private investment companies.
- No assignment of the contract may be made without the consent of the other party to the contract.
- The investment advisor, if a partnership, shall notify the other party to the contract of a majority change in the membership of the partnership.

An investment advisory contract may provide for compensation based on a percentage of the average total value of the funds managed over a definite period of time. If an investment advisor is a partnership, no assignment is considered to be made if a death or withdrawal represents only a minority interest of the partnership or the admission of new members to the partnership is only a minority interest.

An investment advisor is prohibited from having custody of securities or funds of a client if the administrator prohibits custody or the investment advisor fails to notify the administrator of the custody.

Agents are prohibited from engaging in dishonest or unethical business practices. These prohibitions apply to both purchases and sales and may or may not be specifically described in a state's securities law. Some practices are easy to identify while others are not. Some of the actions that have been held to be fraudulent, dishonest, or unethical, are

- Failing to state important facts or making inaccurate statements concerning commissions, markups, or markdowns.
- Telling a customer that, if a security is registered with the SEC or state securities administrator, it means that it has been approved by the regulator.
- Making recommendations on the basis of material inside information about the issuer not available to the public.
- Rendering incorrect market quotations to clients or engaging in false trades or market manipulation.
- Sharing in the profits or losses in a customer's account

  - Without the written consent of the customer
  - Without the written consent of the agent's employing broker/dealer
  - In an amount not related to the agent's personal investment in the account

- Exercising discretion without first obtaining prior written permission from the customer.
- Telling a customer that a security will be listed on an exchange without any knowledge that such listing is to occur.
- Selling securities prior to the effective date of a new securities issue.
- Guaranteeing a profit in a customer's account or guaranteeing that the customer will not lose money on a transaction.
- Promising to perform services for a customer without being qualified or without really intending to perform such services.
- Borrowing money or securities from a customer even with their permission.
- Not telling a customer that commissions and taxes on a transaction may be larger than usual.
- Making transactions not recorded on the employer's records without disclosing such actions to the employer and receiving written permission.
- Not making the employer aware of a customer's written complaint.
- Soliciting orders for securities which are unregistered and nonexempt.
- Participating in market manipulative transactions such as "wash sales," which create a misleading appearance of active trading in a security.
- Misrepresenting the status of a customer's account to the customer.
- Telling a customer that dividends from a mutual fund will always exceed interest earned on a savings account.
- Accepting orders for a customer from a third party without first obtaining written authorization.
- Commingling the agent's funds with customer funds. The term **commingling** refers to a situation in which an agent deposits customer money into his own personal checking account.
- Making unsuitable recommendations or transactions such as

  - Churning customer accounts, recommending "excessive" transactions.
  - Not making reasonable inquiry of customers as to their financial situation, needs, and objectives.
  - Not explaining important facts and risks to customers.
  - Recommending transactions without reasonable grounds.

Under the Uniform State Securities Act, an agent is prohibited from engaging in the following activities since they are fraudulent, dishonest, or unethical business practices:

- Guaranteeing a customer against loss, misrepresenting a return on a security, employing any device to defraud or performing any act that would operate as a fraud on any person.
- Paying commissions to an investment advisor without disclosing this to the customer. Any potential conflict of interest must be disclosed to the client.
- Backdating records such as confirmations or order tickets, making untrue statements of a material fact, or failing to state a material fact. Records cannot be backdated even one day.
- Recommending tax shelters to persons in low tax brackets.
- Engaging in securities transactions based on inside information or material nonpublic information. It is a violation under the Uniform Securities Act to trade any security based on inside information, including US government securities, municipal bonds, limited partnerships, and common stock.

- Stating that the administrator has approved an offering, found a registration to be true and complete, or passed on the accuracy or adequacy of a prospectus.
- Attempting to obtain a written agreement from a customer that he will not sue the agent or broker/dealer even though the sale of securities is in violation of state law. Any agreement of this type is null and void under the Act.
- Deliberately failing to follow a customer's instructions.
- Selling speculative common stock to clients with income objectives.

SUITABILITY

For an investment to be suitable for a customer, the investment must meet the customer's investment objectives, financial situation, and needs. For an older person seeking current income with safety of principal, an agent might recommend US government securities or high-quality municipal bonds. The agent should *not* recommend to the older person investments such as speculative growth stocks, tax shelter investments, precious metals, or options.

Assume an agent recommends that a customer purchase $12,000 worth of a mutual fund. The recommendation exceeds the customer's available cash position. The customer is forced to sell the security prior to settlement date since he does not have the available funds to pay for the purchase. In this example, the agent has made an unsuitable recommendation. Assume an agent has discretionary authority over a customer's account. The customer's investment objective is current income only. The agent invests $14,000 in a speculative security that pays no interest. The agent has engaged in an unsuitable transaction.

An agent, when recommending a securities transaction, must inquire as to whether the customer can pay for the purchase by settlement date. To recommend purchases beyond a customer's ability to pay for them is a clear violation of the Uniform Securities Act.

In certain instances, an agent may make a suitable recommendation to a customer. However, the customer requests that an order for another security be executed. The agent feels that the security the customer wants to purchase is not suitable. The agent, in this case, can execute the order, but it would be wise to obtain a written statement from the customer. The written statement should make clear that the transaction was unsolicited and not recommended by the agent.

Assume an agent recommends a suitable investment to a customer and the customer decides to purchase the security. Three days after the purchase, his spouse calls and wants to cancel the trade. She states that her husband has lost his job and cannot pay for the trade. Since it is an individual account, the agent cannot sell the security without instructions from the husband. The agent is not allowed to give the husband a personal check to pay for the purchase. Also, the agent cannot arrange a loan for the husband to pay for the trade.

Assume an agent calls a customer and offers the customer a security for the customer's portfolio. The customer offers resistance to the purchase of the security. The agent cannot, in order to convince the customer to purchase the security

- Guarantee the customer against loss in the transaction.
- Offer to repurchase the security at a fixed price in the future.
- Offer to repay the amount of the commission to the customer if the transaction is not profitable.

All of those actions would be clear violations of the Uniform Securities Act. The agent could explain the features of the security in an attempt to demonstrate suitability to the customer. However, the final decision on whether or not to purchase the security belongs to the customer.

REGULATORY OVERSIGHT

The Uniform Securities Act is administered by a specified administrative agency. The administrator and his officers and employees are prohibited from using for their own benefit any information which has not been made public.

The administrator may make public or private investigations within or outside the state if he believes it necessary to determine whether the Act has been violated or to aid in enforcing the Act. If he so desires, he may require a person to file a statement in writing, under oath, as to the facts and circumstances concerning a matter under investigation and may publish information concerning any violation of the Act or rules or orders under the Act.

If a person refuses to obey a subpoena, the appropriate court, on application of the administrator, may order the person to appear before the administrator and produce requested evidence or else be held in contempt of court. If an individual has claimed his privilege against self-incrimination, he may not be prosecuted or subject to any penalty or forfeiture. He, of course, is not exempt from prosecution and punishment for perjury or contempt committed in testifying.

If it appears that a person has engaged or is about to engage in an act or practice that violates the Act or any rule or order under the Act, the administrator may bring action in the appropriate court to enjoin the act or practice and enforce compliance with the Act. A permanent or temporary injunction, restraining order, or writ of mandamus may be granted and a receiver or conservator appointed for the defendant or the defendant's assets. The administrator may not be required by the court to post a surety bond.

CRIMINAL PENALTIES

A person who willfully violates the Uniform Securities Act, on conviction, may be fined not more than $5,000, or imprisoned not more than three years, or both. No person may be imprisoned for a violation if he proves he had no knowledge of the rule or order. No indictment may be returned under this Act more than five years after the alleged violation. The administrator may refer evidence concerning willful violation to the attorney general or proper district attorney, who may institute appropriate criminal proceedings.

CIVIL LIABILITIES

Any person is subject to civil liabilities if he or she offers or sells a security

- In violation of specified sections of the Act or rule or order under specified sections
- By means of any untrue statement of a material fact or omission to state such a fact necessary to make statements made not misleading

A person subject to civil liabilities is liable to the person buying the security from him. The buyer may sue either at law or in equity to recover the amount paid, together with interest at 6% per year, costs, and reasonable attorney's fees, less the amount of any income received on the security. If he no longer owns the security, he may sue for damages. Damages are the amount that would be recoverable on a sale less the value of the security when the buyer disposed of it, and interest at 6% per year (rescission of the contract).

Those persons subject to civil liabilities include not only the individual selling the security, but also

- Every person who directly or indirectly controls a seller who is liable.
- Every partner, officer, or director of such seller or person performing similar functions.
- Every employee of such seller who materially aids in the sale.
- Every broker/dealer or agent who materially aids in the sale.

These individuals are liable jointly and severally unless they can prove that they did not know and, by exercising reasonable care, could not have known of the existence of the facts on which the liability is alleged to exist.

A person may not sue under the civil liability section of the Uniform Securities Act more than two years after the contract of sale, and a person may not sue

- If the buyer received a written offer, before the suit when he owned the security, to refund the consideration plus interest at 6% less any income received on the security, and he did not accept the offer within thirty days of its receipt
- If the buyer received such an offer when he did not own the security unless he rejected the offer in writing within thirty days of its receipt

Therefore, if an entity or individual violates the Uniform Securities Act, the entity or individual could be subject to

- Criminal penalties
- Civil penalties
- Administrative penalties

Criminal penalties could result in imprisonment or fines. Civil penalties could result in fines or injunctions. Administrative penalties could be censure, fines, suspension of licenses, or a bar from the securities industry.

JUDICIAL REVIEW OF ADMINISTRATIVE ORDERS

Any person aggrieved by a final order of the administrator may obtain a review of the order in the appropriate court by filing in court, within sixty days after the entry of the order, a written petition requesting that the order be modified or set aside. A copy of this petition is served on the administrator, who then certifies and files in court a copy of the filing and evidence on which the order was entered. After this, the court has exclusive jurisdiction to affirm, modify, enforce, or set aside the order. The court may order additional evidence to be taken, and the administrator may modify his findings and order on the basis of such additional evidence. Unless the court so orders, the commencement of proceedings does not operate as a stay of the administrator's order.

Assume the administrator suspends an agent in Pennsylvania for thirty days for violations of the Uniform Securities Act. The agent immediately appeals the order to the appropriate court (Pennsylvania Court of Appeals). The Pennsylvania Court of Appeals would have jurisdiction to affirm, modify, enforce, or set aside the order. The fact that the agent has filed an appeal does not operate as a stay of the administrator's order. This means the penalty of suspension is in effect unless the Pennsylvania Court of Appeals orders a stay of the administrator's order. In other words, the Court could order that no penalty go into effect until they had an opportunity to review the matter. Assume the Pennsylvania Court of Appeals reviews the matter and modifies it by requiring only a ten-day suspension. The agent would only have to serve a ten-day suspension instead of a thirty-day suspension.

SCOPE OF THE ACT

The Scope of the Act section of the Uniform State Securities Code defines what "in this state" means concerning offers and acceptances of offers to buy or sell securities. The Act applies to an offer to buy or sell and acceptances of offers to buy or sell provided

- They originate from a state.
- They are directed to anyone in the state.
- They are accepted in a state.

The entire transaction will be subject to the Act if any part of an offer is considered "in this state." Assume a customer who lives in Massachusetts receives a soliciting telephone call from an agent in Vermont. The statutes of Massachusetts would apply because the solicitation was received in Massachusetts. However, if the agent in Vermont was operating fraudulently, the state of Vermont could institute action against him on the theory that a state should not be used as a base of operations for defrauding persons in other states. An administrator can investigate the activities of a broker/dealer or investment advisor within or outside of their state. The administrator does not need the permission of another state's administrator to conduct an investigation.

Under the Uniform Securities Act, an advertisement in a regular newspaper or periodical is not an offer in any state other than the state of publication. A person could place an advertisement in the *New York Times* and have it freely circulated in other states without being considered offers in other states. Radio and television programs are considered to be offers only in the state from which they originate. In other words, they are treated in the same manner as a newspaper or periodical.

Under the Uniform Securities Act, an offer to buy or sell is not made in a state when

- The publisher circulates any bona fide newspaper or other publication of general, regular, and paid circulation, either not published in the state or having more than ⅔ of its circulation outside the state.
- The offer is broadcast on a radio or television program originating outside the state but received in the state.

CONSENT TO SERVICE OF PROCESS

Every applicant for registration and every issuer proposing to issue a security in that state must file with the administrator, in prescribed form, an irrevocable consent appointing the Administrator to be his attorney and to receive service of any lawful process in any noncriminal suit, action or proceeding which arises under the Act after the consent has been filed. Service may be made by leaving a copy of the process in the office of the administrator. For such service to be effective, the plaintiff must send notice of the service and a copy of the process by registered mail to the defendant.

If a person (including a nonresident) engages in conduct prohibited or made actionable by the Act and has not filed a consent to service of process and personal jurisdiction over him cannot be otherwise obtained in the state, the conduct is considered equivalent to his appointing the administrator to be his attorney to receive service in any noncriminal suit.

ADDITIONAL CONCEPTS—UNIFORM SECURITIES ACT

The following points are presented to increase a person's understanding of the provisions of the Uniform Securities Act. They are purposely not presented in any particular order.

- Under no circumstances can a prospective customer be told that dividends from a particular stock or mutual fund will always be greater than interest earned on a savings account. The customer cannot be told this even if past history supports such a claim. Remember, past performance in the securities industry is never an indication of future performance. A prospective customer cannot be assured by an agent relating to a particular rate of return on a security investment. Common stocks and mutual funds can decrease in value and an investor can lose principal. An investor cannot lose principal on a savings account.
- A broker/dealer, agent, investment advisor, or investment advisor representative who violates the Uniform Securities Act may be subject to

  - Criminal penalties
  - Civil liabilities
  - Suspension or revocation of their registration
  - Disgorgement of commissions

- The Uniform Securities Act states that an agent may share in the profits and losses in a customer's account provided

  - Such sharing is approved by the customer.
  - Such sharing is approved by the agent's employing broker/dealer.
  - The extent of the sharing is limited to the agent's proportional contribution to the account. In other words, if an agent contributes 50% of the funds to the account, he can share in 50% of the profits and losses in the account. The agent and the customer cannot mutually agree on a different profit- and loss-sharing percentage.

- Assume an agent makes an intentional omission of a fact relating to the sale of a security. Under the Uniform Securities Act, the intentional omission would constitute **fraud** if a reasonable person would attach decision-making importance to the information that was omitted.
- Under the Uniform Securities Act, the administrator can require a qualification examination for a person, which can be written, oral, or both.
- An agent can state that the administrator has registered the security. The agent can also state that he is a registered agent in the state. However, the agent can never imply or state that the security or the agent has been approved by virtue of the registration.
- Under the Uniform Securities Act, the following are considered to be securities even if they are exempt securities:

  - US government bonds
  - Shares of stock in closely held companies
  - Limited partnership interests in a new movie entitled *Discussions of the Uniform Securities act*
  - Certificates of interest in an oil well
  - Certificates of deposit for a security

  However, the following are *not* considered to be securities under the Uniform Securities Act:

  - Condominium units purchased exclusively for residential purposes
  - Collectibles such as diamonds, paintings, rugs, or precious metals

- Under the Uniform Securities Act, assume no denial is in effect and no other securities-related proceedings are pending. In this case, an application filed for registration of a broker/dealer automatically becomes effective thirty days after the application is completed.
- Assume Mr. Kilpatrick has had his agent's registration revoked for violating the Uniform Securities Act. The administrator may deny any future application by Mr. Kilpatrick for registration as

  - An agent
  - A broker/dealer
  - An investment advisor
  - A financial and operations principal

- An investment advisor representative
- Under the Uniform Securities Act, the term **guaranteed** means guaranteed as to the payment of *principal, interest,* and *dividends.*
- An individual or corporation is not considered to be an investment advisor if it gives advice only about annuity contracts. The term **annuity contract** means fixed annuity contracts that are not securities. Variable annuities are securities.
- Under the Uniform Securities Act, the term **market manipulation** includes making false trades, giving false quotations, and disseminating false information. However, commingling a client's funds with the agent's funds is not market manipulation. Commingling and market manipulation are both prohibited under the Act, but are defined differently.
- Under the Uniform Securities Act, a person can sell securities for more than one broker/dealer only if that person becomes registered as an agent of each broker/dealer.
- Under the Uniform Securities Act, a registered agent cannot offer to sell securities in a pending underwriting. The agent cannot sell unregistered, nonexempt securities unless the underwriting has become effective.
- Assume a customer has $1 million of net worth. The customer's investment objective is income only. A registered agent has discretionary trading authority for the account. Discretionary trading authority allows the agent to make purchase and sale decisions for the account. The agent purchases $6,000 of a noninterest-bearing speculative bond issue. Under the Uniform Securities Act, the agent has effected an unsuitable securities transaction for the customer. Even though an agent has discretionary authority over a customer's account, the agent still must purchase securities that are suitable for the customer.
- Under the Uniform Securities Act, an investment advisor's compensation may be based on a percentage of the average total value of funds managed over a definite period of time. Investment advisors cannot share in the capital gains generated in a public customer's account. This rule does not apply to an investment advisor managing a private investment company.
- Under the Uniform Securities Act, if a person knowingly makes a misleading filing with the administrator, that person may be fined not more than $5,000 and imprisoned not more than three years, or both.
- An investment advisor is a person who advises others on securities for compensation. "Person" includes corporation, partnership, etc. The term **investment advisor** under the Act excludes banks. The definition of investment advisor also excludes a lawyer, accountant, teacher, or engineer whose performance of advisory services is solely incidental to the practice of their profession. A broker/dealer who gives investment advice is not considered to be an investment advisor under the Act, provided such advice is incidental to the conduct of its business and receives no special compensation for such advice. Also, a publisher of a bona fide newspaper or magazine with a regular and paid circulation is not considered an investment advisor under the Uniform Securities Act.
- Any person who makes an untrue statement of a material fact in connection with the sale of a security has violated the Uniform Securities Act.
- An administrator, under the Uniform Securities Act, may deny or revoke a registration if

  - An agent or investment advisor representative has been convicted within the past ten years of a felony or misdemeanor involving a security or relating to the securities business.
  - An agent or investment advisor representative has willfully violated provisions of the Uniform Securities Act.
  - An investment advisor or broker/dealer has engaged in unethical or dishonest practices.

SERIES 63 PRACTICE QUESTIONS AND ANSWER EXPLANATIONS

PRACTICE QUESTIONS 1

1. Which of the following securities would be suitable for an eighty-year-old widow with an investment objective of current income?
   a. US government bonds
   b. Blue chip growth stock
   c. An exploratory oil and gas program
   d. A speculative growth stock with good appreciation possibilities

2. With respect to securities, the word *guaranteed* under the Uniform Securities Act means
   a. Guaranteed as to performance results
   b. Guaranteed as to price
   c. Guaranteed as to payment of principal, interest, or dividends
   d. Guaranteed as to the accuracy of statements

3. The term *broker/dealer* under the Uniform Securities Act includes
   a. An issuer
   b. A person with no place of business in the state that does not direct more than fifteen offers to sell or buy into this state in any twelve-consecutive-month period
   c. Any person engaged in the business of effecting transactions for the account of others or for his own account
   d. An agent

4. A newly formed company issuing securities for the first time would normally register its securities by
   a. Qualification
   b. Description
   c. Announcement
   d. Notification

5. All of the following are correct concerning investment advisors **except:**
   a. They may have to register any agent or investment counselor they employ.
   b. They must register with all states if they have assets of $25 million or more.
   c. They may be subject to recordkeeping requirements in some states.
   d. They may have to file advertising literature with the administrator in some states.

6. Soliciting orders for unregistered nonexempt securities is
   a. Prohibited under the Uniform Securities Act
   b. Manipulation
   c. A wash sale
   d. A matched order

7. All of the following are considered securities under the Uniform Securities Act **except:**
   a. A collateral trust certificate
   b. A debenture
   c. A fixed annuity contract
   d. Treasury stock

8. Any individual, other than a broker/dealer, who represents a broker/dealer or issuer in effecting or attempting to effect purchases or sales of securities is
   a. An agent
   b. A registered salesman and principal
   c. A broker/dealer
   d. An underwriter

9. All of the following statements are correct concerning agents, under the Uniform Securities Act, **except:**
   a. *Agent* refers to a person who represents an issuer in an exempt transaction.
   b. If an agent recommends a security to a customer, this security must be suitable for the customer in relation to his investment objectives.
   c. If an agent receives inside information concerning a particular company, the appropriate action for the agent would be to report the news to his supervisor and ask his supervisor for advice as to what to do.
   d. An agent cannot promise a customer that any security investment will always result in a profit, and to do so is misleading and unethical.

10. If the administrator finds that any registrant or applicant for registration is no longer in existence or has ceased to do business as a broker/dealer or agent, he may:
   a. Issue a "cease and desist" order.
   b. Cancel the registration or application.
   c. Revoke the registration.
   d. Cancel or suspend the registration.

11. Telling a customer that a security registered with the Securities and Exchange Commission (SEC) or a state securities administrator has been approved by virtue of such registration is
   a. Permitted if the security has been registered and approved by both agencies and achieved a certain level of earnings for the past three years.
   b. A misleading statement and prohibited under the Act
   c. Permitted with the approval of the administrator
   d. Permitted with the approval of the SEC

12. The administrator, by order, may deny, suspend, or revoke any registration if he finds that the applicant or registrant
   a. Has been convicted within the past ten years of any misdemeanor involving a security or any felony
   b. Has willfully violated any provisions of the Code
   c. Has engaged in dishonest or unethical practices
   d. All of the above

13. An issue in registration under the Securities Act of 1933 may be registered by
   a. Qualification
   b. Notification
   c. Announcement
   d. Coordination

14. A security listed on the New York Stock Exchange (NYSE) is a(n)
   a. Exempt transaction
   b. Security that must be registered in every state
   c. Exempt security
   d. None of the above

15. During a securities investigation, the administrator may
   I. Subpoena books, papers and correspondence deemed relevant to the inquiry
   II. Require a registered agent to file an affidavit pertaining to all the facts and circumstances concerning the matter being investigated
   III. Subpoena witnesses

   a. I only
   b. II and III
   c. I and III
   d. All of the above

16. It is lawful to make which of the following representations in connection with the sale of a security?
   a. That the administrator has found the registration statement to be true and complete
   b. That the administrator has registered the security
   c. That the administrator has passed on the accuracy or adequacy of the prospectus
   d. That the administrator has approved the offering

17. If an agent obtains a written agreement from a customer that he will not sue, even though the sale of securities is in violation of state law, this agreement is
   a. Legal
   b. Legal, but only in a civil case
   c. Legal, but only in a criminal case
   d. Null and void

18. The purpose of the Uniform Securities Code (Uniform Securities Act) is to
    a.   Protect investors from financial loss
    b.   Protect investors from salesmen
    c.   Protect investors from fraud
    d.   All of the above

19. Which two of the following properly describe the administrator's scope of authority?

    I. He can subpoena witnesses only if they live in the state.
    II. He can subpoena witnesses even if they live outside the state.
    III. He must wait for a violation of the Act to occur before he can begin an investigation.
    IV. He can begin an investigation if he feels a violation will occur even if it has not yet occurred.

    a.   I and II
    b.   III and IV
    c.   II and IV
    d.   I and IV

20. If an agent sells a security to a customer, the security must be
    a.   Listed on a national securities exchange
    b.   Registered with the SEC
    c.   Registered or exempted from registration in each applicable state
    d.   None of the above

21. Market manipulation includes

    I. Disseminating false quotations or information
    II. Buying a security on one exchange and selling it short on another
    III. Creating a misleading appearance of trading in a stock

    a.   I only
    b.   I and II
    c.   I and III
    d.   All of the above

22. An offer to sell, under the Uniform Securities Act, includes all of the following **except:**
    a.   An attempt to dispose of a security
    b.   A gift of nonassessable stock
    c.   An offer to sell an investment contract
    d.   Solicitation of an offer to buy a security

23. The administrator may have jurisdiction for a violation of the Act if
    a.   The transaction occurred in the state, regardless of where the agent or customer resides
    b.   The transaction occurred in the state, but only if the agent resides in the state
    c.   The transaction occurred in the state, but only if the customer resides in the state
    d.   The transaction occurred in the state, but only if the agent and customer reside in the state

24. It is a violation of the Act for an agent to

    I. Backdate any records
    II. Misrepresent a return on a security
    III. Pay commissions to an investment advisor without disclosing this to the customer
    IV. Guarantee a customer against loss on a purchase

    a.   I, II, and III
    b.   II, III, and IV
    c.   I, III, and IV
    d.   All of the above

25. Commingling (mixing) customers' funds with the agent's own funds is
    a.   Acceptable
    b.   A prohibited business practice
    c.   Allowed since it simplifies recordkeeping
    d.   Allowed only for a specific period of time

26. The term *investment advisor*, under the Uniform Securities Act, includes
    a. A person who publishes a financial newspaper with a paid circulation
    b. Anyone who directly or indirectly gives advice to clients for compensation on securities
    c. A lawyer who gives investment advice incidental to the practice of his profession
    d. A person who acts as agent for a bank or trust company

27. Which of the following practices is unethical or prohibited under the Uniform Securities Act?
    a. Giving a customer an inaccurate market quotation
    b. Telling a customer that account balances are higher than they actually are
    c. Telling a customer that a commission on a transaction is lower than the amount actually charged
    d. All of the above

28. It is a violation of the Uniform Securities Act to
    a. Employ any device to defraud
    b. Make an untrue statement of a material fact or fail to state a material fact
    c. Perform any act that would operate as a fraud upon any person
    d. All of the above

29. The term *agent* includes which of the following under the Uniform Securities Act?

    I. Any individual other than a broker/dealer who represents a broker/dealer or issuer in effecting or attempting to effect purchases or sales of securities.
    II. A secretary of a salesman who is authorized to accept orders.
    III. A bank, savings institution, or trust company.

    a. I only
    b. I and II
    c. I and III
    d. All of the above

30. Which of the following securities are *exempt* under the Uniform Securities Act?

    I. A City of Duluth bond
    II. A City of Chicago bond
    III. A City of Toronto bond
    IV. An issue of a federal savings and loan

    a. I and II
    b. III and IV
    c. I, III, and IV
    d. All of the above

31. The Uniform Securities Code attempts to protect the investing public by
    a. Licensing and regulating dealers and salesmen
    b. Providing civil remedies to purchasers of securities and providing disciplinary and criminal penalties for unlawful acts
    c. Requiring registration of securities
    d. All of the above

32. When may the intentional omission of a fact in a securities transaction constitute fraud?
    a. Only in the case of a new issue of securities
    b. Only if the information was known beyond all doubt to be factual
    c. If a reasonable person would attach decision-making importance to the omitted information
    d. Any time the information is known by less than twenty-five persons

33. Agents can share in any gains and losses in customer accounts if the sharing is
    a. Approved by the customer
    b. Approved by the broker/dealer
    c. Equal to the agent's contribution
    d. All of the above

34. It is unlawful for any investment advisor to take or have custody of any securities or funds of any client if

    I. The administrator, by rule, prohibits custody.
    II. The investment advisor fails to notify the administrator that he has or may have custody.
    III. He is acting as a broker/dealer as well as an investment advisor.

    a. I and II
    b. I and III
    c. II and III
    d. All of the above

35. If the administrator summarily suspends or revokes a broker/dealer's registration, that broker/dealer
    a. Is not notified of the order but has the right to a hearing
    b. Receives notification of the order but has no right to a hearing
    c. Receives notification of the order and the right to a hearing
    d. Is not notified and has no right to a hearing

36. During a telephone conversation with Mrs. Jones, her agent is told that if American Telephone stock should decline, Mrs. Jones would be interested in acquiring some of these shares. Mrs. Jones leaves on a two-week vacation and, during that period, American Telephone declines markedly in price. Her agent should
    a. Buy 100 shares for Mrs. Jones since he has been told of her desire to acquire these shares.
    b. Attempt to contact Mrs. Jones and, if this is not possible, buy 100 shares for Mrs. Jones since he has been told of her desire to acquire these shares.
    c. Purchase a number of shares of this security consistent with the average amount of money usually invested by Mrs. Jones.
    d. Attempt to contact Mrs. Jones and, if this is not possible, do nothing.

37. Which of the following would be considered an agent of a broker/dealer?
    a. A clerical person with no authority to accept orders
    b. A secretary of a salesman who is authorized to accept orders
    c. A secretary to a vice president of the broker/dealer
    d. An officer of the broker/dealer who does not effect or attempt to effect purchases or sales of securities

38. All of the following practices are considered unethical under the Uniform Securities Act **except:**
    a. Borrowing money or securities from a customer with the branch manager's approval
    b. Soliciting orders for unregistered nonexempt securities
    c. Recommending tax-sheltered investments to a person in a low-income bracket
    d. Splitting commissions with another registered agent who works for the same broker/dealer

39. Stock sold to a bank registered in the state represents a(n)
    a. Exempt security
    b. Regulated security
    c. Exempt transaction
    d. Regulated transaction

40. All of the following statements concerning the registration of an agent are correct **except:**

    a. An agent's registration to sell securities in any state is good only for a certain period of time, which is different for each state, and after that period of time, must be renewed.
    b. If an agent leaves one broker/dealer to go to another, the agent must notify the administrator of the change in employment, but it is not necessary for the broker/dealer to notify the administrator of the change.
    c. An agent can solicit business in a state only if both the agent and the broker/dealer are registered in the state.
    d. An agent is allowed to sell only securities that are properly registered in a state or qualify for an exemption from registration.

41. The term *broker/dealer* under the Act includes

    I. Any person engaged in the business of effecting transactions for his or her own account
    II. A bank, savings institution, or trust company
    III. An issuer selling its own securities to the public

    a. I only
    b. I and II
    c. I and III
    d. All of the above

42. Which of the following are considered "fraudulent or dishonest business practices" under the Uniform Securities Act?

  I. Churning customer accounts
  II. Guaranteeing customers a profit or a specific result
  III. Informing a customer that certain transactions will involve larger-than-ordinary commissions, tax, or transaction costs
  IV. Bringing customer written complaints to the attention of the agent's broker/dealer

  a. I and II
  b. III and IV
  c. I, III, and IV
  d. II, III, and IV

43. An investment advisor's compensation on a customer's account may be based on
  a. A percentage of capital gains and losses in the account
  b. Any terms as long as they are in writing and mutually agreed to
  c. The average value of funds managed over a period of time
  d. Any of the above

44. An agent recommends a security to a customer. The customer decides not to buy at the present time and wants to watch the security for a while. The security moves up in price, and the agent cannot contact the customer. The agent could do which of the following under the Act?
  a. Execute the buy order for the customer immediately.
  b. Buy the stock for the firm's investment account and transfer it immediately to the customer.
  c. Execute the buy order for the customer and give him the right to reject the trade if he so decides.
  d. None of the above

45. The sale of securities within a state is considered an
  a. Exclusive transaction
  b. Inclusive transaction
  c. Interstate transaction
  d. Intrastate transaction

46. All of the following violate the Uniform Securities Act **except:**
  a. A broker/dealer's failing to send a customer a prospectus in a new public offering
  b. A broker/dealer's failing to send a confirmation to a customer
  c. A broker/dealer's selling unregistered nonexempt securities to nonexempt persons
  d. A broker/dealer's engaging in a securities transaction in which no commission or markup is charged to a customer

47. An agent can share in the profits and losses in a customer's account according to the Uniform Securities Act under which of the following conditions?

  I. The agent's sharing is limited to his proportional contribution to the account.
  II. The sharing is approved by the agent's employing broker/dealer.
  III. The sharing is approved by the customer.
  IV. The agent and customer mutually agree to the proportion of the profits and losses the agent will be entitled to.

  a. I and II
  b. III and IV
  c. I, II, and III
  d. II, III, and IV

48. Which of the following is considered to be a broker/dealer under the Uniform Securities Act?
  a. A savings bank
  b. An issuer selling its own securities to the public
  c. A bank executing orders for its trust accounts
  d. A person engaged in effecting transactions in securities for the account of others

49. The requirement that securities recommended to customers fit the customer's objectives, financial situation, and needs refers to the concept of
  a. Buyer beware
  b. Estate planning
  c. Guaranteeing customers against loss
  d. Suitability

50. All of the following are considered to be securities under the Uniform Securities Act **except:**
   a. Investment contracts
   b. Selling interest in farmlands or animals
   c. Warehouse receipts
   d. Individual retirement accounts

PRACTICE QUESTIONS 1—ANSWER EXPLANATIONS

1. **(a)** The most suitable security for this person is clearly US government bonds.

2. **(c)** The term *guaranteed* means guaranteed as to the payment of principal, interest, or dividends.

3. **(c)** A broker/dealer is any person engaged in the business of effecting transactions for the account of others or for his own account.

4. **(a)** A newly formed company would normally register by qualification since it would not meet the requirements for notification.

5. **(b)** Investment advisors with client assets of $25 million or more are registered only with the SEC. They are subject to federal regulation but not to state regulation.

6. **(a)** For a person to solicit orders for a security, the security must be registered or exempt from registration under the Act.

7. **(c)** A fixed annuity contract is an insurance company product and is not considered a security under the Act.

8. **(a)** An individual who represents a broker/dealer or issuer in effecting or attempting to effect purchases or sales of securities is an agent.

9. **(a)** The term *agent* under the Act does not refer to a person who represents an issuer in an exempt transaction.

10. **(b)** The administrator can cancel a registration or application if the applicant is no longer in business or has ceased to do business.

11. **(b)** It is misleading and prohibited under the Act to state that the administrator has approved a security by virtue of registration. It is allowed to state that the administrator has registered a security.

12. **(d)** The administrator can deny, suspend, or revoke a registration for all of the reasons stated.

13. **(d)** An issue in registration under the Securities Act of 1933 may be registered by coordination. In this case the issuer "coordinates" a federal and state registration at the same time by giving the state securities division copies of the federal registration material.

14. **(c)** A security listed on a national securities exchange such as the New York Stock Exchange is an "exempt security" under the Act.

15. **(d)** During a securities investigation, the administrator has broad powers under the Act. The administrator may perform each of these actions.

16. **(b)** It is lawful under the Act to state that the administrator has "registered" a security. However, a person can never state that the administrator has approved a security.

17. **(d)** Any agreement to limit a customer's rights, if the Uniform Securities Act is violated, is null and void.

18. **(c)** The purpose of the Uniform Securities Act is to protect investors from fraud.

19. **(c)** The administrator can subpoena witnesses in or out of the state and can begin an investigation before a violation has taken place.

20. **(c)** For an agent to sell securities to a customer under the Uniform Securities Act, the security must be registered or exempt from registration in each applicable state.

21. **(c)** Choices I and III are market manipulation, which is prohibited under the Act. Choice II defines arbitrage.

22. **(b)** A gift of *nonassessable stock* is not an offer to sell under the Act. Nonassessable stock means that the stockholder cannot be assessed for the par value of the shares at a later date. A gift of assessable stock would not be considered a gift and must comply with the provisions of the Act.

23. **(a)** If a violation of the Act has taken place in the state, the administrator may have jurisdiction regardless of where the agent or customer resides.

24. **(d)** All of the actions, if performed by an agent, would violate the Uniform Securities Act.

25. **(b)** The term *commingling* refers to an agent who mixes customer funds with his own funds. For example, the agent deposits a customer's check into his own personal checking account. Commingling customer funds with the agent's funds is prohibited under the Uniform Securities Act.

26. **(b)** An investment advisor is a person who directly or indirectly gives advice to clients for compensation. The term *investment advisor* does not include lawyers, teachers, accountants, or engineers who give investment advice incidental to their profession. Publishers with paid circulation and persons acting as agents for banks are not investment advisors under the Act.

27. **(d)** All of the three are prohibited under the Uniform Securities Act.

28. **(d)** All of the actions are violations of the Uniform Securities Act.

29. **(b)** A bank, savings institution, or trust company is not considered an agent under the Act. Both I and II would be considered agents under the Uniform Securities Act.

30. **(d)** All of the securities listed are exempt securities under the Act.

31. **(d)** The Uniform Securities Code (Uniform Securities Act) attempts to protect the public by all of the actions listed.

32. **(c)** The *intentional omission* of a fact in a securities transaction could constitute "fraud" if a reasonable person would attach decision-making importance to the omitted information.

33. **(d)** For an agent to share in gains and losses in customer accounts under the Uniform Securities Act, all of these conditions must be met.

34. **(a)** It would be unlawful under the Act for an investment advisor to have custody of securities or funds of a client, if the administrator by rule prohibits custody or if the investment advisor fails to notify the administrator that he has or may have custody.

35. **(c)** If the administrator suspends or revokes a broker/dealer's registration, that broker/dealer receives notification of the order and the right to a hearing.

36. **(d)** An agent cannot buy a security without the customer's permission. If a customer wants an agent to buy a security without contacting the customer, written discretionary authorization must be given to the agent.

37. **(b)** A secretary or administrative assistant would be considered an agent and must be properly registered, if he or she has the authority to accept orders from clients.

38. **(d)** Splitting commissions is allowed between registered agents under the Act. The other three practices are unethical practices and prohibited under the Act.

39. **(c)** Stock sold to an institutional buyer such as a bank registered in the state represents an exempt transaction.

40. **(b)** Both the agent and broker/dealer are responsible for notifying the administrator of a change in employment of an agent under the Uniform Securities Act.

41. **(a)** The term *broker/dealer* under the Act does not refer to a bank, savings institution, or trust company and does not refer to an issuer selling its own securities to the public.

42. **(a)** Churning customer accounts and guaranteeing profits or specific results or returns to customers are actions prohibited under the Uniform Securities Act.

43. **(c)** An investment advisor's compensation may be based on the average value of funds managed over a period of time. An investment advisor's compensation cannot be based on capital gains and losses generated by the account.

44. **(d)** The agent would be prohibited from performing any of those actions under the Uniform Securities Act.

45. **(d)** The sale of securities within a state is an *intrastate* transaction.

46. **(d)** If no commission or markup is charged to a customer, a violation of the Uniform Securities Act has not occurred.

47. **(c)** Sharing in profits and losses in a customer's account requires approval of the customer and the broker/dealer, and the sharing is limited to his proportional contribution to the account.

48. **(d)** A broker/dealer under the Act is defined as a person who effects transactions in securities for the account of others or for the broker/dealer's own account.

49. **(d)** The term *suitability* means that securities recommended to customers fit the customer's investment objectives, financial situation, and needs.

50. **(d)** Individual retirement accounts are not considered securities under the Uniform Securities Act.

PRACTICE QUESTIONS 2

1. Agents who violate the Uniform Securities Act are subject to

    I. Criminal penalties
    II. Civil penalties (civil liabilities)
    III. Suspension or revocation of their license

    a. I only
    b. II only
    c. III only
    d. All of the above

2. A registered agent may engage in which of the following under the Uniform Securities Act?

    I. A transaction in an exempt security
    II. An exempt transaction
    III. A transaction involving a registered security

    a. I only
    b. II and III
    c. I and III
    d. All of the above

3. Which of the following are considered securities under the Uniform State Securities Act?

    I. Listed stock options
    II. Preorganization certificates
    III. A certificate of interest in an oil lease for the Dry Hole Oil Drilling Company
    IV. An interest in a real estate investment trust

    a. I and II
    b. III and IV
    c. I, II, and III
    d. All of the above

4. Assume an agent has his registration revoked for violating the Uniform Securities Act. Under the Uniform Securities Act, the administrator can deny a future application by that agent for registration as a(n)

    I. Investment advisor
    II. Broker/dealer
    III. Agent
    IV. General securities principal
    V. Financial and operations principal

    a. I and II
    b. III, IV, and V
    c. II, III, and IV
    d. All of the above

5. The term *sale* or *sell* under the Act includes

    I. A disposition of a security for consideration
    II. A stock dividend if nothing of value is given to stockholders
    III. An exchange of stock in a merger transaction that is approved by stockholders according to its articles of incorporation

    a. I only
    b. I and II
    c. I and III
    d. All of the above

6. The term *agent* under the Act includes a person who

  I. Sells registered securities to the general public
 II. Sells securities that are listed on a national securities exchange
III. Represents an issuer in an exempt transaction
 IV. Represents an issuer in effecting transactions in which no commissions are paid

  a. I and II
  b. III and IV
  c. I and IV
  d. II and III

7. If an executive officer sells shares of his own company's stock to his employees and no commission is paid to the executive officer for soliciting purchasers, then the executive officer under the Act
  a. Must be registered as an agent
  b. Does not have to be registered as an agent
  c. Must be registered as a broker/dealer
  d. Must be registered only for this transaction

8. State securities laws are commonly referred to as
  a. Irrelevant laws
  b. Prudent man rules
  c. Blue-sky laws
  d. Legal list laws

9. The president of XYZ discloses material nonpublic information about his company to his brother-in-law. The president's brother-in-law immediately purchases 10,000 shares of XYZ. The brother-in-law has
  a. Acted in a perfectly acceptable manner under the Act
  b. Acted on inside information in violation of the Act
  c. Not violated the Act because he did not solicit the information from the president of the company
  d. Not violated the Act because he is a close relative of the president

10. Which of the following are prohibited business practices under the Act for an agent to engage in?

  I. Borrowing money or securities from a customer
 II. Failing to bring customer's written complaints to the attention of the agent's employing broker/dealer
III. Failing to inform a customer that certain transactions will involve larger-than-ordinary commissions, tax, or transaction costs
 IV. Deliberately failing to follow a customer's instructions

  a. I and II
  b. III and IV
  c. I, III, and IV
  d. All of the above

11. A registration of securities by coordination becomes effective in a state
  a. At the time of the filing of the registration statement
  b. At the time the federal registration becomes effective
  c. Ten days after the filing of the registration statement
  d. Fifteen days after the filing of the registration statement

12. If an agent decides to appeal an administrator's order by filing for review of the order with the appropriate court, this must be done
  a. Immediately
  b. Within thirty days after the entry of the order
  c. Within sixty days after the entry of the order
  d. Within three years after the entry of the order

13. Every registration of a broker/dealer, agent, and investment advisor, under the Uniform Securities Act
  a. Is effective for an indefinite period
  b. Automatically registers the person under federal securities laws
  c. Implies approval of that person's competence by the administration
  d. Expires on December 31 unless renewed

14. Which of the following securities are subject to the antifraud provisions of the Uniform Securities Act?

    I. Corporate stock
    II. US Treasury bills
    III. Oil and gas limited partnerships
    IV. Municipal bonds

    a. I and II
    b. III and IV
    c. I, III, and IV
    d. All of the above

15. Which of the following are considered as factors in determining whether a specific investment is considered a *security* under the Act?

    I. Whether the person makes a money investment in a common enterprise
    II. Whether third-party management exists
    III. Whether the person has an expectation of profits

    a. I and II
    b. I and III
    c. II and III
    d. All of the above

16. Exempt securities are exempt from which of the provisions of the Act?

    I. Advertising filing requirements
    II. Registration requirements
    III. Antifraud provisions

    a. I and II
    b. II and III
    c. I and III
    d. All of the above

17. If an officer of a federal bank sells securities issued by that bank and receives no commission, he must be registered as

    a. A broker/dealer
    b. An agent
    c. An investment advisor
    d. None of the above

18. All of the following securities are exempt from registration under the Act **except:**

    a. An initial public offering of a cable TV company
    b. A government security
    c. A municipal bond
    d. Common stock of a railroad company

19. Which of the following would be defined as an exempt transaction under the Uniform Securities Act?

    a. The sale of real estate limited partnerships to the public
    b. A registered investment advisor purchasing securities from a broker/dealer
    c. The sale of mutual fund shares to a public customer
    d. An unregistered broker/dealer buying securities from an issuer for its own account

20. An employee of an investment company tells you he will lose his job if he cannot sell back to you the security he bought last year at $60 a share. The stock is presently selling at $40 a share. You should

    a. Buy it back and substitute another security.
    b. Buy it back at $60 per share.
    c. Do nothing.
    d. Buy it back.

21. Which of the following securities must be registered under the Act?

    I. Public utilities
    II. Debentures issued by a bank
    III. Investment contract
    IV. Limited partnerships

    a. I and II
    b. III and IV
    c. I and III
    d. II and IV

22. An elderly lady receives money from an insurance policy on the death of her husband. She is on a limited budget. Which of the following securities would you recommend that she invest in?
    a. Blue-chip growth stock
    b. Insured certificate of deposit
    c. Speculative growth stock
    d. Options

23. The criminal penalties for willful violations of the Uniform Securities Code are
    a. A fine of not more than $5,000 or imprisonment for not more than three years, or both, upon conviction
    b. A fine of not more than $5,000 or imprisonment for not more than five years, or both, upon conviction
    c. A fine of not more than $5,000 or imprisonment for not more than one year, or both, upon conviction
    d. A fine of not more than $5,000 or imprisonment for not more than three years, or both, upon indictment

24. What is a *consent to service* under the Uniform Securities Act?

    I. An agreement that actions arising out of or founded on the sale of any securities in violation of the code may be commenced against the person executing the consent by filing a copy of the process with the administrator.
    II. Each agent agrees to be bound by any legal action or subpoena served on the administrator even though not served on the agent himself.
    III. Each agent agrees to serve the administrator one day each year.
    IV. An agreement that the dealer will do his best to service the public.

    a. IV only
    b. I and II
    c. I, II, and III
    d. II and III

25. You have just concluded a lengthy presentation on a security. Your client demurs and says he is not ready to buy at this time. You should
    a. Immediately launch into a presentation on a similar security.
    b. Try and "hard sell" the security to the customer.
    c. Stop and not offer the client anything else.
    d. Stop and offer him the security again the next day and every day until he purchases it.

26. Which of the following are exempt securities under the Uniform Securities Act?

    I. Securities issued or guaranteed by a bank or savings and loan institution
    II. Securities issued by an insurance company authorized to do business in the state
    III. Securities listed on the NYSE, American Exchange, or Midwest Stock Exchange, as well as any other exchange the administrator recognizes.
    IV. Securities issued by a nonprofit organization.
    V. Securities of the federal credit union authorized to do business in this state.
    VI. Securities guaranteed by a railroad that operates on an interstate basis.

    a. I, II, IV, V, and VI
    b. I, IV, and VI
    c. All except VI
    d. All of the above

27. An individual who regularly splits commissions with a broker/dealer on executed transactions and solicits customers is
   a.   An agent
   b.   Also a broker/dealer
   c.   An investment advisor
   d.   None of the above

28. An individual receives commissions from both a broker/dealer and an issuer. He is considered an agent of
   a.   The broker/dealer
   b.   The issuer
   c.   Neither
   d.   Both

29. Which of the following terms are synonymous?

   I.   Salesman, agent
   II. Dealer, salesman
   III. Dealer, agent
   IV. Broker, agent

   a.   I and II
   b.   III and IV
   c.   II and III
   d.   I and IV

30. The term *agent* does not include an individual who represents an issuer in
   a.   The sale of one-year commercial paper
   b.   The sale of common stock in a Canadian mining company
   c.   Transactions with an underwriter
   d.   Any transaction for the benefit of the issuer

31. John Public, who is not registered as an agent, has advertised and sold unregistered common stock of XYZ at $20 per share, using $18 to pay the issuer for the stock. Which of the following statements is correct?
   a.   As long as he is an agent for the company and makes full disclosure, he need not be registered as a securities dealer or salesperson.
   b.   Mr. Public has violated the Act since he was not registered.
   c.   The transaction is exempt.
   d.   Mr. Public can legally make this sale if he is an employee of the issuer.

32. Which of the following are unlawful practices under the Uniform Securities Act?

   I.   A sale in which there is a guarantee against risk or loss
   II. Excessive trading in a customer's discretionary account
   III. Sales in which unreasonable delays are created in delivering securities to customers
   IV. An offer in which an agent represented that the security will be listed, without a basis in fact.

   a.   I and II
   b.   III and IV
   c.   I, III, and IV
   d.   All of the above

33. Which of the following are fraudulent or prohibited activities?

   I.   Using the dividends paid in the last twelve months to determine the current yield on a common stock
   II. Implying that registration of a security means approval of the security
   III. Selling speculative common stock to a client with income objectives

   a.   I only
   b.   I and II
   c.   II and III
   d.   I and III

34. All of the following are types of registration of securities under the Uniform Securities Code **except:**
   a.   Coordination
   b.   Qualification
   c.   Notification (filing)
   d.   Description

35. All of the following are securities under the Act **except:**
   a. A preorganization certificate
   b. A proxy
   c. An option on a foreign currency
   d. A transferable share

36. Which of the following is defined as a security under the Uniform Securities Code (Uniform Securities Act)?
   a. Real estate bought exclusively for residential purposes
   b. Collectibles
   c. Individual retirement accounts
   d. Certificate of deposit for a security

37. Which of the following terms are synonymous?

   I. Broker, salesman
   II. Broker, dealer
   III. Broker, agent
   IV. Dealer, agent

   a. I and II
   b. III and IV
   c. I and III
   d. II and IV

38. Which of the following statements concerning agents are true?

   I. *Agent* refers to a person who represents an issuer in an exempt transaction.
   II. If an agent recommends a security to a customer, this security must be suitable for the customer in relation to his investment objectives.
   III. If an agent receives inside information concerning a particular company, the agent cannot disclose it to customers or other persons and cannot use it in the marketplace.
   IV. An agent can promise a customer that any security investment will always result in a profit.

   a. I and II
   b. III and IV
   c. II and III
   d. I and IV

39. Which of the following is an exempt security?
   a. Stock sold to a sophisticated investor such as an insurance company
   b. A nonissuer transaction effected through a broker/dealer pursuant to an unsolicited offer to buy
   c. Securities of Eastern Federal Savings and Loan Association
   d. A sale by a trustee in bankruptcy

40. A *private placement* is defined under the Uniform Securities Act as
   a. Any transaction pursuant to any offer directed to not more than fifteen persons in the state during any period of twelve consecutive months
   b. Any transaction pursuant to an offer directed to not more than fifteen persons in the state during any period of eighteen consecutive months
   c. Any transaction pursuant to an offer directed to not more than ten persons in the state during any period of twelve consecutive months
   d. Any transaction in the state during any period of eighteen consecutive months

41. All applicants for registration as an agent must
   a. Pay a fee.
   b. File an irrevocable consent to service of process.
   c. File an application for registration.
   d. All of the above

42. If the administrator summarily suspends or revokes the registration of an agent, the agent

    I. Receives the right to a hearing
   II. Receives notification of the order
  III. Does not receive the right to a hearing
  IV. Does not receive notification of the order

    a. I and II
    b. II and III
    c. I and III
    d. None of the above

43. You, as an agent, make a sale of securities to an insurance company. Which of the following is correct?
    a. The securities are exempt.
    b. The transaction is exempt.
    c. The agent is exempt.
    d. None of the above

44. Which of the following practices may an agent properly engage in?
    a. Perform investment advisory services so long as they are incidental to his conduct as an agent.
    b. Solicit orders for unregistered securities so long as he is properly registered.
    c. Effect a transaction in a state where the agent is not registered, although the broker/dealer is properly registered.
    d. Represent a broker/dealer who is not licensed in a state so long as the agent is licensed in that state.

45. Which of the following acts is deemed an unethical business practice?
    a. Exercising discretionary power in a customer's account after first obtaining prior written authorization.
    b. Executing a transaction on behalf of a customer with the customer's authorization.
    c. Executing orders for the purchase of securities by a customer, not registered by qualification or coordination but which are exempt.
    d. Sharing in profits or losses in the account of a customer without written authorization of the customer and the broker/dealer carrying the account.

46. A broker/dealer, with its place of business in New York, places an ad in the *Wall Street Journal*. The *Journal* is freely circulated in all fifty states. Which of the following is true?
    a. An offer is being made in New York.
    b. An offer is being made in every state but New York.
    c. An offer is being made in all fifty states.
    d. No offer is being made.

47. Your client, Dr. Jones, has $300,000 to invest but will need the money for a specific purpose in two years. Which of the following investments would you recommend for him?
    a. A blue-chip growth stock
    b. AA-rated corporate bond maturing in twenty years
    c. Government securities maturing in two years
    d. A portfolio consisting of a variety of common stocks

48. All of the following are considered securities under the Act **except:**
    a. Real estate condominiums and cooperatives
    b. Individual retirement accounts
    c. Multilevel distributorship arrangements
    d. Merchandise marketing schemes

49. All of the following are exempt from the registration requirements under the Act **except:**
    a. Municipal securities
    b. Government securities
    c. Common stock of a railroad
    d. An initial public offering of a start-up company

50. All of the following fall under the definition of a *security* under the Act, since they must be registered, **except:**
    a. Commodity option contracts
    b. Municipal bonds
    c. Transferable shares
    d. Investment contracts

PRACTICE QUESTIONS 2—ANSWER EXPLANATIONS

1. **(d)** Agents who violate the Uniform Securities Act are subject to criminal penalties, civil penalties, and suspension or revocation of their license. The administrator could also order an agent to give back (disgorge) a commission received on a transaction that violated the Act.

2. **(d)** A registered agent can engage in all of the transactions.

3. **(d)** All of the choices listed are considered securities under the provisions of the Uniform Securities Act.

4. **(d)** The administrator could deny a future application by an agent for any of those registration classifications for violations of the Uniform Securities Act.

5. **(a)** A disposition of a security for consideration is a "sale" under the Uniform Securities Act.

6. **(a)** The term *agent* under the Act does not refer to III and IV.

7. **(b)** In this example, the executive officer does not have to be registered as an agent under the Act. The executive officer is selling stock in his own company to employees, and no commission is paid to the executive officer.

8. **(c)** State securities laws are commonly referred to as "blue-sky laws."

9. **(b)** Acting on material nonpublic information is a violation of the Uniform Securities Act relating to any security. The president's brother-in-law has clearly violated the Act. The president of XYZ has also violated the Act, but the question did not relate to the president's actions.

10. **(d)** All of the actions stated are prohibited business practices under the Uniform Securities Act.

11. **(b)** A registration of securities by coordination becomes effective at the time the federal registration becomes effective.

12. **(c)** An appeal to an administrator's order must be filed with the appropriate court within sixty days after the entry of the administrator's order.

13. **(d)** Every registration of a broker/dealer, agent, and investment advisor under the Act expires December 31 unless renewed.

14. **(d)** All securities are subject to antifraud provisions of the Uniform Securities Act.

15. **(d)** All of these factors are used to determine whether a specific investment is considered a security under the Act.

16. **(a)** Exempt securities are exempt from the advertising and registration requirements of the Act. No security is exempt from the antifraud provisions of the Uniform Securities Act.

17. **(d)** The officer of the bank is exempt from registration.

18. **(a)** Choice a. is not an exempt security under the Uniform Securities Act. The other three choices are exempt securities.

19. **(d)** A broker/dealer (registered or unregistered) who buys securities from an issuer for its own account is engaging in an exempt transaction.

20. **(c)** In this example, the proper course of action is to do nothing. Securities must be bought and sold at their current market value.

21. **(b)** Investment contracts and limited partnerships must be registered under the Act. Public utility shares and debentures issued by banks are exempt securities.

22. **(b)** Choice b. is clearly the best choice for this person to invest in given her financial situation and needs.

23. **(a)** Choice a. defines the criminal penalties under the Uniform Securities Act for willful violations.

24. **(b)** A consent to service is defined in choices I and II. The consent to service basically means that the person will defend any actions brought against him in the state in which he has filed the consent to service.

25. **(c)** It is a violation of the Uniform Securities Act to employ hard-sell tactics in order to overcome any objections of a client.

26. **(d)** All of the securities listed are exempt securities under the Uniform Securities Act.

27. **(a)** Agents who execute securities transactions through broker/dealers split commission with that broker/dealer. For example, if the commission on a customer transaction is $125, the agent might receive $45 and the broker/dealer keeps $80.

28.   **(d)**   If an agent receives commissions from both a broker/dealer and an issuer, he is considered an agent of both.

29.   **(d)**   The term *agent* is synonymous with salesman and broker.

30.   **(c)**   The term *agent* under the Act does not include an individual who represents an issuer in transactions with an underwriter (exempt transaction).

31.   **(b)**   To sell securities to the public, an agent, such as John Public, must be registered.

32.   **(d)**   All of these actions are unlawful practices under the Uniform Securities Act.

33.   **(c)**   Choices II and III are prohibited activities under the Act.

34.   **(d)**   All three methods of registration of securities available under the Uniform Securities Code are coordination, qualification, and notification (filing).

35.   **(b)**   A proxy is not a security under the Act.

36.   **(d)**   A certificate of deposit for a security is considered a security under the Act. This is not to be confused with a bank certificate of deposit. A bank certificate of deposit is not considered a security under the Act.

37.   **(c)**   The term *broker* is synonymous with salesman or agent.

38.   **(c)**   Choices II and III are correct statements. In choice I, the term *agent* does not refer to a person who represents an issuer in an exempt transaction.

39.   **(c)**   A security issued by a bank or savings and loan association is an exempt security.

40.   **(c)**   The definition of a *private placement* under the Uniform Securities Act is any transaction pursuant to an offer directed to not more than ten persons in the state during any period of twelve consecutive months.

41.   **(d)**   Under the Uniform Securities Act, all applicants for registration as an agent must file an application, pay a fee, and file a consent to service.

42.   **(a)**   An agent who has his registration suspended or revoked by summary process receives notification of the order and receives the right to a hearing.

43.   **(b)**   The sale of a security to an insurance company is an exempt transaction.

44.   **(a)**   An agent can perform investment advisory services without being registered as an investment advisor, provided the services are incidental to his practice as an agent.

45.   **(d)**   Choice d. is an unethical business practice.

46.   **(a)**   The ad placed in a newspaper is considered an offer only in the state where the paper has its place of business (New York).

47.   **(c)**   The best choice for the customer is government securities maturing in two years.

48.   **(b)**   Individual retirement accounts are not considered securities under the Uniform Securities Act.

49.   **(d)**   New companies must normally register under the Act by qualification.

50.   **(b)**   Municipal bonds are exempt securities under the Uniform Securities Act.

PRACTICE QUESTIONS 3

1. Which of the following statements is true under the Uniform Securities Act?
   a. Any broker/dealer who gives investment advice is considered an investment advisor even though such advice is incidental to the conduct of his business and he receives no special considerations for such advice.
   b. A publisher of a financial magazine with a paid circulation is considered to be an investment advisor.
   c. Lawyers, teachers, engineers and accountants who perform advisory services incidental to the practice of their profession are not considered to come within the definition of *investment advisor*.
   d. The term *investment advisor* includes banks.

2. Which of the following constitutes market manipulation?

   I. Disseminating false information
   II. Giving false quotations
   III. Making false trades

   a. I and II
   b. II and III
   c. I and III
   d. All of the above

3. An agent's depositing customer money into his own checking account is an example of
   a. Refunding
   b. Commingling
   c. Free riding
   d. None of the above

4. Which of the following are considered approved acts of an agent?

   I. Backdating confirmations one day
   II. Representing that a bond yields 6% when it actually yields 0.6%.
   III. Paying to an investment advisor a percentage of the commissions generated in a client's account without disclosing this to the client
   IV. Guaranteeing a customer against loss and agreeing to split all profits when the customer provides all of the investment funds

   a. I and II
   b. III and IV
   c. I, II, and IV
   d. None of the above

5. Under the Act, the terms *offer*, *offer to sell*, and *sale* and *sell* include
   a. A stock dividend in which nothing of value is given by stockholders for the dividend
   b. Any bona fide pledge or loan
   c. Any act incident to a class vote by stockholders pursuant to a merger
   d. None of the above

6. An agent has made suitable recommendations to a customer. The customer rejects the recommendations. The customer requests that an order be executed in a security that is not a suitable investment in the agent's opinion. Which of the following is true?
   a. The agent is prohibited from executing the order.
   b. The agent can execute the order only if sufficient funds are in the account when the order is entered.
   c. The agent is required by law to execute the order.
   d. The agent can execute the order, but it would be wise to obtain from the customer a written statement indicating that the transaction is unsolicited and not recommended by the agent.

7. Under the Act, an agent must disclose personal knowledge concerning a material public fact about an issuer to a customer in connection with the sale of an issue
   a. If the investor is not employed by the issuer in such a position as to have knowledge of material public facts
   b. Whether or not the broker/dealer with whom the agent is registered permits the agent to discuss the material fact
   c. If the fact that such disclosure would make other statements made by the agent misleading under the circumstances
   d. All of the above

8. Under the Uniform Securities Act, an administrator must accept an appropriate cash deposit instead of a surety bond for a(n)
   a.   Broker/dealer
   b.   Investment advisor
   c.   Agent
   d.   Issuer

9. Which of the following statements is true under the Uniform Securities Act?
   a.   A misrepresentation or a fraudulent practice by an agent in the sale of US government securities will never fall under the jurisdiction of the state securities commission under any circumstances.
   b.   All securities sold by an agent must be registered in the appropriate state.
   c.   An agent's registration may never be revoked without the opportunity for a hearing.
   d.   An individual may not sell securities to or buy securities from a duly licensed broker/dealer or his agent.

10. Isolated nonissuer transactions are exempt from the registration provisions of the Act if they are effected
   a.   Only by a broker/dealer
   b.   Only on a stock exchange
   c.   Only by a registered agent
   d.   By a person owning the securities selling to an unregistered broker/dealer

11. Assume an agent recommends that a customer purchase $14,000 of a mutual fund. Four days later the customer sells $7,000 of the fund in order to make a personal loan. The agent has probably
   a.   Committed a fraudulent act
   b.   Made an unsuitable sales recommendation
   c.   Induced trading in a customer's account
   d.   Churned the customer's account

12. Under the Act, an investment advisor may share in the profits and losses in a customer's account provided
   a.   It applies only to realized capital gains and not unrealized gains or paper profits.
   b.   It is prohibited under the Act relating to public customers.
   c.   The investment advisor subtracts his advisory fee from his share of the profits earned.
   d.   The investment advisor and the customer maintain a written contract.

13. If a registered representative sells unregistered nonexempt securities to a client
   a.   The registered representative risks criminal penalties to himself.
   b.   The registered representative's broker/dealer may be sued.
   c.   The broker/dealer may be sued if the client loses money, but if it is a gain, the client will keep it.
   d.   All of the above

14. Private placements under the Uniform Securities Act
   a.   Are not governed, they are covered under the 1933 Act
   b.   Have an exemption that is narrower in scope than the federal exemption
   c.   State that if you qualify under the 1933 Act, the transaction is automatically qualified in every state
   d.   Are not governed—they are covered by the Securities Exchange Act of 1934

15. A new customer is not willing to discuss his present financial status. The agent should
   a.   Sell him only securities from the legal list
   b.   Accept only unsolicited orders until more information about the customer is known
   c.   Not allow any transactions in the account
   d.   Sell the customer any type of security

16. If a person not registered in a state knowingly makes a misleading filing with the administrator, he
   a.   May be fined $5,000
   b.   May be fined $3,000
   c.   May be imprisoned for five years
   d.   None of the above since the person is not registered

17. Which of the following is always an exempt security under the Uniform Securities Act?
   a.   Common stock of a Canadian mining company
   b.   Preferred stock of a bank holding company
   c.   Equipment trust certificate of a trucking company operating interstate
   d.   Interest in a limited partnership

18. Which of the following is true regarding surety bond requirements?
   a. A surety bond in excess of $50,000 must be required by the administrator.
   b. A surety bond must be required by the administrator if the broker/dealer's net capital exceeds $100,000.
   c. A surety bond is not required by rule for investment advisors.
   d. Only agents are required to post surety bonds.

19. An agent not registered is employed by and represents a broker/dealer that is registered. Who has violated the Uniform Securities Act?
   a. The agent
   b. The broker/dealer
   c. Both
   d. Neither

20. The right of a purchaser to recover consideration paid for the illegal sale of a security is
   a. Rescission
   b. Tombstone
   c. Safe harbor
   d. Blue sky

21. If a customer places an order for 100 shares of a security and the agent intentionally places the order for 200 shares, the agent may have effected
   a. A discretionary transaction.
   b. An unauthorized transaction.
   c. A transaction excessive in size
   d. All of the above

22. An agent who commits a fraudulent violation of securities laws may be

   I. Expelled from the industry permanently
   II. Fined
   III. Imprisoned
   IV. Suspended

   a. I and III
   b. II and IV
   c. I, III, and IV
   d. All of the above

23. A corporation is not an investment advisor if
   a. It is located outside of the state and advises only for a fee.
   b. It charges less than $100 a year in advisory fees.
   c. It gives advice only about annuity contracts.
   d. It gives advice only about mutual funds.

24. If the status on an agent changes, who is responsible to notify the administrator?
   a. Employer
   b. Agent
   c. Both
   d. Neither

25. A person is excluded from the definition of a *broker/dealer*, under the Uniform Securities Act, in all of the following instances **except** when he or she:
   a. Is an issuer
   b. Has a place of business in the state and only effects transactions in securities with financial institutions
   c. Is agent for a broker/dealer
   d. Is agent for an issuer

26. An agent's recommendation for the purchase of municipal securities to a customer interested in fixed income and who the agent knows is in a relatively low tax bracket would in most cases be

    I. Unsuitable and unethical
    II. A securities felony
    III. Grounds, in extreme cases, for suspension or revocation of the agent's license
    IV. Outside registration jurisdiction

    a. I only
    b. IV only
    c. I and III
    d. II and III

27. If a person intentionally violates the Uniform Securities Act by making a misleading filing with the administrator, the maximum penalty is
    a. Censure
    b. A fine up to $100 and imprisonment up to one year
    c. Suspension of up to ninety days
    d. A fine up to $5,000 and imprisonment of not more than three years or both

28. How often does the administrator have the right to inspect a broker/dealer's books?
    a. Semiannually
    b. Quarterly
    c. Monthly
    d. As often as deemed prudent by the administrator

29. If a security is already registered under the 1933 Act, which type of registration can a state use?
    a. Notification
    b. Qualification
    c. Coordination
    d. Indemnification

30. Under the Uniform Securities Act, an agent is prohibited from which of the following practices?

    I. Guaranteeing a customer against loss
    II. Borrowing money or securities from a customer
    III. Backdating order tickets
    IV. Misrepresenting a return on a security

    a. I and II
    b. III and IV
    c. I, III, and IV
    d. All of the above

31. All of the following are exempt securities under the Uniform Securities Act **except:**
    a. Bonds issued by Watsahatchee State Bank
    b. Shares of stock issued by the Blue Moon Local Bus Corporation
    c. Revenue bonds issued by the Mississippi Delta Conservation Authority
    d. Bonds issued by the Withering Widows Pension Plan

32. If Mr. Max, who lives in State Y, sees an advertisement of a bond in a newspaper published in State Z and makes an offer to buy to a seller in State Z, has an offer been made in State Z?

    I. No. Newspaper ads are not offers outside of the state where they are published.
    II. Yes, if the seller in Z directs an acceptance to the person offering from State Z.
    III. No, if the seller in State Z does not accept the offer from State Y.

    a. I only
    b. II only
    c. II and III
    d. All of the above

33. A customer inherits 3,000 shares of XYZ common stock. The registration statement on XYZ common has expired. If the customer wants to liquidate this stock

    I. He may sell them in any isolated, nonissuer transaction without registering the stock.
    II. He may sell them to a broker/dealer in an exempt transaction.
    III. Both he and the securities must be registered.
    IV. The securities must be registered prior to any offer or sale.

    a. I and II
    b. II only
    c. III and IV
    d. IV only

34. The term *investment advisor*, under the Uniform Securities Act, means all the following **except:**
    a. The publisher of a market letter
    b. A broker who charges for investment advice
    c. A person who sells security analysis
    d. An accountant who charges for constructing a portfolio of tax-sheltered investments

35. An agent in State A solicits a client in State B while the client is in State C. Which of these states' administrators has (have) jurisdiction?
    a. A and C
    b. B only
    c. A and B
    d. A, B, and C

36. The administrator may deny or suspend any registration based on which of the following factors?

    I. Experience
    II. Training
    III. Knowledge of the securities business
    IV. The public interest

    a. I and IV
    b. II and III
    c. I, II, and III
    d. All of the above

37. If a security is purchased by a broker/dealer for his own account
    a. No agent is involved.
    b. Such a trade is not exempt.
    c. The broker/dealer is acting as an agent.
    d. The broker/dealer is purchasing the security for investment and not for short-term resale.

38. ABC stock is sold to a bank registered in the state. This represents a(n)
    a. Exempt transaction
    b. Exempt security
    c. Regulated security
    d. Regulated transaction

39. An administrator would not deny an application for registration of an investment advisor solely for
    a. Lack of any knowledge of the securities business
    b. Lack of any training in securities or investments
    c. Lack of experience
    d. Several felony convictions for securities fraud

40. Which of the following would exonerate the seller from a civil suit due to an illegal sale made in a state?
    a. The buyer has already disposed of the security.
    b. The seller offers to buy back the security (offer of rescission).
    c. The security sold pays income of less than 5%.
    d. The seller offers to pay all commissions and fees incurred by the buyer.

41. Under the Uniform State Securities Act, an administrator may

    I. Subpoena books and records of a broker/dealer.
   II. Subpoena witnesses who live out of state.
  III. Begin an investigation if he feels the Act is about to be violated even though the violation has not yet occurred.
  IV. Summarily suspend the registration of an agent pending a hearing.

    a. I and II
    b. III and IV
    c. I, II, and IV
    d. All of the above

42. Isolated nonissuer transactions are exempt from the registration provisions of the Act if they are effected
    a. Only by an investment advisor
    b. Only in the over-the-counter (OTC) market
    c. Only by an officer of a broker/dealer
    d. By a person owning the securities selling to an unregistered broker/dealer

43. Agents can sell securities in a registered offering prior to the effective date
    a. Only if a nominal amount of shares are sold
    b. Only if the issue has been previously registered under the Act
    c. Under no circumstances
    d. Only if permission is obtained from the issuer

44. Which of the following statements is true under the Uniform Securities Act?
    a. A person registered with the National Association of Securities Dealers (NASD) is automatically registered in every state.
    b. An investment advisor who has a place of business within a particular state need not register in the state if they sell securities only to insurance companies.
    c. If a person knowingly makes a false statement on an application for registration status, this represents grounds for denial of the registration.
    d. If a broker/dealer's registration is terminated, all of the broker/dealer's agents can continue to legally sell shares since the agents' registration is not affected.

45. All of the following are exempt securities under the Act **except:**
    a. Securities listed on the New York Stock Exchange (NYSE)
    b. Securities issued by banks
    c. Securities issued by the government of Canada
    d. Oil and gas drilling programs

46. Which of the following statements is true under the Uniform Securities Act?
    a. Any broker/dealer who gives investment advice is considered an investment advisor even though such advice is incidental to the conduct of his business and he receives no special consideration for such advice.
    b. A publisher of a financial magazine with a paid circulation is considered to be an investment advisor.
    c. Lawyers, teachers, engineers, and accountants who perform advisory services incidental to the practice of their profession are not considered to come within the definition of *investment advisor.*
    d. The term *investment advisor* includes banks.

47. Under the Uniform Securities Act, a person may sell securities for more than one broker/dealer
    a. Only if speculative securities are sold for each broker/dealer
    b. Only if that person becomes registered as an agent for each of the broker/dealers
    c. Only if completely different types of securities are sold for each broker/dealer by that person
    d. Only if blue-chip securities are sold for each broker/dealer

48. Which of the following are unethical business practices for an agent to engage in?

    I. Commingling customer funds with the agent's funds
   II. Misrepresenting to a customer the status of his account
  III. Giving inaccurate market quotations to a customer
  IV. Guaranteeing a profit in a customer's account

    a. I and II
    b. III and IV
    c. I, II, and IV
    d. All of the above

49. The term *person* under the Uniform Securities Act refers to a(n)

   I. Individual
  II. Corporation
 III. Government or political subdivision of a government
 IV. Partnership

  a. I and II
  b. III and IV
  c. I, III, and IV
  d. All of the above

PRACTICE QUESTIONS 3—ANSWER EXPLANATIONS

1. (c) Choice c is correct concerning investment advisors.

2. (d) All three actions are examples of market manipulation and are prohibited under the Uniform Securities Act.

3. (b) Commingling occurs when an agent deposits customer money into his own checking account and is prohibited under the Uniform Securities Act.

4. (d) All of the actions listed are violations of the Uniform Securities Act.

5. (d) All of the actions listed are not considered offers or sales under the Uniform Securities Act.

6. (d) The agent can execute the order but should attempt to document the fact that the order was unsolicited.

7. (d) In each of these examples the agent must disclose a material public fact about an issuer to a customer in connection with a securities sale.

8. (d) Under the Uniform Securities Act, the administrator may require investment advisors, broker/dealers, and agents to post a surety bond. However, issuers are not required to post a surety bond under the Act.

9. (c) An agent will always be given the opportunity for a hearing if his license has been revoked in a summary suspension.

10. (d) The correct statement is d., since isolated nonissuer transactions are exempt transactions under the Uniform Securities Act.

11. (b) This was an unsuitable recommendation since the customer needed the funds in a few days to pay a loan.

12. (b) Sharing in profits and losses in customer accounts by investment advisors is prohibited under the Uniform Securities Act for public customers.

13. (d) All of the statements are true. Securities sold within a state must either be registered or exempt from registration to comply with the Act.

14. (b) The Uniform Securities Act's private placement exemption is narrower in scope than the federal exemption.

15. (b) Choice b. is clearly the best answer. Recommending securities to customers without any knowledge of their financial status is prohibited under the Uniform Securities Act.

16. (a) The maximum fine that may be imposed for violations of the Uniform Securities Act is $5,000.

17. (c) Choice c. is an exempt security by definition. Preferred stock in a bank holding company is not by definition an exempt security, since the issuer is a holding company and not the bank itself.

18. (c) Choice c. is correct as stated.

19. (c) Broker/dealers are responsible for the actions of their agents and must ensure that all agents are properly registered. Both have violated the Act.

20. (a) The term *rescission* under the Uniform Securities Act means the right of a purchaser to recover consideration paid for the illegal sale of a security. In other words, an action is taken to rescind the sale and make the purchaser "whole" with regard to the funds.

21. (d) Intentional violations of the Act are serious matters. In this case, all of the statements are true.

22. (d) All of the penalties could be imposed for a fraudulent violation of the Uniform Securities Act.

23. (c) The term *annuity contracts* refers to a fixed annuity contract, which is an insurance product. If a variable annuity is sold to a client, the fact that it is a "variable annuity" must be clearly stated.

24. (c) Both the agent and his employer are responsible for notifying the administrator of a change in the agent's status.

25. (b) The broker/dealer in choice b must be registered under the Act since he has a place of business in the state.

26. (c) This recommended transaction is unsuitable, unethical, and grounds, *in extreme cases*, for suspension or revocation of the agent's license.

27. (d) The maximum penalty upon conviction for a person who intentionally violates the Uniform Securities Act is $5,000 fine or imprisonment of not more than three years, or both.

28. **(d)** The administrator may inspect a broker/dealer's books at any time to ensure compliance with the Uniform Securities Act.

29. **(c)** Registration by coordination is available if a security is already being registered under the Securities Act of 1933.

30. **(d)** All of these practices are prohibited under the Act.

31. **(b)** Shares in a local bus company are not exempt by definition. Transportation companies operating in interstate commerce are exempt.

32. **(b)** Choice II is correct. State Z has jurisdiction relating to the transaction.

33. **(a)** Choices I and II are correct since they are both exempt transactions.

34. **(d)** The accountant is not an investment advisor since he is acting within the scope of his profession.

35. **(d)** In this example, all three administrators have jurisdiction. However, administrators work together to avoid duplication of effort in most cases.

36. **(d)** The administrator may deny or suspend a registration based on all of these factors.

37. **(a)** A broker/dealer buying for his own account would engage in a "principal" transaction. No agent would be involved in a principal trade.

38. **(a)** Stock sold to a bank under the Uniform Securities Act represents an exempt transaction.

39. **(c)** An administrator would not deny an application of an investment advisor solely for lack of experience.

40. **(b)** A civil suit can be avoided on an illegal sale of a security if the seller offers to buy back the security (rescission).

41. **(d)** The administrator can do all of the choices under the Act.

42. **(d)** Choice d. is correct as stated.

43. **(c)** Agents cannot sell securities prior to the effective date of a registered offering.

44. **(c)** Choice c. is correct as stated.

45. **(d)** Oil and gas drilling programs are clearly not exempt securities under the Uniform Securities Act.

46. **(c)** Choice c. is correct as stated.

47. **(b)** A person must be registered as an agent for each and every broker/dealer for which he is acting as an agent.

48. **(d)** All of the actions are unethical business practices under the Act.

49. **(d)** The term *person* under the Act refers to an individual, business enterprise, or government agency.

PRACTICE QUESTIONS 4

1. Assume an individual has passed the Uniform Agent State Law examination (Series 63). The individual has filed an application in a particular state. The individual may
   a. Solicit mutual fund transactions only
   b. Solicit new accounts
   c. Not make any securities solicitations until the application is approved
   d. Solicit over-the-counter transactions only

2. It would be a violation of the Uniform Securities Act to trade which of the following securities on the basis of inside information?

   I. US Treasury notes
   II. Common stock
   III. Limited partnerships
   IV. Municipal bonds

   a. I and II
   b. III and IV
   c. I, III, and IV
   d. All of the above

3. Common stock listed on a national securities exchange such as the American Stock Exchange is an example of a(n)
   a. Riskless investment
   b. Exempt transaction
   c. Exempt security
   d. Restricted security

4. Assume an agent and a firm (broker/dealer) are properly registered in State A. The agent wants to solicit orders in State B. Which of the following statements is true under the Uniform Securities Act?
   a. The agent only must be properly registered in State B.
   b. The firm only must be properly registered in State B.
   c. Both the agent and the firm must be properly registered in State B.
   d. Neither the agent nor the firm need be registered since they are properly registered in State A.

5. An elderly person has very limited resources and wants to invest some of the proceeds of a $12,000 insurance policy. An agent in this case, under the antifraud provisions of the Uniform Securities Act, should recommend which of the following?
   a. Put or call options
   b. Several securities listed on the NYSE
   c. Bank insured certificate of deposit
   d. Speculative new issue of common stock

6. Which of the following is an example of an exempt security under the Uniform Securities Act?
   a. The sale of securities to an elderly investor
   b. The unsolicited purchase of common stock by a customer
   c. Common stock listed on the American Stock Exchange
   d. Common stock in a new biotech company

7. All of the following are examples of market manipulation under the Uniform Securities Act **except:**
   a. Making false transactions
   b. Giving false quotations to customers
   c. Giving false information about a security
   d. Commingling client funds with the agent's funds

8. Assume Mr. Smith, the president of Domicile Depot, reveals material inside information to an agent about his publicly traded company. Under the antifraud provisions of the Uniform Securities Act, the agent should

   I. Notify all of his customers to sell the stock immediately
   II. Notify the firm's trading department so they can sell the stock
   III. Not disclose the material information about the company
   IV. Engage in no securities trades based on the material inside information

   a. I and II
   b. III and IV
   c. II and III
   d. I and IV

9. Assume an agent has discretionary authority over a customer's account. The customer's investment objective is current income only. The agent invests $10,000 in a speculative security that pays no interest. Under the antifraud provisions of the Uniform Securities Act

   a. The agent has engaged in a completely unauthorized transaction.
   b. The agent has engaged in a suitable transaction.
   c. The agent has engaged in an unsuitable transaction.
   d. The agent has engaged in a fraudulent transaction.

10. Which of the following are exempt securities under the Uniform Securities Act?

   a. US Treasury bonds
   b. A municipal bond issued by the state of Indiana
   c. A sewer district bond issued by a municipality
   d. All of the above

11. An agent sells securities to a customer and the transaction is in violation of the Uniform Securities Act. The agent has the customer sign an agreement that states the customer is fully aware of the violation and waives his rights to sue or arbitrate. This type of agreement is

   a. A valid agreement for civil claims only
   b. A valid agreement for criminal penalties only
   c. A valid and binding agreement for all claims
   d. Null and void

12. All of the following are securities under the Uniform Securities Act **except:**

   a. Common stock in a closely held corporation
   b. Limited partnership interests
   c. Condominium units purchased for residential purposes only
   d. Certificates of deposit traded on a foreign security

13. All of the following are securities under the Uniform Securities Act **except:**

   a. US government bonds
   b. Certificates of participation in an oil well
   c. Limited partnership interest in a new movie, *The Tiger Queen*
   d. Fixed annuity contracts

14. ABC Broker/Dealer has violated provisions of the Uniform Securities Act. ABC Broker/Dealer could be subject to

   I. Civil liabilities
   II. Criminal liabilities
   III. Suspension or revocation of the broker/dealer's registration
   IV. Returning (disgorgement) of commissions

   a. I and II
   b. III and IV
   c. II, III, and IV
   d. All of the above

15. Mrs. Trump calls an agent after seeing a confirmation that her husband bought $20,000 of common stock in his personal account. She tells the agent that her husband lost his job and cannot pay within the three-day settlement period. Mrs. Trump asks the agent to immediately cancel the trade. Under the Uniform Securities Act, the agent cannot

   I. Arrange a loan for the Trumps to pay for the trade.
   II. Immediately cancel the transaction.
   III. Give the Trumps a personal check to pay for the trade.
   IV. Immediately sell the security and send the check for the proceeds, which includes the profit.

   a. I and II
   b. III and IV
   c. II, III, and IV
   d. All of the above

16. The administrator can deny or revoke a registration for violations of the Uniform Securities Act committed by

    I. Agents
   II. Broker/dealers
  III. Investment advisors

    a. I only
    b. II only
    c. III only
    d. All of the above

17. A person who has a pending registration as a securities agent can sell products that are not considered securities. Therefore, under the Uniform Securities Act, a person with a pending application can sell
    a. Bonds
    b. Mutual funds
    c. Fixed annuity contracts
    d. Common stocks provided the order is unsolicited

18. Assume an agent calls Mr. Smith and offers him certain securities. Mr. Smith gives the agent some resistance. Under the Uniform Securities Act, the agent can, without violating any provisions of the Act
    a. Offer to buy back the securities at a fixed price for a certain period of time.
    b. Guarantee a certain amount of a new securities issue if Mr. Smith buys the securities.
    c. Return the commission to Mr. Smith if the transaction is not profitable within thirty days.
    d. Explain to Mr. Smith why the agent feels the securities are suitable and features about the securities.

19. Criminal penalties may be imposed under the Uniform Securities Act if an agent
    a. Agrees to be subject to the Act in writing
    b. Willfully violates provision of the Act
    c. Is properly registered and acts in the client's best interest
    d. Is registered with a broker/dealer who has violated the Act

20. An agent, Mr. Cashman, tells all of his customers that dividends from the XYZ Mutual Fund will always be greater than interest received on a savings account. Which of the following statements is true concerning Mr. Cashman's claims or predictions?
    a. If the customer understands mutual funds, Mr. Cashman's actions are permitted.
    b. If the fund's past history supports Mr. Cashman's claim, Mr. Cashman's actions are permitted.
    c. If both dividends and capital gains generated by the fund over the past ten years has exceeded interest received on a savings account, Mr. Cashman's actions are permitted.
    d. Mr. Cashman's claims are prohibited under the Uniform Securities Act.

21. Assume Ms. Whitman is not registered as an agent or a broker/dealer. Ms. Whitman makes an untrue statement of a material fact relating to the sale of a security to a client. Which of the following statements is true?
    a. Ms. Whitman is not subject to the Uniform Securities Act.
    b. Ms. Whitman has not violated the Uniform Securities Act if the sale was made to an institutional buyer.
    c. Ms. Whitman has violated the Uniform Securities Act only if she was directly paid a commission relating to the sale.
    d. Ms. Whitman has violated the Uniform Securities Act.

22. A broker/dealer's application for registration will automatically become effective, assuming no proceedings are pending under the Uniform Securities Act
    a. Thirty days after completion of the application
    b. Forty-five days after completion of the application
    c. Ninety days after completion of the application
    d. Six months after completion of the application

23. The administrator can revoke a registration of an agent, broker/dealer, or investment advisor for all of the following reasons **except:**
    a. He has engaged in unethical or dishonest practices.
    b. He has been convicted of a misdemeanor relating to the securities business.
    c. He has willfully violated the Uniform Securities Act.
    d. He has been charged with a felony but not convicted.

24. Assume an underwriting is pending in a state but has not been cleared for sale. Under the Uniform Securities Act, a registered agent may offer to sell these securities to a client
   a. Only with the client's written permission
   b. Only if the agent tells the customer that the securities are not yet registered
   c. Only if a registration statement has been prepared in the home state
   d. Under no circumstances

25. All of the following statements concerning investment advisors are correct under the Uniform Securities Act **except:**
   a. Investment advisors with client assets of $25 million or more are subject to federal regulation only.
   b. Investment advisors with client assets of less than $25 million are subject to state regulation only.
   c. Investment advisors are subject to a state's antifraud laws even if they are not registered with the state.
   d. Investment advisors never have to pay any fees to any state if they are registered with the SEC.

PRACTICE QUESTIONS 4—ANSWER EXPLANATIONS

1. **(c)**   A person cannot solicit securities transactions until his application has been approved.

2. **(d)**   It is a violation of the Act to trade any securities based on inside information.

3. **(c)**   Common stock listed on a national securities exchange is an exempt security.

4. **(c)**   Both the agent and a broker/dealer must be properly registered to solicit orders in a state.

5. **(c)**   Choice c. is clearly the proper recommendation for this person with limited resources.

6. **(c)**   Common stock listed on a national securities exchange is an exempt security.

7. **(d)**   Choice d. defines commingling. Choices a., b., and d. are examples of market manipulation.

8. **(b)**   If an agent receives material inside information, he must not disclose it. He cannot engage in securities transactions based on the material inside information.

9. **(c)**   This is an unsuitable transaction, since the agent did not attempt to meet the customer's investment objectives.

10. **(d)**   All of these securities are exempt under the Uniform Securities Act.

11. **(d)**   Any contractual attempt to have a customer waive his rights under the Act is null and void.

12. **(c)**   Real estate purchased exclusively for residential purposes is not a security under the Act.

13. **(d)**   Fixed annuity contracts are insurance products and not securities under the Act.

14. **(d)**   All of the following penalties could be imposed on a broker/dealer under the Act.

15. **(d)**   An agent could not perform any of these actions under the Act.

16. **(d)**   The administrator can deny registration to agents, broker/dealers, and investment advisors for violations of the Act.

17. **(c)**   The person could sell only fixed annuity contracts, since they are not securities.

18. **(d)**   Choice d. is the proper answer since the other three choices are violations of the Act.

19. **(b)**   Criminal penalties may be imposed on persons who willfully violate provisions of the Act.

20. **(d)**   It is a violation of the Act for a person to state that a return from a security will always be greater than interest received on savings accounts.

21. **(d)**   It is a violation for a person to make untrue statements of material facts relating to the sale of securities under the Act.

22. **(a)**   The effective date, assuming no pending proceedings, for a broker/dealer's application for registration is thirty days after completion of the application.

23. **(d)**   Revocations of registration of agents, broker/dealers, or investment advisors may be done for violations of the Act. A person charged with a crime may be found not guilty, or the charges could be dropped.

24. **(d)**   Securities may not be sold in a new issue prior to the effective date by an agent.

25. **(d)**   Choice d. is not correct. Even though an investment advisor is not registered with a state, he is still subject to antifraud laws and fees imposed by a state.

INDEX